D0146007

DATE DUE

HIGHSMITH #45114

THE MAKING OF BELIZE

Globalization in the Margins

ANNE SUTHERLAND

BERGIN & GARVEY
Westport, Connecticut • London

Library of Congress Cataloging-in-Publication Data

Sutherland, Anne.
  The making of Belize : globalization in the margins / Anne
Sutherland.
    p.   cm.
  Includes bibliographical references (p.   ) and index.
  ISBN 0–89789–579-7 (alk. paper). — ISBN 0–89789-583-5 (pbk. :
alk. paper)
    1. Belize.   2. Belize—Economic conditions.   3. Belize—Social
conditions.   I. Title.
  F1443.S88   1998
  972.8205–dc21   97–48627

British Library Cataloguing in Publication Data is available.

Library of Congress Catalog Card Number: 97–48627
ISBN: 0–89789–579–7
       0–89789–583–5 (pbk.)

First published in 1998

Bergin & Garvey, 88 Post Road West, Westport, CT 06881
An imprint of Greenwood Publishing Group, Inc.

Printed in the United States of America

(∞)™

The paper used in this book complies with the
Permanent Paper Standard issued by the National
Information Standards Organization (Z39.48-1984).

10 9 8 7 6 5 4 3 2 1

Copyright Acknowledgments

The author and publisher gratefully acknowledge permission to reprint from the
following material:

Excerpts from *The Independent.* 1996. "Judge Dreadful? Chris Blackhurst and
Phil Davison Report on Death-Row Battles in a Former British Colony." December
1, pp. 1, 17. Reprinted by permission of *The Independent,* London.

Excerpts from "Like Baboons Without a Sanctuary" by Adalbert Tucker. Read at
the SPEAR Conference, October 1996. Reprinted by permission of Adalbert
Tucker.

Contents

A photo essay follows p. 90

Preface

This book is dedicated to my mother, Lois Peyton Hartley Sutherland Young, who made me see Belize through her intensive love for the place. When we first went to British Honduras in 1971, my mother was 60 years old, had already raised 7 daughters, and had 13 grandchildren. We stayed at the house of two sisters, Armead and Irene Gabrouel. The large house of white clapboards had a red tin roof and shutters everywhere. It had spacious rooms with 12-foot ceilings. Armead Gabrouel sat me down in the tea room, served tea with little sandwiches and a cookie, and introduced me to the other English ladies. We discussed the weather and the latest hanging. Born in Belize, where they had lived for all of their 64 and 66 years, the Gabrouel sisters considered themselves English even though they had never been to England. Their father was a British colonial secretary.

The colonial British Honduras of the Gabrouel sisters was already on the wane, and the country was just beginning to think of itself as a nation. My mother was one of the early expatriate Americans who came to Belize, swept up in the heady excitement of a frontier place with an abundance of land and a paucity of people.

After that first visit to British Honduras, she decided to buy land and live there. Ford Young, another early pioneer and a real estate agent, agreed to show her land from his airplane for a $25 fee. In one hour she flew over the entire country. Next to the Mennonites, in August Pine Ridge in the north of British Honduras, was 4400 acres for sale at $10 an acre. The land, on the Rio Hondo, was dotted with coconut trees, breadfruit, date palms, mangos, avocados, citrus, orchids, bromeliads, and flocks of colorful birds. A frugal woman, my mother decided to buy all of it. That way she saved the $25 airplane fee.

Determined to set up a colony at August Pine Ridge for young people disenchanted with life in the United States, she returned to Texas and bought a yellow station wagon for $400 at an auction of the Texas State Highway Department. She cut off the top with a welding torch and stacked 18 foam rubber double-bed mattresses in the back of it, plus 23 pillows, 36 double-bed sheets, 40 pillowcases, 50 towels, 18 plastic mattress covers, 2 shower curtains, enough dishes for 24 people, 24 quarts of oil for the car, 100 pounds of dog food, 2 dogs, 3 plastic dishpans, a saw, a pick, and 3 axes.

The car looked like a fat bumble bee with the mattresses jutting out the top. All the way through Mexico, people kept asking her, "What are you doing?" "Where are you going?" "Are you selling mattresses?" At the Mexican-Belize border the customs officials searched the sawed-off yellow station wagon carefully because they couldn't imagine anyone bringing in so many mattresses without hiding something in them. But my mother did not fit their image of a smuggler, so they finally waved her through.

In 1971, August Pine Ridge was a village of 500 people living in thatched Mayan marl cottages. They grew corn, beans, tomatoes, and marijuana in their milpas scattered around the jungle. In the night small planes landed on abandoned air strips near the Rio Hondo, but the people in August Pine Ridge ignored the smugglers. There were no factories, no traffic, no television, and the air and water were clean. Nearby, at Shipyard, the Mennonites, some 10,000 strong, had cleared the jungle and turned it into tidy, square farms. They had their own school where lessons were taught in German, operated a sawmill, and made concrete blocks.

When my mother arrived in August Pine Ridge, Ladiz Ramos, a Yucatec Maya, asked her if he could buy the yellow station wagon.

"Why?" she inquired.

"It has the top cut off." He straightened and announced, "I'm going to have the first taxi service in August Pine Ridge." So Ladiz bought the car and welded on a top from another junked car. It didn't fit right, but he had a taxi to take people into Orange Walk. He was so small he had to sit on cushions to see over the steering wheel. For years the yellow station wagon traveled the roads between August Pine Ridge and Orange Walk. The car made a living for Ladiz and saved lives. When a young Mennonite man was bitten by a fer-de-lance in the back bush, Ladiz rushed him to the clinic in Orange Walk in time to get the lifesaving serum.

The houses my mother built at August Pine Ridge soon began their natural process of crumbling into the jungle, and the colony never really materialized. So, a few years later, she decided to build a house on Caye Caulker with wood from her land. The Mennonites felled trees on her land—pine, mahogany, bullet trees so dense that you could not drive a nail through the wood, and ziracote, striated with colors. They cut the lumber at their sawmill, trucked it to Corozal, and put it on the boat to Caye Caulker. When they got to Caye Caulker, they threw the lumber overboard into the sea because the water was too shallow for a loaded boat. The boards floated to shore and people on the island walked into the water to help haul it to shore.

On Caye Caulker, my mother met and married Nelson Young, a Creole fisherman descended from a long line of boatbuilders, English pirates, mestizos who fled Yucatan during the Caste Wars, and ex-slaves. He was self-educated, intelligent, and 20 years younger than she. He had never lived in any world besides the island, and he had been put to work when he was 12. Nelson's father, Peter Young, had two households, one with his wife, Miss Mitch, and another with her niece from Belize City, Dominga. Peter said that he had 30 children he recognized—6 by Miss Mitch, 15 by Dominga, 6 by Alexandra (another common-law wife), and 3 others "somewhere."

Marta Young was one of Dominga's daughters. She was 19 years old when she married Frank Bazzell, an American living on the island. He was in his forties and was the only person on the island who had a lending library of paperback books. The first time I met Marta was on the ferry to Caye Caulker. She had brown skin and dark brown hair, and she had a blond eight-month-old boy, Charlie, who was the spitting image of Frank Bazzell. But Marta was also interested in the British soldiers who came to the island for R & R and in the boys her age, and finally she went back to live with her mother.

Dominga had a house in Belize City where she had raised her 15 children and countless grandchildren. She always had foreigners staying there, too. In the living room, there would be 11 children sleeping on the floor, their bodies wrapped in sheets. The mother of five of them lived in New York. Every time the mother had a child, she brought it down from New York for Dominga to raise. Dominga didn't seem to mind taking care of them.

On trips to Belize City, my mother usually stopped by Dominga's house to visit. In those days, you had to travel to Belize City to go to a bank or the dry goods store, or to make a phone call. Everything took a long time to get done, so she had to spend the night in the city. She always stayed in the Hotel Minerva, an old two-story wood hotel, cheap and dingy, built before the turn of the century. Perched on the corner of Haulover Creek and the Swingover Bridge, across from Mom's Cafe, it was the center of the town's activity until the day it went up in flames and burned to the ground. One day, as they were sitting in the kitchen over coffee, Dominga mentioned that Marta had a new baby—a baby Dominga would have to raise. So at age 65 my mother decided to adopt and raise him. My Belizean brother, Simeon, is now 21 years old.

Through my mother's myriad Belizean friendships and family, I learned to know people and life in Belize and became infected with her limitless enthusiasm for the country. Today, at the age of 86, her skin as dry and splotched as parchment paper, but armed with two new knees and other medical miracles, my mother keeps returning to Belize to live. When she flew off this last time, excited at the prospect of building another house at Bacalar Chico, she left me with only one request, delivered in her usual colorful language: "Anne, just bury me where I drop."

1

Making Belize

Belize, an obscure British colony known as British Honduras until independence in September 1981, is now a well-known, though still relatively new, nation. Most Americans and Europeans are familiar with Belize primarily as a major ecotourist destination, one of the tourist meccas of Central America. American government officials know Belize as a tax haven for American citizens and a crossroads for the Colombian drug cartel's traffic through Central America.

Anthropologists Richard and Sally Price have characterized Belize as the ultimate postmodern nation, with "one of the lowest population densities in the world, an extraordinarily rich ethnic and linguistic mix, a sizeable and diverse set of recent immigrant groups, abundant forest and marine resources, significant potential for eco-tourism, an important role as conduit in the international drug trade, and a strong colonial heritage" (Price and Price 1995, 98).

The recent "discovery" of Belize by foreigners is a product of what it lacked in the past. Aldous Huxley's famous and somewhat bilious statement, "If the world had any ends, British Honduras would certainly be one of them. It is not on the way from anywhere to anywhere else. It has no strategic value. It is all but uninhabited" (1934, 32), gives an idea of the unimportance of Belize. Nestled in a small nook of Central America, Belize would be under water were it not for a limestone shelf, porous with caves and underground streams, that juts into the ocean, covered with a shallow layer of soil. Mangrove swamps, normally situated in water on

Figure 1.1
Belize and Surrounding Areas

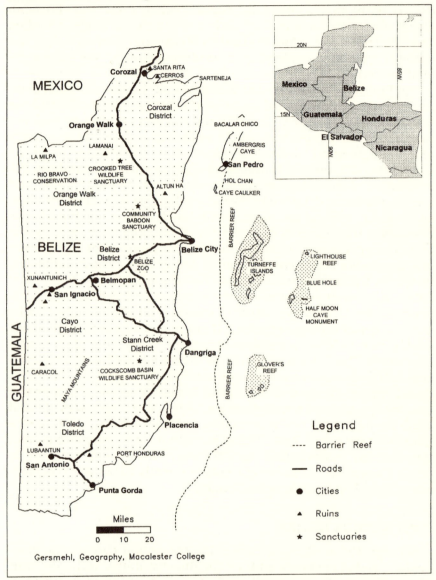

Source: Anne Sutherland, "Tourism and the Human Mosaic," in *Urban Anthropology and Studies of Cultural Systems and World Economic Development* 25, no. 3 (1996): 259–281. Reprinted by permission of *Urban Anthropology and Studies of Cultural Systems and World Economic Development.*

the coast, can be found as far as 30 miles inland, an indication that Belize is barely above water. Low-lying, mosquito-infested, and dotted with small, colorfully named villages such as Blossom Bank, Cowpen, Gallon Jug, Indian Church, Revenge, Crooked Tree, Burrell Boom, Double Head Cabbage, and Guinea Grass, the country remained undeveloped, underpopulated, and undiscovered for centuries.

The Prices may be right that Belize has all the elements of a postmodern nation. It is linked to the world through the media and the latest technology, such as electronic transfers of money and the Internet. It has a mosaic of people moving in and out of the country and a fragmented, diverse ethnicity. It is influenced by strong transnational movements and ideas such as environmentalism, liberalization of the economy, democracy, international tourism, and the international drug trade. But all of this has happened recently, since about 1980 at the most, and it has happened without Belize developing the elements of modernity. Bypassing modernity means more than going from kerosene lamps straight to cellular phones in one generation. The country never acquired a modern economy based on industrial mass production of goods. It has been, until today, a colonial economy based on import and export trade, and import-substitution agriculture. A colony until 1981, it never had a modern democratic government. It never had a history book about itself (until 1976) or a modern system of higher education with a university. Then in the early 1990s, Belize moved from being a social, cultural, and economic backwater in the region to a transnational culture integrated with global forces, acting as a bridgehead into other parts of Central America. Belize surprised everyone and went straight into postmodernism. Without having developed a modernist economic base, Belize moved into the postmodern communications-technological age. The move from being nowhere to being somewhere, from being a colony directly to being a postmodern nation, has a "makebelize" quality.

POSTMODERN BELIZE

Because Belize skipped modernity, the nation entered the postmodern global economy with all the disadvantages and only some of the advantages of a small, undeveloped country: no industry or manufacturing base; a poor infrastructure of roads, electricity, telecommunications, education, waste disposal, and port facilities; and very rudimentary agricultural production, insufficient to feed the population without reliance on food imports. As a colony, Belize exported raw materials such as mahogany, logwood, chicle, and, later, sugarcane, and it imported most of its consumer goods, including approximately one-fourth of all food. In the 1980s, private U.S. business investments and economic assistance succeeded in developing some production of basic export foods and goods. U.S. Agency for International Development (USAID) and international loans were obtained for the construction of the infrastructure. The Northern and Western highways were graded and paved, a new telecommunications system was put into place, a sewer system and a new marketplace were built in Belize City, and port facilities were upgraded. However, the elites in the country still fly to Miami and Houston for shopping and medical treatment, while the less well-off die of treatable diseases in Belize. The threat of contaminated water and the spread of AIDS are growing as fast as the housing developments for recent Chinese immigrants along the highway from the Philip Goldson Airport to Belize City.

Two important factors have come to play a large role in the globalization of Belize: the introduction in the 1980s of media images through radio, televison, and video movies, and in the 1990s the use of new technologies to create a computerized global banking system with the possibility of an electronic transfer of money (Appadurai 1992). Media images from the United States link the local population to the rest of the world while the finanscapes are facilitating the operations of both the original group of businessmen and the tax evaders and land speculators of recent arrival, allowing them to be linked to their investments outside Belize. There is in Belize a transnational culture that combines a history of cultural fluidity, a tolerance of difference, and an economy based on migration. It has a frontier Casablanca atmosphere with an openness to new ideas and a willingness to break the rules, making it a haven for charlatans, adventurers, and scalawags.

How did this tiny nation, situated on the marginalized borders of the global periphery, become a globalized nation so fast? What are the forces of change that have propelled Belize into the twenty-first century? What niche will this nation occupy in the global economy? Will it always be a poor cousin to the big players? Will it stagnate or self-implode, or could it become a site of creative cultural change, finding a small but vibrant niche in the world economy?

GLOBALIZATION

For the last few years, particularly since the end of the Cold War in 1989, scholars such as Immanuel Wallerstein (1974), Roland Robertson (1992), and Ulf Hannerz (1992) have been speculating on the increasing globalization of the world into one system. Globalization refers to the forces of integration and communication that increasingly lead to a smaller world, as well as the forces of disintegration and fragmentation that increasingly produce more conflict and human misery. Globalization is hardly a new phenomenon, having been in process since the mercantilism of the sixteenth century. What is changing is the increasing speed of global processes, increasing consciousness of globalization, and the phenomenal impact of these processes on every individual on the globe.

Global integration refers to the forces bringing people closer together, making distances of time and space smaller, and allowing greater access to the goods and events circulating the world. It refers to increasingly linked economic transactions in global markets and world trade, and to a technological revolution that has spawned an explosion of knowledge, knowledge that is available almost instantly, virtually anywhere. It includes the questioning of our own broad cultural interpretations and basic assumptions about life (the Enlightenment narrative) due to an increased movement of people (e.g., migration, immigration, tourism), on a scale larger than ever before in human history, that allows for greater contact with other cultures. At the same time, in other parts of the world, Western Enlightenment ideas of peace, democracy, and freedom, as well as ecological, feminist, and human rights issues, are now widely disseminated into the global consciousness.

Integration does not mean homogenization or "McDonaldization" of the world, because differences persist even when access to information is greater and shared experiences of world events are more common. In addition, there are forces of fragmentation, things pulling people apart, occurring at the same time as forces that make the world a smaller place. These include the increasingly greater divide between rich and poor, and global inequities due to the high concentration of resources in a few places, contaminated water, and lack of food. Linked to these inequities is the globalization of disease—AIDs and other immunoviruses—and the return of tuberculosis, cholera, dysentery, malaria, and plague. Globally we are more aware of the divisive issues of gender, class, ethnicity, and race, and of the fragility of environmental resources. Dangers from water, noise, and air pollution on a massive scale, resulting from overpopulation and urbanization, have created crises in major Third World cities such as Mexico City, Bangkok, and Cairo. There is concern about an increase in militarism and war through more and more weapons in the hands of more and more people.

Although these globalizing trends have been the subject of much discussion among scholars, the press, and businessmen, no one really knows where it is all leading. The global experience is bringing fundamental changes in the transnational movement of people, cultures, information, and capital, but we know that these changes are understood and practiced in many different ways at the local level and that the processes of interaction between the global and the local levels can take many forms. Anthropologists, for example, are trying to understand the connection between globalization processes and the creation of social forms and cultures. One of the most interesting attempts to study the connection between globalization and culture is the work of Arjun Appadurai (1996). He identifies the central problem of global interactions today as the tension between cultural homogenization—cultures becoming more and more alike through improved communications—and cultural heterogenization—the basic and importance differences between cultures becoming accentuated; but he and others (Wilk 1995; Friedman 1990; Robertson 1992) argue that while people, economies, and technology are increasingly globalized, this does not imply that they are increasingly homogenized. Samuel Huntington (1993), a political scientist at Harvard University, argues that the basic differences between the grand civilizations (Christian, Muslim, Asian) will increasingly lead to more conflict around the world. The major issues of the twenty-first century, he proposes, will be this "clash of civilizations." Furthermore, he urges us not to confuse modernization, which is taking place rapidly, with Westernization, which he says is not happening everywhere (in parts of the Middle East and Asia, for example, where there is strong resistance to Westernization). This last point was picked up by Benjamin Barber, who argued in the *Atlantic Monthly* (1992) that the global cleavage is "Jihad vs. McWorld," or Islam against Westernization.

The new global scholars also criticize the core-periphery model of the world developed by Immanuel Wallerstein in his theory of world systems. The core-periphery model of the world asserts that the globe consists of core developed areas (i.e., Europe and the United States) that have spread their influence via technology and have consolidated economic and political power through colonialism.

The periphery (i.e., the rest of the world) is left with little development: a lack of control of its own resources, which are sucked up by the core; and little power in the political arena. Critique of the core-periphery organizational schema of the world has generally focused on its lack of fit with global realities today and its inadequate analytical value. A few scholars have demonstrated that as a model it was completely flawed from the beginning. John and Jean Comaroff (1992, 181–213), for example, have shown that in the heyday of British colonialism, Africa was not a periphery; rather, it was precisely where the values and practices associated with colonialism (e.g., Victorian ideas of Christian marriage, monogamy, and fidelity) were created and formed—it was, at that time, the core of colonialism. As colonialism formed into a social system, it was exported back to England, where it had an enormous impact on British culture, particularly the working classes on whom it was imposed.

Jack Weatherford (1988), writing about the impact of the meeting of Europe with the New World (the "discovery" of America), has argued persuasively that the making of sixteenth- and seventeenth-century Europe was the product of this discovery and the infusion of the gold, silver, food products, and goods coming from the Americas. His contention is that the most creative cultural and economic explosions of that time took place precisely in the borderlands of the core—in Brazil and the Caribbean, with the plantation system and the production of sugar, and in North America, with the melding of Iroquois and Puritan cultures. This idea has recently been further expanded to include sugar plantations as early prototypes of the factory that later developed in Britain and the disciplined slave gangs of the Americas as a successful test bed for new forms of discipline for British industrial labor (Walvin 1997). This same thesis of creative cultural construction—new ideas and new goods, new political forms and new music—at the borders of the core and in the periphery is the thesis of Paul Gilroy's study of the Black Atlantic, the new black cultures created and fashioned in the Americas as a outgrowth of shipment of black Africans to the New World as slaves (1993). Far from being a sideshow, Atlantic slavery was the main drama of nascent Western capitalism and state formation.

Arguing against the core-periphery model of the world, Arjun Appadurai (1990) proposes five viewpoints, or landscapes, from which to look at "global cultural flow." These five landscapes of global cultural flows are not fixed in any one site on the globe and do not necessarily reside either in the core or in the periphery. The rapid flow of technological advances over the globe he refers to as *technoscapes*. The seamless movements of global capital, investments, and monies without regard to national boundaries create *financapes*. The global distribution of the media (television, videos, movies) creates *mediascapes* that instantly disseminate ideas, languages, and images from one part of the globe to another. Ideologies and master narratives, or *ideoscapes*, include globalized notions of democracy, freedom, human rights, environmentalism, feminism, and liberal economics as well as Eastern philosophies,

Rastafarianism, martial arts, and homeopathy. Finally, *ethno-scapes* are created by the increased geographical movement of people that has produced a shifting landscape of persons (whether they be tourists, businesspersons, environmentalists, refugees, migrants, or immigrants) who nevertheless retain links with other places, links of identity or ethnicity. Such "transnational migrant circuits" produce a continuous circulation of people, money, goods, and information (Clifford 1994) whereby Belizeans in New York and Los Angeles are linked to Belizeans in Belize through sophisticated telecomunications (telephone, Internet, fax) and finanscapes (cash remittances, black market economy, consumer goods).

One of the central paradoxes of ethnoscapes today is that they have become globalized in primordial, essentialized terms, with ethnicity and identity emerging as the "hot" ideas of our time, in contrast to the "cold" ideoscapes of the market and democracy. Feelings of intimacy and connectedness through common skin color, language, and kinship have catalyzed political sentiments of ethnicity (e.g., in Bosnia, Rwanda, and Quebec) that spread over vast and irregular spaces as groups move but stay linked to each other. As people and ideas flow readily in and out of states; as technology and media images cross all borders, instantly changing conceptions of time and space; and as money flows within an infrastructure of its own, tensions develop from the disjunctures in the flow of different scapes. These tensions may be between the state and finanscapes (e.g., Caribbean nations and International Monetary Fund structural adjustment programs), between different ethnicities and ideoscapes (e.g., China and international human rights standards), between mediascapes and local values (e.g., values portrayed on soap operas and local customs), or between combinations of scapes with people and the state.

CULTURE AND ETHNOGRAPHY

Anthropologists no longer focus on the study of people located in one fixed place. Increasingly they are trying to understand the ways that local historical experiences flow both into and from complex transnational structures. These transnational structures of economic goods and services, media images, information and technology, and ideas are available to virtually everyone on the globe, making it possible for most people to be cosmopolitans as well as locals in their acquisition of knowledge. Some of these structures or processes may originate in the global arena and flow into the local. Others begin at the local level and flow to the global (Appadurai 1996, 64). In either case, the critical building blocks of these processes will be the new global ethnoscapes for which they have meaning (Appadurai 1996, 65).

Thus, for anthropologists culture no longer is an inert local substance that people have, and ethnographers can no longer be content with a thick description of the local and the particular. Culture is still a description of differences between people, but it is recognized as a much more shifting, fluid, interactive kind of difference. It is a difference that includes new kinds of collective expression (identities, movements, tourist images) and imagined possibilities. And these collective expressions (or, as Durkheim would have said, collective representations) are situated within an awareness of powerful large-scale social realities (ideologies of democracy and capitalism, media images of social mores in other parts of the globe, ethnic conflicts). More people everywhere are aware of a wider set of possibilities for living their lives than ever before, possibilities that are taking them outside their own locality to imagined worlds they have not necessarily experienced. Any ethnography must situate an understanding of the local context in that wider, deterritorialized, imagined world.

Belize is a particularly fascinating example of these processes and flows between local and global, partly because of its own niche in the world and partly because of the newness of its making. Mediascapes, which came to Belize only in the 1980s, bringing images of reality from all parts of the globe, have given a global dimension to local ideas of ethnicity, national identity, the state, the environment, and "others" (e.g., American tourists, Central American refugees, Chinese "economic" citizens). Improved communications between Belizeans, so rudimentary until the 1990s, are putting the diverse groups within the country in contact with each other for the first time. And while new financial scams seem to pop up daily, the economy is still based on monocrops, such as bananas, exported to a protected market in Europe. Belize's historical position as a cultural and economic borderland has provided the country with some of its greatest assets (an unspoiled environment) and charms (a diverse society), and also is a source of many of its difficulties (a barely nascent economy). However, Belize is now being made, or remade, in a globalized, deterritorialized world where new forms of social life can be imagined and created.

PART I

An Ethnographic History

2

Political Economy and Cultural Mosaic

In 1986 a Maya named Francisco Cruz Reyes was digging a well to water his *canuco* (a milpa on a patch of fertile soil, left by Maya settlements) behind my house at Bacalar Chico, at the north end of Ambergris Caye, when his shovel struck something hard. He uncovered the grave of a Maya man buried in the fetal position, his bones wrapped around an unbroken painted vessel. Although aware that the Maya had occupied all of Belize, I still did not expect to find them in my backyard. A group of archaeologists from Texas exploring the lagoon side of Ambergris Caye came to see the grave and named it Ek Luum, meaning "black earth" in Mayan. They located other sites indicating the presence of Maya communities, including one they called Chac Balaam, which was at the Bacalar Chico Canal separating Mexico and Belize.

The next year they returned for the dig, bringing students and volunteers to work the two sites and making our house the lab and base camp. Francisco built them a cooking cottage behind the house and cleared 2 acres of land for 15 tents to house the volunteers—lawyers, teachers, a filmmaker, an advertising executive—who were paying the archaeologists for allowing them to escape the rat race at home by spending a few weeks digging in dirt, being eaten by mosquitoes, bathing in the sea, and sleeping on the ground.

At Chac Balaam they uncovered a cylindrical vase glazed with blue, red, and green, the surface covered with three monkeys with protruding faces and long, curled tails. Mainly what they discovered was that the northern coast of Ambergris Caye, a place now so remote, was once a center of civilization. The archaeologists estimate that at the time of the Mayans, there were about 10,000 people living next to a valuable salt mine in the lagoon; canoes loaded with salt bound for the highlands left daily. All along the Caribbean coast Maya traders came from the Yucatan—from Tulum, Chichen Itza, and Coba—to Bacalar. Ek Luum was a workers' village where pots were made and salt was collected. Chac Balaam was a ceremonial center with 300 burials that contained jade earrings, polychrome pots, and necklaces of conch pearl and jaguar teeth. San Juan, farther down in the Bay of Chetumal, was a trading post where the Mayans brought the oceangoing dugout canoes (about 50 feet long) into the Bay of Chetumal through the Bacalar Chico Canal and changed to river canoes to take the trade goods from Yucatan to Guatemala. The mile-long canal through Ambergris Caye was dug by the Maya by A.D. 600 so they could reach the security of the lagoon and change to smaller canoes that could navigate the rivers into Guatemala.

The Maya past and the Maya present came together when disaster struck during the last week of the dig. One of the smoke-fires built to drive away the clouds of mosquitoes at the site flared up and burned Francisco's *canuco*—his banana trees, fruit trees, vegetables, everything. Francisco's livelihood was destroyed. To the archaeologists, the banana and fruit trees were worth nothing—they left with what they were after, history and artifacts—but they were all Francisco had. After the fire, Francisco left his house and the land at Bacalar, never to return. As with other Maya today, his struggle to make a living is constant.

The Maya of the past present one of the great conundrums of the ancient world. A highly complex, successful civilization, they used sophisticated agricultural techniques such as raised fields and the highly effective milpa shifting-cultivation system that was sufficient to support a dense population estimated to be 3 to 5 million by the Classic Period (A.D. 300–900). The Maya were consummate traders who developed extensive trade routes throughout the Yucatan, Belize, and Guatemala. Their knowledge of the sun, moon, and stars was sufficient to develop an extremely accurate calendar and knowledge of celestial events. Their architecture is staggering in its beauty and complexity: centers of commerce, ball courts, fortresses for defense, administrative buildings, tombs in the form of pyramids, and residences surrounding their city-states. (See Figure 2.1.)

The Maya had a city-state form of government with regional centers that cooperated and competed with each other. They recorded their history on stelae, murals, and monuments in a hieroglyphic

Figure 2.1
Archaeological Sites in Belize

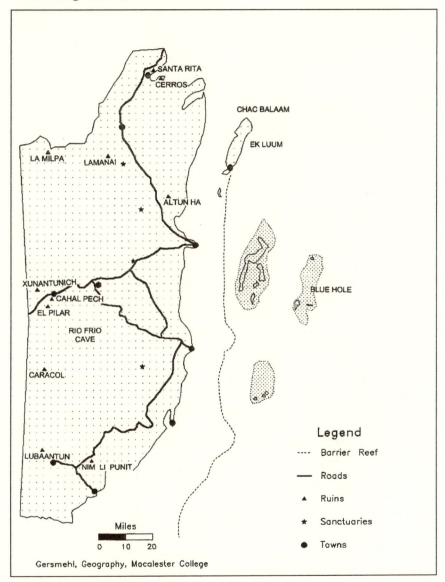

Reprinted by permission of Carol Gersmehl.

writing that is still being deciphered by scholars. The Early Classic Period (A.D. 300–600) was the period in which the Maya civilization took shape and its political, social, and commercial patterns were formed. This was the period in which Tikal was built. During the Late Classical Period (A.D. 600–900) Maya civilization reached its height, and cities such as La Milpa, Altun Ha, Caracol, Lamanai, Lubaantun, and Xunantunich were built in Belize. It is estimated that at this time the cayes of Belize had a population of 30,000 Maya (Guderjan 1993) and the Belize area, about 400,000 (Barry 1992, 77). Excavations at Caracol have revealed a city-state larger and more populous than the one at Tikal and with writings indicating that the Maya of Caracol conquered Tikal at one time. At this time the population was so dense that virtually none of the primary rain forest could have remained; and the hills and valleys along the Belize River already showed signs of erosion into the canals.

In the north of Belize, Santa Rita and Cerros, on the Bay of Chetumal, controlled major trade routes along the coast and down the Rio Hondo and New River to Lamanai. In the middle of Belize, temples and monuments were built at Altun Ha, where the jade head of the Sun God was found; at Xunantunich, with its incredible stucco frieze; and at Cahal Pech, overlooking the Belize River valley. Further south, at the beginning of the Mountain Pine Ridge of the Maya Mountains, is Pacbitun, where a wealth of elite artifacts was found, including musical instruments made of carved and molded pottery. In the Chiquibul Forest to the south, Caracol is a huge complex only recently excavated, the largest known Maya urban center in Belize. Caracol had no major water source, so the Maya there built a huge reservoir system to provide water to the surrounding area. Lubaantun, in Toledo district in the south, is a ceremonial center whose stone structures are made entirely without mortar; there the Crystal Skull, carved from a cube of rock crystal, was found in 1926 by the archaeologist F. A. Mitchell-Hedges. Lubaantun was a primary area for the production of cacao, a product very important to the Maya both as a food item and as a form of "money" or exchange item for trade.

In A.D. 900 the Maya civilization went into decline. Monuments were no longer built, population declined and moved, cities showed signs of abandonment, and the forests began to regrow. For the next 500 years, until the Spanish arrived, there were areas that thrived—for example, Chichen Itza and Tulum. No one knows exactly what happened to the Maya, and although there are theories about famines, wars, breakdown of political order, and pestilence— any one or more of which could be true, as they were in Europe— we may never know the whole story on the ancient Maya.

We do know that the Maya have persisted. Civilizations may collapse, but people live on and make new lives. Today the Maya population has increased, and they are farming their milpas, building their houses, and raising their families in some of the same ways they have for hundreds of years. They are not gone, but they occupy a new status, one that is much impoverished. While the tourist industry promotes with fanfare La Ruta Maya and the celebration of ancient sites in the Yucatan, Belize, and Guatemala, the Maya quietly carry on with their lives. It is always somewhat jarring when great play is given to the Maya as an ancient people while the living Maya are ignored or trampled in the rush toward archaeology, just as Francisco, a living Maya, was swept aside by the archaeologists.

POLITICAL ECONOMY

Belize was a British colony from 1862 until its independence in September 1981. In the preface to Cedric Grant's book on the making of modern Belize (1976), W.J.M. Mackenzie wrote that British Honduras had none of the main features of colonialism and imperialism: loot and land. There was no gold nor silver, therefore no mines; no large labor force, therefore no enslavement of Indian labor; no good agricultural land and no agriculture apart from scattered milpas, therefore no plantations with African slaves (Grant 1976, ix–x). When the British arrived in the eighteenth century, the population was already so sparse from the spread of European diseases that even the small labor force needed to cut mahogany had to be provided by slaves from the Caribbean islands.

Belize was an economic borderland of the main European powers in the New World. Colonial British Honduras never garnered the attention bestowed on the other British colonies in North America, the Caribbean, Africa, and India. Because it was essentially a depopulated area, there was hardly any economic advantage to the British in staying there. Nevertheless, this was their foothold in Central America, and they stayed.

Although Belize's history has always been based on trade, even during the Late Classical Period of the Maya civilization, when trade routes were developed through the Belizean cayes into the interior, it was in the seventeenth century that Belize's present style of trade economy developed. At this time the British came to the Mosquito Coast of British Honduras mainly because their pirate ships could get fresh water and fruits along the coastline and hide in the mangrove islands before moving back onto the high seas of the Caribbean to plunder Spanish galleons. British and Spanish shipwrecks dotted along the coast of Belize attest to the frequency with which battles took place (Foster 1987). From the beginning, trade in contraband and piracy positioned Belize as a kind of semilegitimate crossroad.

After the accidental discovery of the value of logwood as a dye in 1655, British pirate bands began to capture Spanish ships loaded with logwood as they were making their way from the Mosquito Coast to Europe (Cook 1935, 7). When such privateering was suppressed by the Treaty of 1667 between England and Spain, the buccaneers—or baymen, as they were called—began to cut the wood themselves. From this point on, it was clear that Britain had a political interest in territorial possession and commerce in Central America, and Belize was the main British settlement. By 1670 there were about 700 whites settled in Belize (Cook 1935, 7). Relations between the buccaneers and the governments of Yucatan, Spain, and England were very tenuous; the buccaneers received no support from anyone. Nevertheless, they persevered even when successive governors of Yucatan sent troops to drive them out. Around 1733 the baymen were routed by Spanish troops from Yucatan, but since the Spanish never left any permanent garrison or colonized the area, the baymen filtered back. A climax to the constant struggle between Spain and the logwood colonists, which included raids by the colonists on Yucatan, came to a peak in 1763 when Spain lost the Seven Years War with England. The resulting Treaty of 1763 contained a clause permitting the British to cut logwood, but it left the settlement within Spanish territory and without political support. (Cook 1935, 12). This meant that an illicit contraband trade between the English colonists and Yucatan was permitted to develop, but within a legal limbo. In Belize there was a period of slow and checkered evolution of organized government by scattered parties of buccaneers until the end of the eighteenth century, when England began to take a more serious interest in governing the region.

The importance of logwood and mahogany increased British interest in Belize. In 1907, the British Honduras coat of arms, granted by royal warrant and now on the Belizean flag, became a testament to the importance of logging. With the motto *Sub Umbra Floreo* (Under the Shade I Flourish), the coat of arms shows a squaring axe and a paddle on the left side and a beating axe and saw on the right, indicating the means of transportation and the tools needed to harvest wood in the interior. At the base is a ship in full sail, transporting the wood to England. The crest is a mahogany tree, and on each side of the crest is a man, one holding a beating axe and the other holding a paddle. (See Figure 2.2.)

Figure 2.2
The Belize Flag

In 1765 Sir William Burnaby, governor of Jamaica, went to Belize to reestablish British settlers in the Rio Hondo area, on the
border with Mexico. He carried with him dispatches commanding
the governor of Yucatan at Merida to allow British settlers to work
the logwood regions in Belize. He also brought with him a "constitution" dubbed Burnaby's Code. This code outlawed, in the following order, profane cursing, theft, and luring away a sailor who
belonged to a ship. It set up a system for collecting taxes, codify-
ing contracts with servants, and appointing officers of the law. It
contained no laws about murder, rape, or physical assault and
was signed by 86 prominent settlers, all men (Burdon 1931,
100–107).

Burnaby's expedition included Lt. James Cook, who made the
trip by land along the Rio Hondo. Cook's *Remarks on a Passage
from the River Balise, in the Bay of Honduras, to Merida* details the
relationship between the Spanish garrison there and the baymen:

I must not here omit observing, how much it is in the interest of the baymen (and which indeed they never fail to avail themselves of) to be on good
terms with the guards of these outposts; this my friend the merchant did,

by making the sergeant and his guard very drunk, that he not only told him where they had discovered a good spot of logwood, but am persuaded, had he discovered a mine as rich as Potosi, he would have made no scruple of informing him of it. (Cook 1935, 5)

Cook's observations give insight into how the baymen managed to coexist with the Spanish authorities during the eighteenth century. This uneasy coexistence came to a climax at the battle of St. George's Caye, when the British consolidated their hegemony in Belize. After that battle, a settler oligarchy, a small group of wealthy logwood and mahogany cutters, used their political power to hold an economic monopoly in the territory (Bolland 1986, 19–21). The slave trade was abolished in 1807 and legal emancipation declared in 1838, but long after these events, a very small number of whites (1 percent of the population) continued to exert tight control of political and economic power. This power was held by the settler elites until the latter part of the nineteenth century, when it was usurped by the big trading companies based in England. By 1875, the predominant landowner of the colony, the Belize Estate and Produce Company (earlier known as the British Honduras Company) owned about half of the privately held land in the colony and since then has been the chief single force in Belize's political economy for over a century (Bolland 1986, 20).

This company completely eclipsed the power of the settler elites and placed it in the hands of a company board of directors orchestrating the economy from Britain. Much of the recent economic history of the Belize could be told by following the vicissitudes of the Belize Estate and Produce Company. In 1947 the company was purchased by the Glicksten family and became part of the J. Glicksten Property and Investment Trust. It still owned an enormous amount of land that it did not use but prevented others from using. The government tried to tax the enormous landholdings during the 1960s, but the company refused to pay the taxes. However, the government acquired more than a million acres of land in lieu of payment of taxes, much of it from Belize Estate and Produce. In 1983 Belize Estate and Produce was bought by Barry Bowen, a wealthy Belizean who held the Coca-Cola franchise and other very profitable businesses. At the time of that purchase, Belize Estate and Produce had only 709,000 acres remaining, of which 500,000 acres, constituting 13 percent of the country, Bowen sold to Coca-Cola in 1985 to be developed as citrus plantations (Barham 1992, 843). The development was due to take place with aid from USAID and the Belize government.

From the beginning, the project was controversial both in Belize and abroad because of the large amount of land owned by foreign investors and the potential environmental implications (Barham 1992, 844). Considerable controversy ensued from the conflict of interests in the sale. Issues of concern were the very cheap price of the land (U.S.$10 per acre versus $500 per acre in other citrus-growing areas of the country) and the involvement of the law firm of Dean Barrow, Minister of Foreign Affairs, and his partner Dean Lindo, the Minister of Agriculture. Their commission for the sale was about U.S.$500,000 on the $5 million transaction. In addition, Barry Bowen, who sold the land, held the exclusive Coca-Cola bottling franchise for Belize. U.S. Ambassador Barnaby, who had a key role in the negotiations, resigned soon after the deal and became a paid consultant for Coca-Cola (Barham 1992, 844–855).

But the biggest controversy emanated from the strong opposition of the Massachusetts Audubon Society and the International Friends of the Earth, which objected to the development of citrus plantations in the jungle. This opposition proved to be overpowering. "The Friends of the Earth organized a 'save the rain forest' boycott of Coca-Cola projects in Europe that, according to one industry expert, was estimated, at its peak, to have cost Coca-Cola as much as $1 million a day in sales in Europe" (Barham 1992, 854). The consequence was a decision to abandon citrus development in the area and turn the land into a reserve called the Rio Bravo Conservation Area.

Trade, extraction of resources for export, import of manufactured goods from outside, contraband, and piracy are the foundation of Belize's "modern" economy. By the end of the nineteenth century, the monopoly of the British import-export business was challenged by white and colored Creoles whose ties were with U.S. businesses. Merchant families who were involved in rum-running from the Caribbean to the United States during Prohibition, for example, became major political and economic figures in the colony (Bolland 1986, 30–31).

By all accounts, these merchant families included some strong women. One famous "contrabandista" during this period was called Lady Smuggler. Captain of her own ship, she made regular trips to Mexico, delivering rum for smuggling into the United States. Today she is the matriarch of a prominent Belizean family; I learned of her exploits from a man who, as a youth, had been impressed as a crew member on her ship. By his account, she was an extremely tough woman feared by the Mexican officials, who nevertheless took her bribes, and by her crew, who never defied her or refused her frequent demands for sex.

Another lady merchant was an Englishwoman who came to Belize in 1922 as the bride of an English sea captain. When I met her, she was a small, white-haired, gentle woman in her sixties. When she smiled, she exposed wooden dentures, held on with bits of plastic material in different shades of brown and pink, that moved when she talked. Her white hair was yellowed on the ends from the tropical sun, and her face, arms, and legs were weathered and lined, but her most striking feature was her feet. Each toe had been broken and twisted at one time in her life, and they stuck out at unnatural angles. The myriad bent and folded toes gave her a strange loping gait. Since the day she arrived in Belize, she had never gone back to England, even when she needed new teeth or to have broken bones fixed. She raised her children on land and worked with her husband at sea until he died. She lives far up the coast, without electricity or running water, in a desolate house her husband began to build but never finished. Every so often she rows seven miles down the coast to town in her dinghy, fighting the waves and the current. Once I admonished her for living so far up the coast, in an area so remote that if anything happened to her, it would be a week before she was found. But she just looked away dreamily and her teeth slipped a few notches. "Ahh," she dismissed me, "but I came here for love."

DIASPORAS

From the retreat of the Maya to the present day, Belize has offered a haven to a series of diasporas, migrations, and displaced peoples. An early diaspora was the deportation from St. Vincent of a group of fierce fighters who had resisted being controlled by both the English and the French. These Garifuna were a mixture of Arawak/Caribs and ex-slaves. How this hybridization took place is a contested issue among some Garifuna, who argue that, in contrast to the Creoles, they were never slaves because they are descended from Africans who were shipwrecked and fled before actually becoming slaves. Another contested issue among the Garifuna is the relative importance they place on their Carib and indigenous heritage versus their African heritage. In 1989 they joined the World Council of Indigenous Peoples (Palacio 1994), but they are also regularly urged in the *Amandala*, Belize's Black-Consciousness newspaper, to identify with their "African brothers, the Creoles."

Historical accounts (Shoman 1994, 72–73; Palacio 1994) indicate that Garifuna heritage has a complex history that can be interpreted in a number of ways. There is general agreement that their origins can be traced to a shipwreck in 1635; many of the African slaves on board escaped to the island of St. Vincent, where they intermarried with Caribs. There is also evidence suggesting that during the seventeenth century, the St. Vincent Caribs raided other islands for both whites and blacks, and brought them to St. Vincent to become slaves of the Caribs. Finally, throughout the eighteenth century, African slaves escaped from nearby islands and joined the Garifuna on St. Vincent.

In any case, the St. Vincent Garifuna took on the Carib gender-based language system, the women speaking Arawak and the men Carib, and a culture based on female-focused households and strong resistance to slavery and colonialism. In 1796, they were defeated in battle and eventually exiled by the English to Roatan, an island off the coast of Honduras. Their descendants are the English-speaking Garifuna, or Black Caribs, who maintain communities along the east coast of Central America from the Miskitos in Nicaragua to the Garifuna in Dandriga and Punta Gorda in the south of Belize.

Other Belizeans are the descendants of slaves brought from Jamaica to harvest logwood, and later chicle and mahogany. In the eighteenth century, logwood was the basis of the baymen society of British Honduras. The cutting of mahogany, which replaced logwood, changed the nature of work groups; men armed with machetes, and under the loose authority of one foreman, were able to flee through the mangroves into vast unpopulated areas where they could hide and live on fish, wild game, and manioc. Only half-hearted efforts were made to recapture them. These ex-slaves who intermingled with the British settlers are now the basis of the bulk of the Creole population in Belize, clustered in Belize City and the Belize district (*SPEAR Reports* 3, 1990).

Belize City is a Creole town. The mosaic of ethnic groups—mestizos, Garifuna, Chinese, Mennonites, and Creoles—mingle in the city, but the Creoles run it. The town has a spirit of defiance and the fluid feel of a port that is exciting. Even today Belize City has the air of a harbor for pirates and soldiers, entrepreneurs and wanderers. It is a colorful town, with busy narrow streets and crowded wooden shanties built one on top of another. In spite of a new sewer system financed through foreign loans, open sewers still line the dirt lanes. Although the government built a new fire station at the Swingover Bridge, a fire on June 17, 1997, that destroyed 20 buildings on Prince and Albert streets, on the other side of the bridge, was like the fire that burned down the Minerva Hotel 20 years earlier. Dry, wooden buildings acted as tinderboxes that went up in flames in a matter of seconds, and the fire department still could not get the water pumps to work so it could put out the fire (*The Reporter* 1997c).

Every day the harbor is full of fishing smacks that have delivered their catches to the market. In the evening you can still see the sand lighters, the last of the large sailing cargo vessels in Belize, their patched sails flapping in the breeze, creak and groan their way to the pier. One sand lighter, *The United*, makes the trip from Belize City to San Pedro every other day with a load of sand, fruit and vegetables, building materials, and jeeps. Every part of *The United* seems to be falling apart: its paint is chipped and cracked; its bow, worn. Yet the sailors maneuver the lighter gracefully up to the dock so that it stops within inches, step off, and tie it up. While three men wrap the mainsail and the jib, other crew members begin shoveling sand from the pier into the lighter with terrific speed and graceful strength, shouting to each other in a lively, argumentative tone. They have been sailing together for 25 years, and although the boat looks decrepit, they are such skilled sailors that they win races year after year.

In the nineteenth century, East Indians were brought to Belize as indentured labor. Although it is claimed that they were present in Belize in the early part of the nineteenth century, most of them arrived in the 1870s and 1880s, brought to Belize after their contracts as indentured servants had expired elsewhere in the Caribbean. Many went to the American settlement in Punta Gorda town or to towns such as Alabama Wharf and Savannah, established by planters from the U.S. South who left in 1868 and set up rice and sugar plantations (Cardenas 1991, 3). Many East Indians were brought to Orange Walk as "coolie laborers," a name that still has a pejorative meaning in Belize, to work on sugar plantations owned by the Belize Estate and Produce Company. They were frequently sold to new employers without their knowledge, a practice that seems to be operating today (Cardenas 1991, 11).

In 1847, war broke out in the Yucatan when Maya farmers rose up against mestizo landlords, shopkeepers, and the Mexican middle class. The Maya prevailed and took over the area, killing or expelling most non-Maya. Their isolation from the rest of Mexico handicapped the Mexican government in its efforts to restore order, and the Maya were able to control the area, with sporadic battles, from 1847 until 1853. The mestizo exodus from the Yucatan brought a large Spanish-speaking population into the northern areas of British Honduras and onto the cayes along the northern coast.

A town called Bacalar Chico, for example, was established on upper Ambergris Caye (it was wiped out in the 1931 hurricane). It consisted of former residents of the border areas of Mexico and Belize. Farther down the coast, San Pedro and Caye Caulker were formed at this time and still consist primarily of "Spanish" people (as they prefer to call themselves). Corozal Town, on the border of

Mexico and Belize, became a haven for those fleeing the Caste Wars, although at one time during the battles it was temporarily taken by the Maya. Farther into Belize, Orange Walk, which probably began as a New River logging camp, swelled with mestizo migrants and was also attacked by the Icaiche Maya military commander, Marcus Canul (Emond 1977).

At more or less the same time, Lebanese and Chinese shopkeepers and traders arrived in Belize City. These few families provided goods from outside for the import-hungry Belizean market. Augusto Quan's hardware store was for many years the best store in Belize City and the only one with the tools, nails, and buckets greatly needed in the colony.

The next major migration to British Honduras was a group of Mennonites who came from Mexico in 1958, in search of inexpensive land and a place that would allow them to live unfettered by laws requiring them to send their children to state schools, pay income tax, or participate in any aspect of life not controlled by the Mennonite elders. In that same year, Mennonite communities were formed in Blue Creek and Shipyard in the north, and at Spanish Lookout in Cayo district in the west (Koop 1991, 17). These communities have grown to about 7,400 today, but they have kept their particular form of Swiss German, their handmade clothing, and their agrarian life. The Mennonites brought cooperative agriculture to Belize. Before their appearance, Belize imported most foods from abroad, including such basics as onions and tomatoes. When the Mennonites began to sell their produce, they created new markets. They raised cows, produced milk and cheese, and sold chickens, eggs, and honey produced by bees they brought into the country. They set up a sawmill and made wooden furniture to sell. The Mennonites created a local economy in foods and furniture that serves the whole country. A few years ago the Belize government asked them to pay an import tax on cows. Given their religious principles against supporting any government with their taxes, over 800 of the Mennonite dairy farmers packed up and moved to Bolivia. The dairy industry, which did not exist before the Mennonites, collapsed until the government finally agreed to abandon the effort to tax them.

The next wave of migrants came in the 1980s when Central American refugees began fleeing the civil wars in Guatemala, El Salvador, and Nicaragua (Palacio 1990, 16). Although refugees from Central America were not a new phenomenon in Belize, this particular group was part of the massive migration of refugees fleeing to Mexico, Costa Rica, and the United States. An estimated 30,000 refugees entered Belize (Palacio 1990), although the official, documented number is only about 5100. Nevertheless, because of the small population in Belize, the ratio of refugees to natives in this particular wave is 1:39, placing Belize tenth in the countries with a high proportion of refugees to natives (Stone 1994, 186).

These refugees formed communities in the Maya Mountains along the border with Guatemala and in "the Valley of Peace" in the Cayo district. The Belize government under the People's United Party (PUP) was very sympathetic to them, partly because of the long-standing feud with the government of Guatemala over claims on Belize and partly because, as an underpopulated country, Belize at that time welcomed cheap labor. The government granted residency permits and citizenship to many refugees in the Valley of Peace during the early part of the migration, slowing down only when the labor market began to reach its limit. The PUP also courted the votes of the new Belizeans, who fit well with the party's interest in stronger Central American ties (Stone 1994, 190).

This refugee population has met innumerable problems, such as obtaining title to land that they farm and finding legal employment. They also have faced opposition from Belizeans, primarily Creoles, who have seen them as a threat to a Caribbean Belizean national identity. The "aliens," as Central Americans are derogatorily called, have been blamed for crimes of violence ("chopping" with a machete), theft, and the rise in drug trafficking, despite evidence that Belizeans are at the top of the drug trade (Stone 1994, 192). The 1984 election that put the United Democratic Party (UDP) in power for the first time was partly a consequence of the African Creole backlash to the PUP's liberal immigration policy (Stone 1994, 194).

Today, in the south of Belize, large populations of mostly illegal immigrants from Central America work in plantation agriculture for wages that most Belizeans will not accept, under the supervision of better-paid Creole and Garifuna workers. Towns where the banana workers live, such as Cowpen, are inhabited by Central American immigrants who receive little or no assistance from the government except for some schools. Cowpen, according to some sources, has the worst living conditions anywhere in the Central American banana industry. These migrants have not integrated with the rest of the community, and are very vulnerable to deportation and reprisals by the banana company.

The impact of an influx of 30,000 Central American refugees in Belize, out of a total national population of 200,000, was even greater because of the continuing heavy emigration of the Creole population to the United States. The result was a dramatic shift in the demographic balance of ethnic groups in Belize, making Spanish-speaking mestizos the largest single ethnic group in the country. The assumption that Belizean national culture is primarily characterized by the African Creole culture of Belize district no longer is consistent with the demographic reality. The presence of so many Central Americans and mestizos has generated anxiety among the African Creoles, who fear the shift from a Caribbean identity to a Central American identity, a shift that threatens their privileged position in Belizean society. The immigrants also raise fears that hark back to the negative historical experience of Belize with the threat of a Guatemalan invasion based on Spanish claims on the territory of Belize.

The latest group of foreigners seeking a haven in Belize—in this case a tax haven—consists of wealthy Americans escaping U.S. tax laws in the 1990s. They join an earlier group of people who left the United States in the 1980s and took up residence in Belize to avoid the increasingly harsh drug sentences of the Reagan years. Many Americans living in Belize have become Belizean citizens.

Chinese from Hong Kong also have taken advantage of the UDP-instituted Economic Citizenship Program, under which they could buy Belizean passports for U.S.$25,000. Hong Kong residents were attracted to the purchase of Belizean citizenship as a safeguard against the return of Hong Kong to China in 1997, but many Taiwanese also took advantage of the program. The purchase of citizenship is a very controversial issue in Belize, with each opposition political party accusing the party in power of "selling" the country to foreigners to put money in its political coffers. An article by Joseph Palacio discussed this controversy, indicating some of the derogitory Belizean attitudes toward the "Chinee."

In 1986, the government announced its economic citizenship programme whereby persons could receive Belize citizenship in return for paying money either as bond or direct cash investment in specific schemes.

The plan was originally meant to attract Hong Kong Chinese in anticipation of the 1997 return to the People's Republic of China. However, the patently mercenary nature of the programme together with the allegations of corruption surrounding it have made it unpopular among a cross-section of Belizeans. Finally, the relatively arrogant disposition of the arrivals, whom the government has been wooing to bring much needed foreign investment, has been upsetting to most Belizeans. (1996, 41–42)

In return for the purchase of citizenship, the Chinese have been given large tracts of government land on which to build their communities. A well-funded, relatively wealthy group, they are building houses, schools, and shops, and buying more land in the Belize River valley. This is a community that probably will not integrate immediately with the rest of Belize. It brings its own workers to build houses, and sets up its own Chinese-language schools. Although it is too soon to gauge the impact of these new immigrants, estimated by recent research to be about 1.5 percent of the population, there are early indications that ethnic tensions between the Chinese and other Belizeans are on the rise (Ropp 1995, 22).

These tensions were brought home to me one day as I flew out of Belize. I sat next to a young Chinese man, the head of a Taiwanese immigration service bringing Chinese from Hong Kong and Taiwan to Belize. He and his wife had bought a cattle farm in the Orange Walk district and settled there, surrounded by a community of friends and relatives. He told me his story.

Two years ago there were 6000 to 7000 Chinese in Belize. The Belize government was friendly, and the Taiwan government paid money to Belize to take in immigrants. But then the Belize government made a rule that you had to be resident for one year before applying for a residency permit which would allow you to work. This rule caused a huge exodus of Chinese from Belize. The Taiwanese want to continue to make money in Taiwan but obtain residency in Belize. They cannot sit in Belize for one year with no source of income. So they are leaving for Costa Rica, the Philippines, and Thailand, where the governments are welcoming them.

Also, the Taiwanese want to have their whole family in Belize, especially the aged parents and grandparents. They want a piece of land to make a community and family compounds, but they don't want to invest in Belize if residency permits are withheld from them. Corozal alone had 500 immigrants, but now there are only 40 to 50 Chinese left in Corozal. They are all leaving.

While he talked in a calm, sad voice, his wife wept during the entire flight from Belize to Houston. They were returning to Taiwan after living in Belize for several years, deeply distressed. An article in the *Amandala* reported that Taiwanese residents,

which number in excess of 1,000 families, do not feel they are appreciated nor are they getting a fair deal for their investments (in the region of U.S.$225 million). They point to the recent mass exodus of families and investors to other countries which work at integration with them and provide better economic and political returns on their investments. (*Amandala* 1997d)

THE BELIZEAN ETHNOSCAPE

The Belizean ethnoscape, in sum, contains myriad cultures, no one of which has ever completely dominated the country. And all of them—Garifuna, Creole, mestizo, Maya, Mennonite, British, and

American—have made Belize a peculiarly tolerant, "anything goes" colony (Sutherland 1992). On any one day, while walking across the Swing Bridge in Belize City, one can see a wide range of ethnic groups and hear Spanish, Creole, Carib, Maya, and Mennonite German spoken, with English as the lingua franca. There is a generous tolerance of difference, of racial mixture, of the need to negotiate in several languages, and an ease with which people switch back and forth between languages. This is not a utopia of racial egalitarianism; rather, there is a general acceptance of a variety of cultures and races as the normal venue that individuals must navigate in their daily interactions.

The culture of British Honduras developed around groups that had fled persecution elsewhere—slaves, Mennonites, victims of the Caste Wars of Yucatan, and indigenous groups such as the Caribs and Maya. They were joined later by Lebanese traders, American businessmen, hippies, religious groups, survivalists, environmentalists, tax evaders, and Hong Kong Chinese. This hybrid mix in a population that still numbers only 200,000 (1990 census) is a maelstrom of multiculturalism and all the tensions such a mosaic creates.

The background of the production of locality presented here is the economic history of trade and colonialism, the adventuresome individuals who gained a foothold in Belize as pirates or logwood cutters without much colonial interest in their well-being. The same colonial boredom with the Mosquito Coast gave various diasporic groups an opportunity to escape wars and persecution, to hide out and survive.

Because of its patchy, disparate, diasporic history, locality in Belize takes different forms in each part of the country, making it impossible to generalize from one region to another. The relationships and context of each community have been formed from its particular history. The Creoles of Belize City port, the mestizos of Orange Walk and Cayo, the Garifuna of Dandriga, and the Maya of Toledo in the past had little contact with each other, very few overlapping relationships, and little in common. This is changing as Belize is being made into a nation.

3

Family Ties on
Caye Caulker

Destination Belize, the slick official visitors' magazine of the Belize
Tourism Industry Association, describes Caye Caulker thus:

> If you're wearing shoes when you arrive in Caye Caulker, you may not be
> for long. A travel-poster, scenic jewel-of-an-island lying just inside the bar-
> rier reef, this caye redefines the words "laid back." Sandy roads, swaying
> hammocks beckon the barefoot look. T-shirts are part of an unwritten
> dress code. Cool Caribbean sea breezes rustle through coconut palms. . . .
> Yes, Caye Caulker is the place. Its lure is relaxation. (1997, 95)

While tourists are beckoned to Caye Caulker for its relaxed, laid-
back ambience, local islanders, of course, are engaged in the work
of making a living, raising families, and negotiating with the world
outside their local lives. The social activities of producing and re-
producing local culture—the relationships, the collective ideas,
self-understanding, sentiment, and ethos—are never part of the
tourist image of a place, nor are they easy to describe. My own en-
counter with this community, based on a 25-year history of visiting, studying, and living there, has provided me with only a loosely
understood sense of the social framework within which specific actions can be placed in context. While each community in Belize has
its own uniqueness, Caye Caulker is the one with which I am most
familiar and can therefore present as an example of community life
in Belize.

This chapter and the next look at the production of locality in
Belize, that is, the context within which Belize is globalizing, the

interactions between people in that context, and the immediate social networks and relationships they maintain. Although this book
is a macro ethnography of Belize in the context of globalization, it
is important to ground the history in the local context. The purpose is to present a historical example of techniques for the production and reproduction of locality, of how the local categories of
people and place are formed and challenged by growth, modernization, and an influx of Belizeans from other parts of the country.

Drawing on a long association with one particular community,
Caye Caulker, I show in this chapter how local contexts and local
subjects have created local knowledge and structures. On Caye
Caulker, families are focal points in persons' lives and are the basis
for an unusual system of independent family localities in which
family relationships, landownership, and acquisition of lobster territories are closely interconnected. While this particular configura-
tion of family and land may not be found elsewhere in Belize, both
the importance of building on family relationships and anxieties
over the use of land are widespread local issues in the country.

GOING TO CAYE CAULKER

In the summer of 1972, to escape the unrelenting heat of northern Belize, where I was heading an anthropological expedition, I
climbed into a sweaty cargo barge, inappropriately named *The Mermaid*, paid U.S.$3.00 for my passage, and chugged out to a small
island called Caye Caulker that lies 21 miles northeast of Belize
City, 11 miles south of Ambergris Caye, and just inside the barrier
reef. Looking down at the ocean over the rail, I could see the sandy
bottom clearly, with patch coral and fish darting under the boat.
The air was warm, moist, and salty. Landing at the back harbor of
the island, I saw a small sandy caye dotted with palm trees and
tin-roofed wooden houses on stilts. The people on the island were
mestizos, a mixture of Spanish and Maya, descended from shopkeepers and peasants who had fled the Yucatan during the Caste
Wars. On Caye Caulker, they had learned Creole and English in
addition to their native Spanish and had become fishermen. They
were deeply tanned from the sun, wiry and strong from day after
day of fishing and hauling lobster traps from the ocean bed.

As I stepped off the boat onto the pier, mosquitoes landed on my
arm in such numbers I could brush them off like bread crumbs on
a table. I walked past a shed where a generator alternately
throbbed and clanked, on past the town garbage dump, festering
in a mangrove swamp, and entered the small village consisting of
two sand lanes. As I moved toward the windward side of the island,

the warm Caribbean breeze became stronger, the mosquitoes thinned out, and I could see the waves breaking on the reef less than a mile out to sea. The sun beat on my head through a clear blue sky. The only sounds were those of the water lapping against piers, the soothing breeze rustling through the coconut fronds, and an occasional pelican splash-landing in the water. People padded by silently on bare feet, nodded disinterestedly, and went about their business.

Caye Caulker felt like total isolation. Here was a fishing village whose only contact with the mainland of Belize was by boat, often a whole day's trip by sail or several hours on the *Mermaid*'s semi-weekly trip. There was no telephone on the island, hence no rapid way to contact the rest of the world. Visitors were obviously rare, because there were no hotels. I spent the night on the veranda of a vacant house, and in the morning I searched the island for a place to buy a meal. I found Annette, one of a handful of resident Americans on the island. She made me a cup of coffee and scrambled eggs in exchange for news from abroad.

She also told me the local behavioral rule of thumb: "Whatever you do, people won't interfere. They're very tolerant—except when you try to tell them what to do." I later discovered what she meant. When Santiago Marin was robbed of an expensive skiff motor, he decided he would have to store the motor under his house instead of leaving it on the boat. Even though he knew the identity of the thief, he shrugged it off with the comment, "He probably needed the money more than I do." The people extended this reluctance to interfere with each other to foreign visitors as well.

Visiting Caye Caulker regularly from 1972 onward increased my interest in the community, so in 1982 I decided to bring students there to undertake a more serious study of the island. Even in 1982 Caye Caulker was a village that to the untrained eye appeared poor, isolated, and undeveloped. The houses, still square wooden plank structures on stilts, were peeling and weathered. Everyone walked around barefoot and wore faded, well-worn clothing. There was now one telephone line (with many extensions), and news from the outside, as well as messages from relatives and friends in other parts of the country, came over Radio Belize.

These appearances were misleading. The peeling paint produced by Caribbean trade winds and the bare feet on sandy lanes belied the real conditions on Caye Caulker. In 10 years Caye Caulker had become one of the wealthier communities in Central America. Furthermore, the wealth was distributed fairly equitably among all the island families. Individuals who were willing to work and had some family support system in place could do extremely well. Even more remarkable was that the island's culture and social organization weathered the sudden wealth without major upheaval. In spite of an influx of major consumer goods, such as refrigerators, gas stoves, washing machines, fast skiffs, and big boat motors; major services such as electricity and plumbing; and contact with several hundred tourists a year from all continents, Caye Caulker looked nearly the same as it had on my first visit 10 years before.

A SUCCESS STORY

What happened in Caye Caulker between 1972 and 1982 was a case study in success, the success of a group of fisherman who, through a locally organized and controlled fishing cooperative, turned their efforts into a lucrative fishing business. Caye Caulker was an example of successful small-scale local development using highly effective strategies to deal with production and marketing of marine resources. The fishermen were fortunate to have rich lobster beds surrounding the island. However, this environment became lucrative to the islanders only because they developed techniques for effective use of lobster traps, established a local cooperative to market the lobster without loss to middlemen, and maintained personal control over their land and the seabed, the source of their income. Caye Caulker developed as an affluent enclave in a poor country.

Briefly, their success can be attributed to the organization of the Northern Fishermen Cooperative Society. The fishermen of Caye Caulker took advantage of the cooperative movement in Belize that was developed in the 1960s by Father Hickey, a Catholic priest. Initially a Caye Caulker cooperative, it was so successful in bringing the fishermen a good price on their produce that it quickly gained national recognition and was joined by fishermen from all over Belize. The success of the Northern Fishermen Cooperative brought affluence to Caye Caulker, but it also has led to a loss of control by the local fishermen. In June 1997, for the first time in its history, no fisherman from Caye Caulker was elected to the board of directors; fishermen from Sarteneja had more votes. In addition, the cooperative is in financial trouble for the first time in its history, with a debt of over U.S.$3 million.

Although the cooperative was the major reason Caye Caulker experienced an economic boom, there were other factors instrumental in Caye Caulker's success. The islanders tried to develop an economy that would draw on the strengths of their sociocultural institutions and values. Strong nuclear family ties combined with tolerance of individual differences, for example, created support networks of extended family members that were stronger than communitywide organizations. Their refugee origins, fishing mode of production, and isolation from the colonial political center in Belize City helped to create a tradition of autonomy, individualism, and self-sufficiency. The islanders also developed flexibility by balancing one area of endeavor with another. Within the range of available resources, people kept open as many options as possible. They began to supplement lobster production with tourism, where they applied their traditions of local control and independence to the use of land and the development of tourist facilities.

After writing a book on these aspects of economic success in Caye Caulker (Sutherland 1986), I did not return there for any significant length of time until 1996, when I found that the lobster fishing had diminished considerably as a result of overfishing due to a large increase in the number of cooperative members. The 1980 census recorded 435 residents, approximately 100 houses, and 175 children in school on Caye Caulker. The population has more than doubled since then and is estimated to be about 1000. The census, however, is notoriously unreliable. Rumor has it that the 1995 census update on Caye Caulker consisted of a list of the census taker's own relatives, whether they lived on Caye Caulker or not. It is not clear whether non-Belizeans were counted, although the number of foreigners who live on Caye Caulker on a semipermanent basis has grown considerably. However, much of the new population consists of Garifuna from Punta Gorda, Creoles from Belize district, and Central American immigrants. The population still contains a majority who would call themselves "Spanish"; nevertheless, it has become considerably more ethnically diverse.

In addition to population growth, the village had greatly expanded. In the early 1980s a few foreigners had built houses southwest of the school, but few islanders lived south of the village. By 1996, the south end of the island was being developed into a new residential area, with lots being sold primarily to non-Belizeans. Today there is a new north-south road, along which houses have already been built, that runs from the main pier to the new airstrip. Most new homes, hotels, and stores are cement structures. There has been an increase in the number of teachers and schoolchildren. The school, which operates on the British system, goes from Infant School through Standard Six. For a secondary education, young people from the island must still go to a "college" in Belize City.

Tourism is now a primary source of income, though lobster fishing continues despite poor yields. There are approximately 20 hotels on the island—still in the low budget range (U.S.$15–35 per day)—numerous restaurants, and three diving operations that offer certification courses and trips to the Turneffe Islands.

Attempts by the Belize government to build an airstrip on the island dragged on for over 10 years, primarily because of local resistance, but it was finally completed and opened in 1992. Both San Pedro and Caye Chapel have had functioning airstrips for at least 20 years. For passengers to the island, the main transportation is still provided by islanders who run skiffs to and from Belize City. "Chocolate" started the first reliable daily skiff transportation to the city. Soon he became so well known among travelers to Belize, that he had to contend with imposters calling themselves "Chocolate." He and others organized the Caye Caulker Water Taxi Association to provide regular, reliable service to tourists and to reduce the bitter competition for passengers among the many boats. The Association now sells tickets, organizes a regular schedule of boats, adds boats at the height of the tourist season (December–February), and provides the skiff captains with a fair rotation.

Transportation has greatly improved, with water taxi service leaving for Belize City four to five times a day (for U.S.$7.50 one way) and regular daily flights to the airstrip. Three airlines—Island Air, Tropic, and Maya—connect Caye Caulker with all the major mainland cities. Caye Caulker is also connected to the Internet, has a telecommunications office with fax service, and is linked by satellite dish to the major cable networks. No longer isolated, it is a major tourist destination for young Europeans and Americans seeking a laid-back budget vacation recommended by the hippie-oriented Insight Guide and Rough Guide authors.

WHO'S IN THE FAMILY

This thumbnail sketch of the changes on Caye Caulker since 1972, based on my own observations, is nevertheless a superficial view from the outside. If we move away from the tourist "gaze," we notice that the people who have lived their lives on Caye Caulker divide themselves into two categories: islanders and non-islanders. This distinction is a very sensitive one that creates friction between the original island families and the relative newcomers who have arrived since about 1980. Within the group of people considered islanders, there is also distinction between kin (or family) and non-kin. Both these distinctions have important economic implications. First, islanders have had preferential access to land, to membership and credit in the fishing cooperative, to lobster territories, and to the Caye Caulker Water Taxi Association. This has given them an economic advantage over the newer arrivals. Second, through their network of kin, islanders have a solid system of social and economic support. These economic advantages are no longer operating as they did before. Today, other Belizeans have obtained land, and have joined (and now manage) the cooperative and the Water Taxi Association. The 1997 election of board members of the Northern Fishermen Cooperative (in which no Caye Caulker fisherman gained a seat) was a landmark in Caye Caulker history. Caye Caulker is no longer a local place; it is a player in the national arena.

These tensions are part of a rudimentary class division between original island families who have generally (but not always) benefited from early access to resources on the island, and the later arrivals, Belizeans from other cayes and the mainland who are still trying to establish a foothold on Caye Caulker. Part of the emerging class distinction is due to the hiring of workers by the family businesses that previously used only family members to help out. Now, the most undesirable and onerous labor is performed by those coming to the island seeking work. One of the consequences of the success of the lobster business and tourism is the change from a family-based exchange of services to paid labor in a market context.

FAMILY TIES

Among the islanders, the extended family is the primary and largest social group. Loyalty to kin or family means tolerance of relatives at all times, and a willingness to offer financial assistance and personal support to family members. Individuals rely on support from kin networks in order to achieve economic self-sufficiency and personal independence. Consequently, there is a congruence between the cultural ideals of self-sufficiency, independence, and noninterference, on the one hand, and the ideals of family loyalty and reciprocity, on the other.

On Caye Caulker, loyalty to kin is not only an ideal, it is a widespread reality as well. Kin have an obligation to help one another when in need and to engage in reciprocal economic exchanges. Relationships between kin are expected to be closer and more dependable than relationships between non-kin. For example, one group of brothers who work together as tour guides will include a brother who is crack addict, when he is capable of working, so he can have some income.

Relatives cooperate in a variety of ways in their work. A young man learns to fish with a father or an uncle. Later he may become the partner of a relative and share in the work and profits from their fishing together. Relatives will loan each other fishing equipment and tools. A father may give his son his first boat and motor. Eventually a man will inherit a lobster territory from a relative or begin one adjacent to that of a relative.

Exchanges of favors, labor, and food are expected between family members, and in general, relatives do not charge for services. There are indications that this general practice is beginning to break down, especially when the service, such as passage to Belize City or a meal at a restaurant, is the basis of a person's livelihood. It is also very common for relatives to eat regularly with each other. Children in particular are fed whenever they are present in a family member's home during a meal. Adult children and relatives who do not, for whatever reason, have a hot meal prepared for the day also regularly eat with parents or relatives. Although food is the most frequent item of exchange on Caye Caulker, child care is an equally important service, especially for the women. Children go freely to the homes of relatives to have a meal or be cared for by a female relative. Finally, family members share transportation to Belize City and back, and while there, they pick up mail or run errands for each other.

Members of extended families on Caye Caulker reinforce these obligations by participating in a system of reciprocal exchanges that provides everyone with some economic and social security. Some family members fail to reciprocate, but the obligation stands, nevertheless. As one man put it:

I know they won't have anything to eat unless I give them this chicken. He promised to come pay me Friday, and I know that he will pay me with money he got selling the lobsters he stole from my traps on Thursday. They're never gonna pay me, but they're still family, see.

Family members interact daily. In addition to being social, most of this interaction is based on a reciprocal exchange of goods and services:

I have just backed [carried] ten coconuts in a gunnysack to Anita (the speaker's husband's nephew's wife), for which I got one pint of coconut oil. Then I stopped by to pass the time of day with my mother-in-law, and she gave me a sack of limes and a breadfruit.

On Caye Caulker, men have always cooperated with each other on projects that require a group. Sometimes, friends and others who are not particularly busy at the time, or who enjoy the company and a shared bottle of rum, will join these work groups, but they have less obligation to do so than family members. For instance, boats have to be hauled up on the beach every three months to be scraped and painted. To haul up a sailboat or a skiff requires the efforts of several men. When a group assembles for this task, it becomes a social event. Work groups also form when a catastrophe strikes or there is some natural disaster. One day a huge storm knocked over one of the outhouses at the end of a pier. Five men formed a work group to lift the outhouse back onto the pier in order to allow access for an old lady.

The influx of new residents on the island and the introduction of wage labor have changed this cooperative system for large projects. Now most island families rely more on hired workers for these jobs than on relatives, particularly for construction of a new house, running a restaurant or hotel, or working on a boat.

Some families on Caye Caulker have become partners in business. The Reyes family is a good example of how a family partnership works. Ramón Reyes owns a hotel and restaurant. He and his brother Eduardo started out as fishing partners, but when the tourist business began to take more and more of their time, Ramón asked Eduardo to help him out. Eduardo commented, "I didn't think twice about working for Ramón even though I don't have to. But I see that it's all in the family, and I know if in the course of a year I need some cash, he will give it to me." However, as salaried jobs have been introduced on the island, this pattern is changing. I have suggested (Sutherland 1986) that reciprocity based on exchanges of goods and services might move to a more cash-based set of economic transactions. By 1996, it was clear that this transition had taken place. For example, with the opening of the airstrip on Caye Caulker, Eduardo had taken a salaried job with Island Air, one of the airlines that service Caye Caulker. Jobs with the telecommunications company, the electricity board, the airlines, and some government agencies were all filled by islanders. Furthermore, the hotel, restaurant, and tour guide businesses were employing many individuals in positions from management to day labor.

Even by 1986, transportation from the island to Belize City was beginning to move from being based on a casual exchange basis to a pay-as-you-go service. Because gasoline for the skiff motors was so expensive, and anyone making a trip to Belize City can charge tourists for a place, islanders began charging each other as well. Close family members still provided transportation as a service, but non-family and sometimes distant relatives were having to pay on a regular basis. Hotel and restaurant work had already started to turn to wage labor. As the tourist trade developed during the

1980s and early 1990s, businesses on Caye Caulker needed more labor, and this attracted a labor force from other parts of the country.

The nature of interaction between members of the extended family is understood by everyone and is an accepted part of island culture. So it is with friends and others beyond the family. Fights do occur, and a returning ex-convict, for example, may be viewed by all with suspicion; but the ideals of tolerance and noninterference, combined with loyalty and aid to family members, still prevail.

FAMILY NAMES, FAMILY LAND

People on Caye Caulker trace descent bilaterally through their father as well as their mother, using the same kin terms that are used in English. The surname is generally that of the father but not rigidly so: most children take their father's last name (whether he was married to their mother or not), although they may, and sometimes do, take their mother's name. Women generally take their husband's surname at marriage.

Thus islanders belong to loosely formed bilateral kin groups that are lumped together under a family surname. The community is composed of a small number of such kin groups, virtually all of whom are interconnected through generations of marriages. Because of the multiple interconnections between kin groups, sorting out people's kin relationships is complicated. The easiest way to discover the relationship between two people is to take account of two variables: the person's surname and the location of the person's residence or household on the island. Sometimes the last name of a person fails to reveal the tie to a major kin group; in that case, the relationship can be determined by where the person lives and through which kin tie he or she obtained land to build a home.

Identification with a family name, participation in a family support network, and acquisition of land on Caye Caulker are closely connected. During the formation of the community, the large kin groups became situated in specific areas of the island. These areas, or localities, have been, and still are, important as spatial arenas for the family networks. Family members visit each other, borrow from each other, and share economic and social support within a specific area of the village.

In 1986, families from one locality did not usually visit other parts of the island. People generally kept to their own locality and carried on their daily activities there. This pattern changed considerably with the growth in population and the opening up of a new site in the north part of the island to young families. Now the older and younger generations visit each evening at one or the other's residences.

The self-sufficiency of the localities is still very obvious on Caye Caulker. Each locality has a pier or two, shared by the kin who live in that area. In this way even inland households have access to the sea and a place to dock their skiff and to clean their catch. The localities of the larger kin groups also have a dry goods store run by one of the families. Someone in the locale may bake bread or make coconut oil that family members (and others, too) can buy. People in family localities often rely on reciprocal exchange rather than cash. If they need to borrow tools or equipment, or require help with building or transporting, they may give a loaf of bread, a bottle of rum, or some fish in return. Families also help each other without payment. For example, they may get together to haul a boat, or they may allow kin to collect breadfruit and sell them without any expectation of return. Each family locality has one or more hotels, rental houses, restaurants, bars, or bakeries for the tourist trade. In 1982 businesses were well distributed throughout the island with each locality supporting most necessary services. Thus, no one had to leave a locality to buy what was needed. Consequently, for the most part, family members did not stray too far from their area. Only on rare occasions, and usually for specific reasons, does one find a Badillo at the southern end of the island or a Marin at the northern end. This pattern is no longer so established, since the proliferation of stores and businesses all over the island, and the move to tourism over lobster fishing as a primary source of work, have loosened movement around the island.

There are eight main family localities on Caye Caulker, based on the original founding families. From north to south, they are the Badillo, Alamina, Herredia, Rosado, Magana, Rodriquez, Marin, Reyes, and Young families. The Badillo and Marin families have the largest localities, but in all cases, although the localities are relatively self-sufficient, there is always some overlapping with families in other locales.

The formation of these family localities is primarily the result of land distribution practices throughout the history of the island. The availability of land for building a house was always limited, but in the past, when subsistence fishing was the only source of income, land was inexpensive. Families could purchase land very cheaply and pass it on to their descendants. New households could thus be established through purchases adjacent to kin localities; since 1986, as the population has grown, this easy access to land has changed. Also, when commercial fishing became very profitable, and tourism became an alternative source of income, land suddenly became very expensive and scarce. Concerned with keeping the land in their families, people have, on the whole, been careful not to allow it to be sold to foreigners. However, this unwritten rule has broken down recently, with land sold to Belizeans and non-Belizeans. Islanders, too, have been buying land outside their localities.

In the past, land was obtained through inheritance. Eduardo and Ramón Reyes' grandfather owned a large section in the middle of the village. He transferred the title to several plots to Eduardo and Ramón, and they in turn have provided their children with land. When islanders purchased land from a non-family member, they tried to buy a piece close to their kin, and islanders who wished to sell land were expected to sell to their kin. Selling land to non-kin was, and still is, viewed as somewhat unscrupulous. There is still a strong feeling among many islanders that kin have a right to their choice of land and that the owner does not have the right to sell to non-kin. The wealthier islanders are buying up land, even at today's prices, and they call on this value system to get preferential access to land coming up for sale.

Another factor that has changed access to land is the government program for distribution of Crown lands acquired at independence from Britain. Because of the demand for lots to build houses, the Belizean government obtained a large tract of land near the cut at the north end on the island, with the aim of distributing it to those who want to live on Caye Caulker but do not have land. This land distribution program has occurred all over Belize and has been very successful at guaranteeing every Belizean a piece of land on which to build a house. Since 1986 both islanders and other Belizeans (over the age of 18) who did not already own land have applied for lots, with islanders given first preference. Applicants were screened by the Land Committee, which consists of members of the Village Council. When an individual's application was approved, there was a raffle to draw a lot. All the lots in the new site north of the village up to the cut were distributed in the 1980s. This area is now a thriving new community, consisting mainly of young families. The new site, having been distributed by lottery, is not organized around extended family localities. Many lots have already changed hands, and continue to be bought and sold. New lots are being distributed north of the cut in the mangrove area, where presumably another community will develop.

The kin relations, values, social categories, access to land, and fishing territories I have described are not obvious to casual visitors to the island. With the changes taking place on Caye Caulker, changes that reverberate nationally and globally, certain tensions have developed, primarily between "islanders" who have lived all their lives on Caye Caulker and the "Belizeans" who have come to live and work there more recently. Islanders view these newcomers as interlopers and outsiders, and the newcomers are resentful of the elitist attitude of the islanders, who, for the most part, are better off. A new class system has emerged just as it has nationwide —"born Belizeans" are juxtaposed against Belizeans who are arrivals from outside the country (Chinese, Americans, Canadians, and Europeans); the lowest category is the Central American immigrants, who are referred to as "aliens."

4

Flapping Around

When I wrote *Caye Caulker: Economic Success in a Belizean Fishing Village* (1986), my niece, then a high school student who had been to Belize several times, read parts of it and commented, "Why didn't you put all the interesting stuff in it? All the gossip, the sex with tourists, and the sleeping around." She was right; I had not written much about what the locals call "flapping around," even though it may be the first thing every visitor notices. Rampant sexual libido is a well-known part of the sun-sea-sex kind of tourism, and Caye Caulker is no exception. Virtually every plane or boat I take from Caye Caulker has a female tourist who was seen off by a Rasta man, a situation giving the impression that a sexual liaison with a Rasta is an essential part of the female neo-hippie experience.

But sexual license has never been restricted to foreign tourists. Islanders have a long history of forming multiple sexual liaisons and households. One longtime resident jokingly claimed that "during the Easter holidays, Belize City upper-class girls often got pregnant while still virgins, though they swam off the end of the piers, fully dressed, with their friends while the chaperones sat ashore under a coconut tree, chatting . . ." (Bz-Culture@psg.com, from trust2@juno.com March 25, 1997). On Caye Caulker aphrodisiacs are a favorite topic of conversation, with the effectiveness of eating lobster and conch high on the list. In the same vein, one resident swore that his libido increased significantly if he drank one quart of rainwater a day; it had to be collected from a roof of galvanized zinc covered with pelican droppings.

In spite of all the talk about sexual activity, which is probably greater than the activity itself, Caye Caulker has its standards of respectability. Nudity, for example, is frowned upon among the locals. Europeans who desire to sunbathe nude are quickly corrected by the local population (staring and laughing usually work), and even at the "cut," which European tourists have tried to make into a nude beach, there is a "No Nude Bathing" sign. Despite the sun-sea-sex tourism on Caye Caulker, the local framework of social mores and sexual relations produces families and community networks that are often not obvious to tourists.

CARIBBEAN REPUTATION AND RESPECTABILITY

It is commonly accepted that in the English-speaking Caribbean there is a dual system of values, labeled "respectability" and "reputation," that operates simultaneously and applies primarily to men (Wilson 1973). Those who seek respectability base their lives on a stable marriage and home, close relations with extended family, investment in education for themselves and their children, community service, and participation in church. The other set of values focuses on forging a "reputation." A man's reputation in the Caribbean is made on the streets and in public bars. In the reputation system of values, a man gains status for his sexual conquests and impregnation of women. With the status gained by frequent sexual conquests (tourist women, in particular) go clever verbal repartee and patter, and a lifestyle of dancing, drinking, and partying with a different woman every night (Wilk 1995).

Reputation can be gained through sexuality and fertility, by mastery of local gossip and verbal performance, but also with the latest New York hip hop, untied pump basketball shoes and a "dread" belt. Acquiring respectability can entail visible public service or a church marriage into a light-skinned family, but may also involve an American college diploma, an imported pure-bred Alsatian or a passion for wildlife conservation and bird watching. (Wilk 1995, 117)

Most studies link this dual set of values of reputation and respectability to colonialism, under which respectability was sought by those who wanted to emulate their masters, whereas reputation was a form of resistance to colonial mores. In Belize this dualism has become part of the national culture not only for Creoles, but for most of the ethnic groups. Also, far from being separate systems, as sometimes has been claimed, in Belize many individual life cycles include both. A young man, for example, may seek reputation in his youth and later settle down to respectability, only to return to reputation in his middle-to-later years, when the children are raised and his wife is old.

How do women fare in this system? Comparison of the "position" of women from one culture to another is notoriously slippery. Of late, non-Western feminists have complained loudly about one kind of feminism (American and European) being set up as an ideal for women in other parts of the world. While not wanting to tread in these murky waters, I would suggest that there are different kinds of freedoms and obligations, and it is hard to assess how women fare in the local context. The freedom to be sexual can turn into the obligation to be sexual, the freedom to work can become the obligation to work, and the obligation to bear children and form a family can ultimately be a source of support and power, as well as one of a woman's most rewarding life experiences. In many ways sexuality is less repressive in Belize than it is in Minnesota (admittedly an unfair comparison), but communication between spouses and lovers is less prevalent in Belize than in Minnesota. In Belize women are strong, but they also are sometimes beaten and treated badly. These are very subjective issues, not resolvable here but of great importance.

SEXUAL RELATIONSHIPS AND DOMESTIC GROUPS

In the area of sexual relationships and the formation of domestic groups or households, Caye Caulker is a synthesis of the Caribbean values of reputation and respectability, and household formation centers around a nuclear or extended family based on a primary conjugal relationship. This is a pattern that combines elements of the English-speaking Caribbean and Latin America, and while it may be a particular construction local to Caye Caulker, there is reason to believe that such a pattern can be found elsewhere in Belize as well. Virginia Kerns (1983), for example, reports this pattern among the Garifuna in the south.

Domestic unions are based on one of three kinds of conjugal relationships: Christian marriage, consensual union without formal marriage, or a "visiting" relationship. Consensual unions are common-law unions in which partners live in the same household, and visiting relationships are conjugal relationships in which partners live in different households. For the most part, "visiting" is very subtle and low-key, the couple meeting in a remote place in an attempt to keep their relationship secret. Some visiting relationships remain in that state for the duration of the couple's life. For example, I know of several visiting relationships that are stable in the sense that the woman lives with her parents and has children with one man only. The man may engage in other sexual relationships, but he seems to be a stable partner in the visiting relationship. When a woman has a child from a visiting relationship, there is pressure for the father to recognize the child. It is good for a man's reputation to demonstrate fertility by recognizing the child, although he may be less than eager to take responsibility for contributing to the child's support. A visiting relationship may become a consensual union if the man is able to support the woman and child by providing a place for them to live.

Consensual unions are very common and accepted, but it is the relationship between consensual unions and Christian marriage that is most interesting in Belize. Christian marriage carries prestige but is not a requirement for a socially acceptable union. A very common developmental cycle for households on Caye Caulker, for example, is for a young couple to start off with a Christian marriage. This marriage may end in separation, in which case each member moves on to a consensual union that is longer-term and more stable than the marriage. Many older couples on Caye Caulker have very long-lasting consensual unions, with the legal wife and/or husband living nearby. (See Figure 4.1.)

Figure 4.1
Current Marital Status, by Age

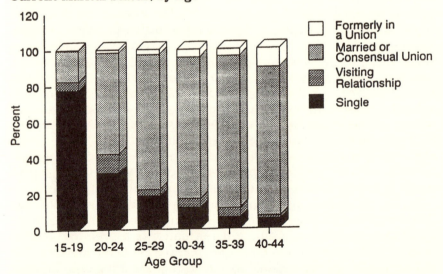

Source: *1991 Belize Family Health Survey.* May 1992. Final Report. Atlanta: U.S. Department of Health and Human Services, Centers for Disease Control.

The Caribbean values of reputation and respectability, described here for Caye Caulker, are also national values. Conjugal relationships are at the heart of the reproduction of families and households, and the sometimes fragile ways that families are formed and interact are not always compatible with the formation of civil society. The complications of associations beyond family are continuous points of tension in the making of the nation. Both educational institutions and government ministries struggle to create some sense of a common identity for Belizeans.

GENDER

According to one study, women constitute 50 percent of the world's population, provide one-third of the official labor force, toil for two-thirds of all working hours, receive one-tenth of the world's income, and own less than 1 percent of the world's property (Lundgren 1993, 365). In many ways, Belize is no exception. Women traditionally have had responsibility for domestic work and raising children, supported by men who are supposed to take responsibility for providing financial support.

In reality, each ethnic group has its own particular history regarding work, and of course situational circumstances may alter the nature of traditional roles to some extent. Garifuna, Creole, and Maya women have always worked both within and outside the household, while the "Spanish" women on Caye Caulker have worked primarily within the household. The availability of jobs on Caye Caulker is bringing about changes in this pattern. Female-headed households are more common in Creole and Garifuna areas, but they exist on Caye Caulker as well. Although it may offend feminist sensibilities, I would suggest that the clarity of the ideal gender roles in Belize has an important consequence, that of reducing tension between the sexes about the obligations of one spouse to the other. Relations between the sexes in Belize benefit from the lack of feminist ambiguity, although they may suffer when one partner does not fulfill his or her role. A good spouse is one who carries out his or her obligations. Tension in the union stems primarily from failure to perform the appropriate duties.

On Caye Caulker a man traditionally provided for a wife and children primarily through fishing. Fishing was, and still is, exclusively men's work, and being a fisherman was a primary identity for a man. Manliness was based on operating a boat, knowing the reef and fishing grounds, and bringing in a good income. Being a responsible family man who does not run around too much, does not beat his wife, and takes care of his children's welfare and education is very important for a man's respectability status. At the same time, a reputation for success at sexual conquest and ability to have children is also viewed as manly. Most men seek both kinds of status.

Men establish tourist-related businesses, such as a bar, shop, or restaurant. They also take tourists to the reef, to Belize City and to San Pedro, handle tourist needs in a hotel, and take responsibility for building the family-owned hotel, restaurant, or shop. Some men, who in the past were full-time fishermen, have turned entirely to tourism. Emilio Novello, who built the first hotel in 1970, claims to be the first fisherman on Caye Caulker to retire and work only at tourism. Beli Martinez and Ramón Reyes and their respective families run a combination hotel, bar, and restaurant. A few men are also known for their ability as boatbuilders or carpenters. The Young family, for instance, has a reputation for producing good carpenters and boatbuilders, highly regarded for their work. All the men in the Young family have also worked as fishermen.

Although many of their jobs are at home and in the kin locality, the men often socialize in public places such as the lanes, bars, and main docks. Building lobster traps, mending nets, and building or repairing houses can be done close to home or in the kin locality. But some of their work, such as fishing, selling produce at the cooperative, and buying supplies in Belize City, requires them to go beyond the kin locality. A fisherman often spends his mornings at sea, the afternoons at home working on projects, and the evenings socializing with other men.

In contrast, a woman's sphere of activity is domestic and focuses on the kin locality. The woman is responsible for taking care of her children, preparing the family's meals, washing clothes, cleaning the house and yard, and looking after the family's religious and educational interests. The greater part of each day is taken up with domestic chores that center on the home. Women have less time than men to visit friends and relatives. Occasionally they can be seen walking their children to school or to church. They are less often seen standing in their yards visiting with neighbors, running errands, or walking to the house next door.

Being a mother is a primary role for a woman. It is also considered normal for women to be sexually active. Although women are expected to form stable unions and have children, the status of a family is not dependent on the sexual purity of its women. Being a mother is not viewed as diminishing a woman's sexuality. It is not unusual for girls and women over 15 to have visiting relationships; however, whereas for men a visiting relationship in addition to a consensual union is viewed as a sign of manliness and something to brag about with other men, women are more circumspect about their reputation in this area. On Caye Caulker men talk to other men about sexual conquests, but this information is not passed on to the women. Women, of course, have their own sources of information. Children, for example, who roam the island more than any adult, are very knowledgeable of sexual activities.

Before the 1980s the only viable source of income for women on the island came from the few teaching jobs at the local primary school. These jobs always went to recent teacher's college graduates—girls who returned from the mainland to teach until they had families of their own. Women who were widowed or abandoned by a husband could make coconut oil and bake bread, but the income from these tasks was meager. These women depended heavily on relatives to help them financially until they could establish another union with a man. Basically, at this time, a female-headed household was not a viable unit on Caye Caulker, because even the financial support of a large group of relatives is very limited. In 1982, one woman remarked, "There are virtually no single women on the island who live without a man, not even living with their own grown children. Likewise, a widower usually seeks another woman to share his space and fulfill his needs."

The division of labor and the complementarity of men's and women's responsibilities in the domestic group make the conjugal unit an important part of every household. Kerns reports that among the Garifuna, 89 percent of households are based on the nuclear family but also contain extended family members (1983, 122); the household focus is primarily on women's work. For the Maya, Wilk reports that households, based on a nuclear family, usually also include a parent, a stepchild or a half brother (1991, 241). In one survey, Maya households averaged just over five persons per household; work groups often consisted of a cluster of related households (1991, 215).

By the early 1980s a major shift in economic opportunities for women was beginning to take place in Belize. During this time, opportunities for work in tourism created the possibility of a higher income for women. The creation of businesses and jobs in tourism did not necessarily change the roles that women and men performed. Men still did the physical labor of building a hotel or shop, and women cooked, served, and cleaned for the tourists. Nevertheless, the cash income that women generated gave them an economic independence that was significant and impacted general relations between the sexes. More girls were able to stay in the place where they grew up and were under less pressure to find a spouse in their teens. Many girls now are well into their twenties before they find a partner, and when they do form their own households, they continue to bring in an income and contribute to the support of their children. In addition, the emergence of income-producing women's work meant that a household could have more varied means of support. When income from fishing is low, women sell coconut pies and *garnaches* (fried tortillas covered with refried beans and hot peppers) from their homes, bringing in supplemental income. Some women began to operate regular businesses, such as a restaurant or hotel. Most depended on their partner's help in these endeavors, and some ran the business jointly; however, men continued to fish and operate a lobster territory, working the tourist trade only during slack fishing times. The responsibility for, and the income from, these tourist businesses often went to the women. Gradually, throughout the 1980s, men began to turn to tourism on a more full-time basis, but only after women had established a strong foothold in the business. Today, there are many more jobs available for women in shops, offices, and travel agencies.

CHILDREN

Children are an important link between households. They carry messages, run errands, and shop for their mothers at the local stores. Children move around the island more freely than adults do, and are an important link in the communication of information and gossip. The amazing speed with which news travels from one end of the island to the other is partly explained by the light-footedness of the children in carrying this news.

In the past, children had an important role in the distribution of food. When a woman decided to offer food for sale, she sent the children to spread the word throughout the village. The children told other villagers and children in the locality, and the children then relayed the information to their mothers. The women passed the information along to their neighbors and friends, again often using their children as messengers. The children took orders for cooked food or went and picked up a meal for a relative. With the opening of restaurants with regular hours, islanders now pick up food directly from the restaurants and are using children less frequently to relay infomation about availability of cooked food. However, children still go door-to-door with pastries and bread baked by their mothers to help supplement the family income.

Children are taught at an early age to be responsible for their own actions, to take care of themselves, and to become independent. For example, if a child is injured, his or her family views the injury as the child's fault, and he or she may be reprimanded for not being careful. Children are expected to learn from experience and trial and error. Three-year-old boys are given fish knives and are expected to learn to be use them without cutting themselves. If they cut themselves, parents explain that it probably will not happen again, now that they have learned what not to do. Even as toddlers, children must learn to avoid the dangers of island life— falling off a pier, touching a Portuguese man-of-war, or stepping on broken glass or a conch shell. Once I watched a mother cleaning fish by the shore. Several times she warned her crawling child not to touch a dead man-of-war on the beach, although she did not explain why. The child's curiosity prevailed, and he was badly stung. The mother continued to clean fish, ignoring the welts and the screams of the child, who, she explained, had now learned never to touch a man-of-war.

Children are expected to stay out of trouble, and injuries are viewed as an indication the child has done something wrong. One girl broke her toe while playing. She did not cry, nor did she tell her father about it, because he would get mad at her. Another time a young boy was badly cut while playing in the bush behind the school. Because he was not supposed to be playing there, the principal scolded him when she found out. Children are often reluctant to go to an adult when they get hurt because they are then scolded.

Perhaps the most striking aspect of adult-child interactions is the teasing children are expected to endure. Children are constantly teased by their parents, siblings, and relatives, mostly in a kind way. They are expected to endure the teasing without necessarily taking it seriously. For example, Cindy and her infant cousin were often in the care of Cindy's 14-year-old sister, Ruth. Ruth teased them by hiding from them, prodding them, or threatening to abandon them. Ruth was delighted when they started to cry. "Want to see them cry? I can make him cry. Ta-ta. Ta-ta." She pretended to leave the room, and her infant cousin's face pruned up, and he finally dissolved into tears. "I love it when he cry. I like his face."

Though the young children almost always get a hug afterward, they are nevertheless immediately teased again. Teasing generally concentrates on four areas: hiding from the child, threatening to leave the child, threat of physical harm, and insults about appearance. Hiding and leaving evoke the most response, insults about appearance are often ignored, and threats of harm are frequently laughed off.

Even very young children learn how to respond to teasing. When adults relate to children by teasing, children are expected to stand up for themselves and trust their own resources rather than the adults. Jessica's little boy, Toby, one and a half years old, was teased one day by an uncle who poked a clothespin at him, laughing cheerfully the whole time. "Toby, hold out your finger. Give me your finger, Toby." He clicked the spring clothespin. Toby, frowning, looked very suspicious and put his hands into tight fists, close to his chest, indicating that he knew what would happen if he stuck out his finger. Everyone laughed heartily at Toby's gesture.

COMMUNITY RELATIONS

Religion arrived on Caye Caulker with the first mestizo settlers, who brought their Catholic faith with them from Yucatan. The first church was built in the 1880s. It was used occasionally when priests from Belize City came to the island, but there were no regular weekly services. Everyone on the island was at least nominally Catholic, but without a priest or much organization, religious beliefs persisted primarily on a personal level. Only since the 1970s have priests begun visiting the island from Belize City on a weekly basis to conduct Sunday worship services. In 1982 a cement block church was constructed, and in 1983 six lay ministers were ordained from among the islanders, after 10 months of study. These lay ministers are now qualified to lead services. The Catholic Church had been the only religious body on the island for nearly a century when Protestant missionaries began arriving, one by one, in the late 1970s. Initially they had little impact; however, the Assembly of God Church gained a foothold on Caye Caulker.

Although its membership is small, the Assembly of God Church brought some significant changes to the island. Because it believes in active conversion rather than noninterference, and because by church doctrine virtually all nonconverted islanders are sinners, there is a clash of values between the converted and the unconverted. For example, the church takes a strong stand against drinking and adultery. According to several men and their wives, their conversion has improved their family lives because the men spend more time at home and do not drink. However, it has also divided families. If only one spouse converts, for example, tension between husband and wife inevitably results. In several cases conversion has strained or caused severed relations between kin as well as lifelong friends; in some cases, it has even resulted in a break in the traditional kinship support networks.

Many Catholics feel threatened or betrayed by the converts, and members of the Assembly of God Church feel some anger toward the Catholic Church because they believe that a personal relationship with Jesus Christ is not possible within the Catholic doctrine. Further, they strongly disapprove of many of the actions of some members of the Catholic Church, such as drinking or carrying on visiting relationships. Some Assembly of God members have severed relations with friends or relatives whose actions they believe are immoral. The Assembly of God Church is the only force that has been able to erode family support networks on Caye Caulker, an indication of its current strength. A woman whose family converted after her daughter was healed at a prayer session aptly described the dilemma of conversion:

We all got saved. . . . It was like a bomb dropped on the Catholic Church. They even called a priest from the United States to convince us to come back. Our best friends turned their backs on us. I remember on my birthday, standing looking out my window with tears streaming down my face, because all my friends left me. But I had found a new friend—Jesus.

This community divisiveness due to the arrival of evangelical churches has been reported in other parts of Belize. Lundgren, for example, indicates that Pentecostal religions are proliferating in Belize,

creating contentious divisions within villages, towns and neighborhoods. One way to draw people into the church is to provide supportive activities for the women. Thus, women's groups of all kinds are forming, forcing women to make choices which divide their communities in ways in which they were not previously divided. I was told that this creates tensions which are not always easy to resolve. (Lundgren 1993, 374)

Missionaries for evangelical churches, whether American or Belizean, are ever present in Belize. Boats traveling between Belize City and Caye Caulker regularly carry a number of "brothers" wearing Ray-Bans and heavy gold rings, and carrying nice luggage. The leader, a missionary from Africa, prays that God and Allah will watch over the passengers.

Both the Catholic and evangelical churches are involved in charity work, but most communities in Belize have other organizations devoted to good works, such as the Lion's Club, the Rotary Club, and DARE. Individuals who participate in these organizations gain respectability in the community. There is now, and always has been, a great deal of infighting in these communitywide organizations. On Caye Caulker, for example, there is still skepticism toward the activities of the Village Council, but it has managed, even if imperfectly, to regulate garbage disposal, maintain roads, and control insects. On Caye Caulker, as in other places, active participation in the Northern Fishermen Cooperative is also an important source of status.

Today, Caye Caulker is connected with the rest of Belize. The Northern Fishermen Cooperative is an established and important feature of the country's fishing industry. Boats to Caye Caulker have a new marine terminal in Belize City that includes a maritime museum, a coffee shop, clean bathrooms, shops, and tickets for passage on a water taxi sold from a booth. According to John Connerley of the U.S. Embassy, this terminal was the last project in Belize funded by the USAID.

Since the beginning of the 1990s, tourist organizations have become important. The Belize Tourist Association now trains tour guides, and the Caye Caulker Water Taxi Association has an office on Caye Caulker as well as a marina in Belize City. Membership in these organizations is crucial for obtaining hotel and water taxi permits. The fierce economic individualism of the men of Caye Caulker is now being tempered by the enforcement of nationally established rules and regulations in these organizations.

PART II

A Nation in the Making

5

The Nation in the Making

The hallmark of modernity is the formation of the nation-state and the priority of nationalism over local or tribal affiliations. The notion of a nation-state developed first in Europe, under conditions in which the territorial boundaries of a people with a common history, language, and territory dovetailed so closely with the formation of the state that the early nation-states contained people of one ethnic background and language, living more or less in one territory. Later modern states—such as India, Indonesia, and most African states—were more complex imagined entities, à la Benedict Anderson (1983), in which the state consisted of many nations coming under its aegis. These later modern states also arose under conditions of colonialism, and therefore were in a dialogue with both their colonial past and many ethnic groups.

Belize represents another, and perhaps a final, phase in the historical process of nation-making, a phenomenon also being experienced in the new states of Central Asia. Like other later modern states, Belize always had diverse ethnic groups or nations in different localities of the colony, and thus is forming under both postcolonial and multicultural conditions. In addition to these frameworks within which it has to stretch its wings, Belize is becoming a state in postmodern times, times marked by instant media-transmitted events, images of the world at large, and a shrinking of distance. Furthermore, Belize is becoming a state just at the time when the concept of the state is being undermined by the forces of globalization. Not only multinational corporations but also transnational organizations such as the World

Bank, the International Monetary Fund, and a multitude of non-governmental organizations (NGOs) operate virtually independently of the state. Supranational and regional political and trade organizations such as the Caribbean Community and Common Market (CARICOM), the Organization of American States (OAS), and the North American Free Trade Agreement (NAFTA) override the traditional roles of the state in economic and trade matters. All of these elements are part of the large-scale imagined possibilities that a state such as Belize can access. The making of a nation in these times has more possibilities than ever before, but whether this proves to be an advantage or a disadvantage depends on how those large-scale possibilities coincide with concrete local worlds and individual life trajectories.

How Belizeans frame their national identity in the present (in museums, the Central Bank, the courts) and imagine the past (in national myths, colonial history, the Westminster system) will create a certain kind of locality. That locality will include collective ideas of ethnicity and identity politics as well as boundary-maintenance questions among the diverse ethnic groups, as well as between Belizeans and tourists, foreign residents, and immigrants. If culture is a useful device for talking about difference, then the mobilization of group identities in the new nation of Belize is about the formation of local Belizean culture.

THE NATION AS IDEOSCAPE

As a former British colony, Belize follows the Westminster system of parliamentary democracy, which puts one political party in power through elections to the House of Representatives. The party is led by a prime minister, and the ministers appointed by the party in power and the government bureaucracy have almost complete control of the daily operation of government. Belize is formally a democracy; in practice, an autocracy. This structure of democratic authoritarianism, a British colonial legacy, oversees a stable country with no history of civil war, violent conflict, or coups d'état—no small feat in such a diverse society located in a geographical region of incessant violence. At the same time, it is run by a very small number of elites who have tight control of the spoils of government and run the country as their personal fiefdom. The cabinet, which consists of numerous ministries, is composed of a substantial number of the members of the House of Representatives, making the cabinet "in effect the legislative as well as the executive power, with the house acting as a rubber stamp" (*Profile of Belize* 1990, 6).

Belize is a young nation whose identity with Britain was very strong right up to independence in September 1981. Many Belizeans were reluctant to become independent, and even decorated their cars and houses with the Union Jack to show their desire to stay with Britain. They wanted the British military to protect them from Guatemala, their highly armed and hostile neighbor to the west, and they wanted the financial aid that Britain could provide. Some also had a genuine affection for the British, an affection that reflected their positive attitudes toward British law and the English language as well as their historical mistrust of the Spanish colonial empire. The independence movement took hold of many Belizeans' imagination nevertheless, and in the end, the transition was relatively painless.

As a stable, democratic country in a politically volatile region, Belize enjoys a strategic position in the globalization process currently racing through the Caribbean and Central America. Located on the Central American mainland facing the Caribbean, Belize has physical and cultural ties to both regions and shares borders with Mexico and Guatemala. The long sovereignty dispute with Guatemala still bubbles up occasionally but on the whole has settled down into a non-issue. British troops left Belize during 1993, with a loss of U.S.$40 million in revenue and of a major deterent to Guatemalan aggression. The fledgling Belize Defense Force now has responsibility for Belize's external and internal security. The political turmoil in Central America in the 1980s, which affected Belize by suddenly increasing the flow of refugees from Guatemala, El Salvador, and Honduras, has subsided somewhat.

During the Reagan years (1980–1988) the American government targeted both the Caribbean basin and Central America as areas for major investment and political concern. U.S. policy in the region focused on promoting pro-American governments and discouraging the creation of socialist governments. The invasion of Grenada in 1983 and the political, economic, and military involvement of the United States in Guatemala, El Salvador, Honduras, and Nicaragua are only the most recent events in a long history of U.S. manuevers in the region. The threat of socialism and communism is now a distant and somewhat unreal memory.

The United States turned its attention to Belize in the 1980s with an eye to ensuring the stability of the fledgling government as well as promoting U.S. business interests. The United States, Belize's principal trading partner and the main source of investment funds, became the largest provider of economic assistance to Belize through the USAID program, which poured money into the economy and infrastructure. The Peace Corps began operations in Belize, and at its peak had more than 100 volunteers in the country. Today the effects of the severely reduced foreign mission budget (state department and aid) are very visible. The Peace Corps is much reduced in numbers, and the USAID and U.S. Information Service no longer exist. Interestingly, the United Nations Development Programme and European Community aid programs continue, and both Taiwan and Japan are larger providers of foreign aid than the United States. The influence of the United States may be affected, though it is still to soon too know how this will play out.

THE WESTMINSTER SYSTEM

Belize has two main political parties, the United Democratic Party (UDP) and the People's United Party (PUP), and holds regular elections that are reasonably fair and democratic. However, once a party is elected and becomes the government, democracy is highly compromised because the system has no built-in checks and balances and no cultural tradition of a democratic civil society or common law to provide protection from abuse of power. This kind of democracy has been called a low-intensity democracy because although it is formally democratic (i.e., elections, opposition party, press, etc.), it lacks the informal institutions and cultural accoutrements of democracy (i.e., civil organizations, media not silenced by intimidation, a nonpolitical judicial system, grievance processes, etc.).

Because of the almost complete power of the party in office, people are reluctant to protest against those in power or even to speak out against them. Retaliation against those who do so is common. There are many examples of a new government canceling contracts with people who supported the previous government and punishing towns and villages that voted for the opposition by leaving them to stagnate without government support. Because of these abuses of power, the electorate has, since independence, created a yo-yo system of government, with each party in power being voted out in the next election.

For 20 years (1961–1981), George Price governed Belize. He was the first premier of the colony, and after independence he was the first prime minister until the elections of 1984. He was described by Graham Greene (1984), who met him briefly, as a likable man, not unlike a parish priest in his demeanor, and in touch with his people, espousing benevolent, elitist ideas of socialism. In spite of Price's popularity, Belizean voters tired of one-party rule, and in 1984 elected a new party, the UDP, to power. Manuel Esquivel became the Prime Minister. The UDP government stood for liberal economic policies, encouraged foreign investment, and was extremely friendly to the United States. Its time in power launched the heyday of American involvement in Belize, with money and Peace Corps volunteers pouring into the country. Five years later, voters disgusted with UDP political scandals and corruption supported the PUP and George Price became Prime Minister once again. Four years later, the UDP returned to power. The next election, due to be held in June 1998, will almost certainly oust the unpopular UDP government and see the return of the PUP under its new leader, Said Musa. In a precursor to this election, the municipal elections for town boards took place in March 1997. The PUP swept into power in virtually all the districts, indicating that people are ready to yo-yo back to it. Each change of government has shifted the spoils of governing from one small group of elites to another, so although elections are fair and democratic, the process of governing is viewed by most Belizeans as corrupt and exploitative. When the party in power becomes too blatantly corrupt, Belizeans vote in the opposition party and the cycle begins again. Already the UDP is attempting to ward off defeat by creating a new list of registered voters that they can control. However, reregistration is plagued with accusations of corruption because it is being handled by a company owned by the Prime Minister's wife (*Amandala* 1997f, 3).

Corruption is built into the system. Belize has been described by many as an elected party dictatorship and police state. The election is significant primarily as a time when each party hands out spoils in the competition to get votes (Moberg 1991). Persecution and victimization of opponents by those in power is led by the ministers of government, but they are by no means the only abusers of party power. The system of party politics filters down to the village level, affecting every home in the nation. When one party takes office, village councils that are of the same party tend to punish individuals of the opposite political allegiance. Members of village councils of the party in power settle political and personal vendettas against village families with whom they are feuding. They use the opportunity, for example, to deny those families access to ownership of land distributed by land committees. Party members are able to do this because they are backed up by the ministries in the capital. Some villages are neglected for the five years of an administration because they elected a village council and mayor of the opposition party.

In June 1993, when the current UDP government was elected to office, it announced that it needed to "clean up" the failures of the last government and reduce the external debt. At the urging of the International Monetary Fund, the government decided to support the inflated Belize dollar and not allow it to be devalued; it fired a large contingent of civil servants (mostly PUP supporters who held their jobs as political spoils); it refused to honor promises that the PUP had made to some of its friends; and it sold the government-owned Banana Control Board and Belize Telecommunications, Ltd., and partially privatized Belize Electricity, Ltd. The state was reduced to control of only the major public authorities, employing 14.5 percent of the workforce. Journalists and PUP politicians and businessmen printed stinging criticisms of these measures (*The Courier* 1995).

By 1996 the corruption in the UDP government had begun to peak. With no processes of consultation with civil groups built into the government structure, and almost complete control of information, the government basically operates in secret. Complaints by the media that the government will neither release information nor allow government employees to talk to the media are met with threats. But with the next election on the horizon, the unpopular Esquivel government is looking to improve its image, for example, by promising pay raises for civil servants. After the last election, infrastructure improvement projects begun by the PUP were halted, but now the government is moving to finish the Hummingbird Highway, a much-needed link to the remote, agricultural south.

Perhaps the most powerful man in Belize is Dean Barrow, who is Minister of Foreign Affairs, Minister of National Security (Belize Defense Force and police), Minister of Immigration and Nationality (customs), Minister of the Media, and Attorney General (courts and legal system). The opposition paper, *The Belize Times*, regularly refers to him as "the Minister of Everything," bringing to attention the concentration of power in one man's hands. *The Times* also accuses him of close connections with a lawyer who, in a high-profile legal case, defended major drug dealers who were caught red-handed with a planeload of cocaine. This so inflamed the outgoing U.S. Embassy Deputy Chief of Mission, Gerard Galucci, that he gave an uncharacteristically angry interview to *The Reporter* in which he said that a government with an official whose family defends drug dealers is a government that is not trying to stop drugs. Barrow is not the only minister associated with the legal defense of drug smugglers. The speaker of the House of Representatives, William Pitts, also defended accused Colombian drug barons in a famous case. His law partner, Wilfred Elrington, is the speaker of the Senate, a nominated body.

Drug connections with the government are not new. Before Dean Barrow became "minister of everything," the Minister of National Security was Elito Urbina, whose son-in-law was indicted for drug smuggling when he was caught with an airplane being loaded with cocaine in Orange Walk. Unfortunately, the police vehicle that was carrying the evidence burned up on the way to the trial in Belize City. Fortunately, the two police officers acting as drivers, who came under the jurisdiction of Minister Urbina, escaped without being roasted. The evidence, of course, went up in flames.

THE COURTS

The judicial system in Belize is intricately linked to the government ministers in power. The system suffers from the small number of lawyers and judges who also become government ministers when their party is in power, creating conflicts of interest and the possiblilty of a miscarriage of justice. When the PUP was in power, Glenn Godfrey was Minister of Tourism and the Environment. Just before his appointment, I attended a trial in San Pedro of a man who was caught by the police with a substantial amount of cocaine. Glenn Godfrey was his defense attorney. Although it was generally known that the man regularly sold cocaine from his house on a busy corner, he was acquitted because in the Belizean justice system, police must act as the prosecution even though they do not have legal training. The cards are highly stacked in favor of a defendant with money, especially the kind of money available from the sale of drugs. Indeed, so far all accused drug dealers have gone free even when caught in possession of large quantities of drugs.

This may be one of the reasons for the frustration of the Chief Justice of the Supreme Court of Belize, Sir George Brown. Sir George, who was knighted in 1991 by Queen Elizabeth II, has handed out some 20 death sentences in Belize over the past few years. Since Belize is a former colony, the ultimate legal arbiter of the courts is the Privy Council in London, and most of the death penalty cases have been appealed to it. The Privy Council, which vehemently opposes the death penalty, has hastily granted stays of execution in every case. According to a 1996 newpaper article in a London paper,

Sir George sees the English lawyers [the Privy Council] as an irritation, an obstacle in his attempt to impose justice on this small impoverished state and its 190,000 inhabitants. With their wigs and traditions and clever,

plummy way of talking, the lawyers are an interfering throwback to Belize's imperial past.

Concern is mounting among lawyers here and in Belize that the unfettered imposition of the gallows has become Sir George's personal crusade.
His style in the courtroom is described as ranting. He brooks no argument, he regards his decision as final. He has also started to claim he is
being assisted by God and has erected loudspeakers in his court to deliver
his fire and brimstone judgments.

"I think the judgment is one which is not directly from me in person,
but through me," Sir George declared. "It is one in which there is an inspiration . . . the divine inspiration," he told the court. "On a day like today,
our judicial process should be heavily impacted upon, not by me, but I
give all this credit to the inspiration which goes to the glory of God." In his
first ever newspaper interview last week, Sir George told the *Independent*
on Sunday he had simply meant to explain that he had prayed before
reaching judgment.

"We can't have a Chief Justice who's not well," one Belize lawyer said.
He was referring to the fact that Sir George is suffering from an unex-
plained illness which has caused seizures, sometimes in court. Under the
front-page headline "The illness of Sir George", the weekly *Belize Times*
wrote in September that Belize was "abuzz" with the news that the judge
had acted strangely during a funeral service a few days earlier.

Asked about his reported illness, he said: "I've been suffering seizures,
generally when I'm totally exhausted." . . . A straw poll in Belize City suggested that most Belizeans, concerned by rising crime, favoured executing
the men on death row. Many criticised the Privy Council for commuting to
20 years the death sentence on Linsberth Logan, who slit his girlfriend's
throat. The Privy Council found that the girl had provoked Logan by saying she had another man. Most Belizeans were also shocked by the release
this year of Ellis Taibo, who had been on death row for two different murders. His first death penalty was reduced to five years after he claimed
"self-defence" because his victim was a homosexual. (Blackhurst and
Davison 1996, 1, 17)

This article, published in England (edited for length here), was
banned in Belize and could not be reprinted in newspapers, although it enjoyed considerable underground distribution for some
time. Finally, it appeared on the Internet in the Bz-Culture group
and became widely available. In November 1997 Chief Justice Sir
George Brown resigned (*The Reporter* 1997d, 1).

SPEAR

To address the problems of a government that makes decisions
without any system of consultation, that has no checks and balances, that hands out the spoils of power to itself, that operates in

secret, that tightly controls all information going to the media, and that is felt by many to be involved in blatant corruption and possibly complicity in the movement of drugs through the country, the Society for the Promotion of Education and Research (SPEAR) held a conference in Belize City in October 1996, called "Putting People Back in Democracy." The director of SPEAR, Dylan Vernon, in a speech on another occasion, summarized the problems SPEAR thinks beset Belize:

When Belize gained independence in 1981, there were expectations of taking control of power, of increasing social and economic well-being and getting a collective sense of direction.

But 16 years after independence, Belizeans are no better off. The government is excessively centralized, there is no improvement in the economy and a decrease in public expenditure on social welfare, education and labor.

There is a rise in poverty, criminal activity, and domestic violence, and NGOs are falling apart just when there is a greater demand for their services. Public officials tied to the drug barons go with impunity. There is need for political reform. Labor costs are high, so cheap labor is imported in the agri sector and even then the impending end of quotas may be the death of banana, citrus and sugar. Although Belize has global consumption patterns, it is not keeping up in the production and export side.

There is a change in ethnic patterns and relations and a reluctance to even talk about ethnic tension. Education is stultified and needs major reform. Belizeans are increasingly frustrated with the situation.

Although Belizeans today are more informed and therefore more aware of the failures of the system, we still have not developed a collective sense of self-worth. There is no unique collective Belizean vision of where we want to go. (Vernon 1997)

Advertised as the first summit of civil society organizations in Belize to discuss the making of a better democracy, the SPEAR conference was a four-day workshop for groups from all over the country. The purpose was to identify problems to be tackled by civil society and to suggest solutions. The problems identified at the conference led to five resolutions: more political participation, improvement of education, integration of youth into the economy, rational (i.e., nonpolitical) distribution of land, and rational use of natural resources.

In a way the conference was a response to more than the development of a civil society that can challenge the government. It was also an attempt to deal with emerging questions about globalization in Belize. Globalization has highlighted the problems of unemployment, gangs, and drug trafficking among youths (Belize City has the Crips and Bloods, imported from Los Angeles by returning Belizeans); it has made accessibility of land and natural resources a critical issue because of the amount of land in nature reserves, owned by the crown, or in the hands of foreigners.

Bridgit Cullerton, of the Belize Enterprise for Sustained Technology, summed up the feeling at the conference:

We feel Belizean; we own this land, but we lack a sense that we can do things. We are very conscious about the words "globalization" and "free trade"; in the present climate in Belize we feel a sense of helplessness, passivity, malaise. Precisely because of the diversity among us and because of our history, economy and colonialism, we as a people try to get a piece of the pie instead of thinking about how to make an impact. We talk about . . . all being Belizean, . . . all one, but in our actions we just try to get a piece of the pie. Some say the NGOs have tried to do good for Belize, but NGOs are more of a face sometimes, and those involved are in it for personal gain. We have to ask what is the good for our country, our beloved Belize. (SPEAR 1996)

LEARNING TO BE LOCAL

As citizens of a new nation, Belizeans are working to form a new national identity—learning how to be Belizean within a newly independent local context. With their identification with Britain on the wane, Belizeans are creating new national identity symbols, myths, and sites. The creation of national identity, of course, has competing voices and is regularly contested. The Battle of St. George's Caye, an important event of national mythological stature, for example, has become the center of a controversy over constituting the past, and the site of the new Central Bank in the old colonial prison has set up a marriage of monetary policy and colonial incarceration.

Some Belizean intellectuals argue that Belize still lacks a sense of itself as a people or a nation. Lita Krohn, the Minister of Culture under the former PUP government, argues that Belizeans lack a knowledge of Belizean history; history textbooks have been published in Belize only since independence. Their sense of themselves as a nation was always incipient, galvanizing only around the Guatemalan military threat. Not until 1975, when the United Nations voted in favor of Belizean sovereignty, "did about half the population get independence fever. The other half drove around with the Union Jack on their car." (Krohn was referring to Graham Greene's [1984, 166] description of the conservative opposition to George Price in 1978.) The reluctance of many Belizeans to give up their status as a British colony stems from the role Britain played in controlling the power of the local elites and in keeping together under one rule a country that was composed of so many competing ethnic interests. Stuart and Myra Haylock, in whose house I stayed many times during the early 1970s, used to argue with me into the night that they wanted British law, British government, and the British army to defend them from Guatemala. As proud of their Scottish heritage as they were of their African roots, they kept pictures of Queen Elizabeth and Prince Philip on the wall. Stuart Haylock took his jury duties very seriously and had attended two hangings because, in British Honduras at that time, the jury that sentenced a man to hang had to watch his execution. Stuart found it a valuable experience in a justice system he clearly admired. The Haylocks (who had survived Hurricane Hattie in 1961 by running from their oceanfront house inland when they saw the great tidal wave coming) were vehemently opposed to independence from Britain.

So how do Belizeans develop a sense of Belizean identity at a time when the world is increasingly globalized? What are the consequences of becoming a nation just as nation-states elsewhere are weakened by global forces? One consequence has been the increasing cosmopolitanization of Belizeans. Belizeans travel more than ever and thus are becoming transnationals. Belizeans are bombarded by foreign media; over 70 percent of them now have direct access to foreign television through cable or rebroadcast. There are nine stations broadcasting American and Mexican programs all day, and any town over 1,000 can have a pirated cable system.

Most Belizeans are fully transnational, family members are in the United States, and the young expect to spend a good portion of their lives abroad. Belize is also inundated with foreigners, not only tourists but also resident expatriates, archaeological groups, students, and scientists studying the environment. Richard Wilk describes Belize as a place that is "full of foreign tourists, resident expatriates, students in search of authentic local experience, traditional medicine, untouched rain forests and ancient ruins" (Wilk 1995, 113).

Under colonialism, the stores in Belize were stocked primarily with imported consumer goods. In those days most imports were from England. Belizeans paid high prices for McVitties biscuits, sweetened condensed milk, salad cream, Smarties, Robertson's marmalade, and dessert nougats. Today most food imports are from the United States, including Pringles potato chips, cheese puffs, breakfast cereals, and detergents. Pricier consumer goods, such as televisions, washing machines, and microwaves, previously unavailable and unaffordable for most Belizeans, now stock the new appliance stores in Belize City. Even the production of food staples such as beef, chicken, eggs, rice, and milk became local only with the arrival of Mennonite farmers in the 1970s. Consumers have always considered imported foods and goods to be superior to Belizean goods. Imported matches, clothes, and canned foods were high status items.

Until recently there was no distinctly Belizean material culture, at least in the public display of goods. In the 1970s and 1980s, I never brought home any locally produced goods from my frequent trips to Belize because there was nothing locally produced to buy. This situation has changed dramatically in a short time. Today the emergence of a public national culture is evident. Not only are there local goods—for example, wood carvings of native fauna, Melinda's hot pepper sauce, and Belizean jams—but local culture is flourishing with Punta Rock (started by Pen Cayetano, described as a Belizean musical genius), authentic Belizean food (stew chicken, rice and beans), a touring national dance troupe, a national theater movement, a historical society that is designating landmarks (e.g., the colonial prison on Gaol Street), Belizean art and poetry, a Kreole language column in the newspaper, national parks, and a national flower and a national animal. There are now history books (e.g., *A Nation in the Making*), national heroes such as Baron Bliss and Philip Goldson (who have buildings named for them), Belize's own atlas, a maritime museum with replicas (made by Simeon Young) of well-known Belizean sailboats with the distinctive shallow draft, and participation in international beauty pageants, including the Mr. Gay Universe competition in El Salvador.

In an article titled "Learning to Be Local in Belize," Richard Wilk suggests that the emergence of an objectified national culture in Belize is an example of what Friedman calls "the production of local difference on a global scale" (1995, 114). This raises important questions for Belizeans: Is the production of local culture something new and transforming? Or is it a cynical creation of a local culture for the international tourist market? Does it create a new cultural order, one that is creolized, commodified, and transnational? To what extent is this emergent national culture really shared by all Belizeans?

Wilk suggests that the emergence of national culture in Belize is indeed new, but that the local and the global have had a long-term relationship that is anything but new. The making of local culture in Belize has always been a response to the global cultural system; what has changed is the global cultural system itself (1995, 118).

According to Wilk, this new global cultural system is one that promotes difference instead of suppressing it, thus the emergence of
cultural associations for different ethnic groups and the ethnic
goods to accompany them. But more important, Wilk argues that
the new global system promotes difference not of *content* but of
form. Global structures now "organize diversity," and while different
cultures continue to be quite distinct, they are distinct in very uniform ways—that is, the dominant global economic and cultural so-
cieties present universal categories and standards (capitalism, free
trade, consumerism, etc.) by which all cultural difference can be defined. Thus, "we are not all becoming the same, but we are portray-
ing, dramatizing, and communicating our differences . . . in ways
that are more widely intelligible." This "globalizing hegemony is to
be found in structures of common difference" (Wilk 1995, 118).

In Belize, the whole concept of the local emerged under mercan-
tile capitalism—first with slavery, then in class stratification in the
context of a superordinate British empire (Wilk 1995, 129), and
after independence in the midst of the late-twentieth-century communications and technology revolution. Standards of beauty (via
beauty pageants), of value (via consumer goods), of competition
(via games), of self (via TV), and of history (via museums) have a
common structure with the rest of the world. Through this common structure Belize joins the global community without necessarily sacrificing its localized meanings. The global structures do
not create homogeneity; rather, they provide a common channel
and a standard by which to measure the local for the debate and
expression of difference (Wilk 1995, 129–130). They take

the full universe of possible contrasts between nations, groups, locales,
factions, families, political parties, and economic classes, and they sys-
tematically narrow our gaze to particular kinds of difference. They organize and focus debate, and in the process of foregrounding particular
kinds of difference, they submerge and obscure others by pushing them
into the background. They standardize a vocabulary for describing difference, and provide a syntax for its expression, to produce a common frame
of organized distinction, in the process making wildly disparate groups of
people intelligible to each other. They essentialize some kinds of differences as ethnic, physical and immutable, and portray themes with mea-
surable and salable characteristics, washing them with the legitimacy of
objectivity. And they use these distinctions to draw systematic connections between disparate parts of the world system. (Wilk 1995, 130)

Belize never had much range for autonomous action under
British colonialism. But today, within a system of global communications, new sorts of communities, identities, and kinds of locality

have become as real as the tribes and kinship systems traditionally studied by anthropologists (Wilk 1995, 130). Whether these communities and identities will form a truly national culture or will continue to be a pastiche of cultures remains to be seen.

THE NEW NATIONAL IDENTITY

An example of a recent national identity project is the building of the new Central Bank, a project financed with borrowed money that will substantially increase the national deficit. The project is rife with the kind of common frame of organized distinction that Wilk suggests is part of the globalizing process.

On the site of the new Central Bank Headquarters building is the old Belize City Central Prison, and as part of its building project, the Central Bank of Belize plans to restore this building, as close to its original nature as possible, and open it to the public as a historic site. The Belize City Central Prison is at least 139 years old. Built between 1856–1857, it is the only remaining large-scale public brick building with this type of architecture; and the only remaining intact British colonial prison, typical of the Caribbean, to be found anywhere in Central and South America. (*The Observer* 1996, A)

For the restoration, the bank is minting a special silver coin. The proceeds from the sale will go toward paying for the restoration of the prison building. The design of the coin is being selected through a competition open to students from all primary and secondary schools countrywide. The design has to focus on environmental protection and cultural preservation issues relative to the country. The theme of the design is "Protect Our World." Thus we have a colonial-era prison being turned into a historic site and tourist attraction with its own memorabilia based on a competition (a transnational ideoscape) on the theme of protecting the environment (another transnational ideoscape). The "real" function of the site will be to create and manipulate monetary policy for the country.

THE BATTLE OF ST. GEORGE'S CAYE

Nothing better illustrates the competing ideologies of national identity than the stories surrounding the battle of St. George's Caye. Two major accounts of this battle are in direct competition to become official doctrine. The first account, which appears in *Belize 1798: The Road to Glory: The Battle of St. George's Caye, A Novel History of Belize*, by Emory King, is a fictionalized account in the format of a three-act play. In his introduction, King explains, fortunately, I am not a qualified historian and, therefore, not bound by the rigid restrictions of the professional. I am an entertainer and a propagandist. The object of my propaganda, pure and simple, is the glorification of Belize in the hearts and minds of today's Belizeans and future generations. . . . The important thing is to learn to love Belize and to protect our unique way of life. (1991, 3)

For King, the battle of Saint George's Caye has become an essential symbol for the beginning of Belize's nationhood. His account more or less follows the traditional view of what happened on September 10, 1798, as recorded at the time in letters from Captain Edwards of the sloop *Happy Return*, Captain Moss of the British schooner *Merlin*, Lord Balcarres, Colonel Barrow, and Admiral Hyde Parker, and in two letters printed in the *Jamaica Royal Gazette* (Burdon 1931). Thus, it focuses on the establishment of British rule, victory over the Spanish, and British tradition in Belize: "This English-speaking, British-oriented land has survived war, pestilence, fire, flood and hurricanes for over 300 years because the people who lived here were determined that they would remain English-speaking and British-oriented. If that changes, Belize will be no more" (King, 1991, 3). This version also emphasizes throughout the cooperation between masters and slaves, and the bravery of the slaves in defending the British against the Spanish. It sets up a national ideology of race that sees blacks and whites working toward the same ends, intermarrying and producing true Belizean children. It downplays race and class divisions.

Emory King's version of the battle differs completely from Assad Shoman's account in *Thirteen Chapters of a History of Belize* (1994). Shoman, one of the founders of SPEAR and a well-known political activist in Belize, focuses on class and race as divisive forces in Belizean society. He disputes the traditional version of cooperation between slaves and masters to fight the enemy, calling it a romanticization of the facts of slavery, which included beatings, escapes, and poor living conditions for slaves. He sees the battle as a symbol of the nation's history of racism and colonialism.

Both versions are culled from the *Archives of British Honduras* (Burdon 1931) and are based on the English/British Honduran perspectives. Spanish perspectives would undoubtedly differ. The Spanish expedition from Yucatan was sent to stop the British invasion of the Mosquito Coast and to solidify Spanish claims to the entire region. The basis of the claims was the papal bull that divided Central and South America between the Spanish and the Portuguese.

On September 3, 1798, the story goes, a Spanish flotilla of 31 ships carrying 2,000 Spanish troops and 500 seamen, commanded by the Governor of Yucatan, converged on St. George's Caye at the mouth of the Belize River. They were met by a British flotilla consisting of one British warship, H.M. Sloop *Merlin*, commanded by Captain Moss, who had 50 men on board; five local sloops—the *Towser, Tickler, Mermaid, Swinger*, and *Teaser*—with volunteer crews of 25 on board each, commanded by masters of merchant vessels; and seven logwood rafts. The total British and baymen force was 350 men. The odds were clearly in the favor of the far more impressive Spanish force.

But the baymen had several factors in their favor. They had communication with the local population, who were out in the sea in numerous small craft, including many canoes, providing intelligence to the *Merlin*. The British flotilla, consisting of small ships, more maneuverable in the shallow waters off the shore, could move quickly and more effectively than the larger Spanish ships. In addition, the British had superior local knowledge of the channels and seabed. When the Spanish flotilla tried to make its way through a channel, the baymen, already aware that they were moving in that direction, quickly moved into positions that allowed them to block the Spanish. For three days the Spanish tried to work their way among the shoals, and finally 14 of the largest Spanish ships bore down on St. George's Caye, towing launches full of soldiers. The baymen had already burned down every building on the caye to prevent it from becoming a base for the Spanish. When the Spanish anchored off the caye to disembark, the *Merlin* and the other small craft attacked, pounding the immobile Spanish vessels for two and a half hours until they cut anchor and retreated. Judging from the number of dead the Spanish buried on Caye Chapel, it has long been speculated that they had many casualties. In addition, there were probably high losses due to malaria, yellow fever, and dysentery. What is startling is that the baymen and the British lost not one man. Reports at the time talk about such enthusiasm of the baymen and their black slaves for a fight that in the middle of the battle, they paddled out in dories to engage the Spanish (Burdon 1931, 25–30, 247–263).

Thomas Paslow, for example, was an Irish colonel of artillery who settled in Belize about 1785. He became a prominent citizen and a magistrate. In the Battle of St. George's Caye, he commanded a craft he had fitted out and maintained. Dressed in a uniform previously worn by King George II, he led his men gallantly through a hail of grapeshot, shouting "Death or Glory!" A saying of his was "The man that will not defend his country is not entitled to the fruits thereof." The Paslow Building in Belize City was named for him (Belize-Culture Group correspondence from Neil Fraser, March 9, 1997).

The battle of St. George's Caye is an important part of the mythologization of the nation and a window into the political economy of Belize. Several aspects of this battle are now mythologized into a historic moment the equivalent of the signing of the Declaration of Independence for the fledgling United States. Both 1776 and 1798 mark the beginnings of nationhood.

Interestingly, neither Emory King nor Assad Shoman comments on features of the battle that, even in 1798, provided a historical foundation for features of national identity today. For example, the names of the baymen's boats—*Towser, Tickler, Mermaid, Swinger,* and *Teaser*—demonstrate that the humorous and slightly risqué naming customs of Belizeans for places, boats, and people has a long, entertaining history. I can only guess at the meaning of *Tickler, Swinger,* and *Teaser,* but a recent boat in my memory, the *Seven-Up,* was so named not because it was the "un-cola" but because the owner claimed he could "get it up seven times a day with no problem, man." Also revealing is the importance of flexible, maneuverable, shallow-draft craft in the Belizean waters and the word-of-mouth system of communication so important in a place with a small population. These aspects of colonial life persist today.

The importance of the battle of St. George's Caye is almost entirely symbolic. For a long time the battle changed neither the legal status nor the actual situation of Belize. The threats of attack from the Spanish still nagged the baymen, who could not know that this would be the last battle the Spanish would fight with them, because Spain was preoccupied with the impending loss of more important colonies. In fact, Belize continued to have a limbo existence and did not become a colony with British protection until 1862 (Dobson 1973, 78).

What comes out in this story of the battle of St. George's Caye is that a small force of Belizeans with excellent local intelligence and knowledge of local waters, and the help of one British ship, was able to turn back a Spanish force of 31 ships and thousands of men, weakened with dysentery, malaria, and yellow fever. Although the Spanish assumed that they would easily land and occupy St. George's Caye, and rout the lightly armed baymen from Belize, their ships were badly damaged by the *Merlin* as they sat helpless in shallow water where they could not maneuver or retreat. Although it is not clear how many Spaniards died or were killed, the climax of the story is that not one bayman or Briton perished, and although this fact deprived the nation of heroes who died in battle, it was wonderful evidence of a poor and raggle-taggle group prevailing over a major colonial power. This is an extraordinary tale, a tale of life in the borderlands where the isolation of the area, the lack of resources, and the localness of it all create an advantage for those there who are faced with the attention of the global scene, in this case the perpetual war between the English and the Spanish.

NEW NATIONAL THEMES

The SPEAR conference on civil society and democracy, which was advertised as an attempt to "put people back into democracy," asked the Belize Theatre Company, the only national theater company in Belize, to present a performance that would symbolize the new national identity. Two men and a woman from the Belize Theatre Company formed a scene that replicated the Belize flag.

The man in the middle, a Garifuna wearing a hat made of ferns, held the state motto, *Sub Umbra Floreo.* He said, "My fellow Belizeans, I want you to think globally, act locally, and stop blaming the system. I'd like you to all think that this country '*da fu all we*' [is for all of us]."

The woman, holding an ax, chimed in, "Mens got to take dere equal share in de society, woman ax could cut through doors, man, we paddle outa dis shit crik to where under de shade we do flourish, oderwise dere gonna be a Rukukukutumtumg."

Then the second man, holding a wooden board [log cutting], said, "We businessmen blamed for the high prices, international this 'n international that, take off the 'inter' and just leave 'national,' else we gan shut down de shops and dere gonna be Rukukukutumtumg." They ended with a "call for peaceful revolutionary action" so that "under the shade we ALL flourish."

The nation of Belize, consciously forming itself in a time of rapid globalization, is searching for an economic niche and an identity. The struggle for a national identity is partly a construct of the political leaders of the state, who have their own agendas regarding race and ethnicity. The question of whose culture and ethnicity will dominate the nation is a highly contested issue. There is also an interest in constructing a national identity that portrays Belize as a relatively egalitarian society of multicultural harmony. This is a commodified identity primarily for the global tourism market, which has a hunger for such an idealized society. The promotion of multicultural harmony, encapsulated in the slogan *Belize da fu all we* (Belize is for all of us), is part of the postmodern condition in Belize.

6

Belizean Ethnicity

Belize is a multicultural nation, a mosaic of cultures, peoples, religions, races, languages, and economic niches. It is a postmodern ethnoscape replete with recent migrations, immigrations, emigrations, and the resultant demographic changes in the country. Ethnicity is an integral part of the emergence of today's local Belizean culture and the localization of today's global culture. In the making of Belize, the move from being nowhere to being somewhere is related to the history (see Chapter 2) of the different peoples who have migrated or escaped to Belize, forming the culture as we know it today.

Today most articles and books on Belize begin with a description of the diverse ethnic groups living there, thus emphasizing Belize as a successful multicultural nation with a strong tolerance of diversity. The particular mix of cultures and groups that developed historically in Belize is a defining characteristic of the nation. *The Nation We Are Making*, the book that is used throughout Belize to teach schoolchildren their history, begins:

Our population is made up of Creoles, Mestizos, Garifuna, Maya, Mennonites; and people with Arab, East Indian, Chinese, European, British or other ancestry, and any number of combinations. Each group brings with it a rich heritage and helps to make our national culture. . . . Belizean Creoles are a mixture of European (mostly British) and African ancestry, sometimes with Amerindian ancestors also. The Garifuna group is a mixture of Africans and Amerindians. Mestizos are a mixture of Spanish ancestry and the Maya. There are three different kinds of Maya living in Belize—Mopan, Kekchi, and Yucatec. Many Belizeans have ancestors from more than one of these groups or are a mixture of one of these groups with another ethnicity. (Nembhard 1990, 18)

This portrayal of Belizean ethnicity emphasizes mixture, hybridity, creolization, *mestizaje*. It does not present ethnicity as a function of primordial or biological ties; rather, it focuses on historical and cultural differences coming together to form a unique Belizean identity. The Belizean identity presented here is a consciousness of a rich hybrid cultural heritage.

In writing about Belize (Sutherland 1996), I have argued that this hybridity-focused ethnic consciousness is the product of specific historical and geographical circumstances in which Belize has long been a haven for groups fleeing persecution elsewhere, including the English pirates from the more powerful Spanish in the seventeenth century, the African ex-slaves from the Caribbean in the early 1800s, the mestizos from the Caste Wars of Yucatan in the 1850s, the Mennonites from Canadian and then Mexican law in the 1950s, the Salvadorans and Guatemalans from the wars of the 1980s, and the Chinese from China's takeover of Hong Kong in 1997. I have argued that Belize developed into the "Casablanca" of Central America, a crossroads nation noted for its small population, backwater location, and laissez-faire approach to the comings and goings of people.

COMPARISON OF AMERICAN AND CARIBBEAN IDEAS OF RACE

Historically, ideas of race in North America have been based on at least three major assumptions. The first is that race is primordial, that is, it is the primary and most fundamental basis of identity; and the reason this is so is that race is biological and immutable. It is sometimes called an essentialist position, in that the essence of one's being and identity is lodged first and foremost in one's racial category. This notion is held by American whites as well as American blacks.

The second assumption is the "one drop of blood" idea that forces categorization of people as either white or black only. A person who has some ancestor who is black is herself black even if 90 percent of her heredity is white. Color categories such as mulatto, brown, and yellow, which are common and relevant in the rest of the Black Atlantic area (which stretches from southern United States to the northeast coast of Brazil), are fundamentally unimportant in the United States. This was not always so in parts of the U.S. South (e.g., South Carolina and Louisiana), where there were "official" communities of mulattoes and categories such as "high yellow," but these have generally become inoperable in recent history.

The third idea follows from the first two. In the United States the elimination of the legal and social segregation of the races was the major political and social issue of the civil rights movement in the 1960s and 1970s. By the 1980s, segregation had broken down enough that the social issue moved to affirmative action and race preferences for minorities in order to further hasten equalization between the races and integration, although residential integration has yet to be achieved except for middle-class blacks. The 1990s, on the other hand, have seen a turn toward more segregation, often at the request of minorities who have experienced integration and now urge separateness to preserve race identity (e.g., separate housing and graduation ceremonies for black college students). In this sense, segregation is still a major focus of race relations and race is still the primordial basis for identity.

American anthropologists were among the first scholars to refute the biological validity of some of these ideas of race. Going back to a long tradition of studying race, as early as the 1920s anthropologists came to the conclusion that people who are classified as members of a "race" (based on skin color, hair type, and facial features) do not constitute a physically or genetically consistent set of characteristics as opposed to another "race," that is, their genetic makeup does not correlate with the supposed racial grouping. For example, American blacks have a gene pool that is closer to the gene pool of American whites than it is to any African gene pools (Marks 1995). In addition, there is almost as much genetic variation between two randomly selected individuals of the same "race" as between those of different "races" (Brace 1996). In spite of decades of this knowledge, Americans still view the difference between races as biological, and a number of American blacks search for their "true" identity in Africa.

In the Caribbean and the Black Atlantic, ideas of race are based as much on culture and language as on skin color. Racial categories are not restricted to the two basic black/white categories but contain many gradations in between (e.g., in Portuguese—*mulato* [mixed with black], *moreno* [dark], *pardo* [brown], *claro* [light], and permutations thereof, such as *moreno claro* [light brown], etc.), indicating much greater recognition of miscegenation than in the United States. Status is determined by shade of color as well as education and money. The Caribbean race issues are not centered on segregation versus integration; they are problems with a ranking system that privileges lighter over darker color, along with the acquisition of power, status, and wealth. These ideas about race have resulted in a different system of social interaction between the races, with different consequences for individual lives.

ETHNIC CONSCIOUSNESS

Belize is a curious mixture of these two prevailing approaches to race in the New World. On matters of race, it is very Caribbean in its recognition of many categories of ethnicity and race, frequent intermarriage between these categories, and complete interaction between the ethnicities. If ideas of ethnicity are the result of specific historical forces, Belize's own history—a mixture of races and cultures to form the unique Belizean identity—is one that reinforces the Caribbean notions of race.

However, as Belize develops into a nation situated in the global ethnic community, there is increasing influence of the primordial thesis, the idea that there is something "natural," given, and ascriptive about ethnicity. The primordial view argues that there is a deeply felt shared sense of we-ness among people in a group who share the same race, language, kinship, gender, or place. A person who takes a primordial position feels that the fact of shared race or kinship or place itself creates a bond and understanding between those people. Nationalism and ethnicity often take a primordial stance, but the expression "it's a Black thing" is also a primordial view. Anthropologists, while recognizing the importance of the affective sense of we-ness, have argued that these ties of race or language are socially situated sets of classifications (i.e., race is a social classification, not a biologically significant relationship), and that the affective ties are produced by the same social situatedness. If you feel ties to all members of your "race," it is because you are taught in specific contexts to feel that tie. Thus ethnicity is a historically constituted form of social classification that is often viewed as a "natural" entity that evokes strong group sentiments and a strong sense of group identity.

The idea that one's identity is primordial is currently experiencing a kind of renaissance in Belize, as it is globally. Some Belizean Creole intellectuals and leaders, for example, are trying to raise consciousness of and pride in the African roots of Creoles and Garifuna. In addition, both the Garifuna and the Maya have their own cultural associations to revitalize their indigenous roots. This new emphasis on ethnic consciousness as a primordial identity defined by roots and race, I believe, is a consequence of the arrival of ideoscapes about race, identity, and experience through the global media (television programs, movies, and music) and through tourists (including environmentalists), international ethnic movements, and Belizean émigrés. European and American tourists bring their own ideas and experiences of race and superimpose them in Belize. Television programs depicting race in the United States—*The Jeffersons*, *The Cosby Show*, and *Oprah*—are among the most widely watched programs in Belize. Belizean émigrés also bring their own experiences of race and ethnicity to bear on the Belizean context. The number of émigrés returning to Belize from New York and Los Angeles in the last few years has steadily increased as many of them retire on pensions that allow them a better quality of life in Belize. Even young émigrés are returning to Belize to work in the improved economic climate and to use experiences and education gained in the United States to their advantage in Belize.

BLACK CONSCIOUSNESS

Among these myriad influences, one that is particularly noticeable, among some of the intellegentsia in Belize City, is the presence of Belizeans who are influenced by the Black Power movement of the 1960s. For example, Evan X. Hyde, the founder of *Amandala*, a Black consciousness newspaper, is a Belizean who as a university student went to the United States at the height of the civil rights agitation. Although the situation for American blacks was not all that similar to Caribbean issues of race, he acquired primordial ideas of race and a focus on segregation and tried to transplant them upon his return to Belize. These 1960s views still predominate in *Amandala*, in the rhetoric of some intellectuals in SPEAR, and among many of the teachers at University College Belize. They often strike Belizean Creoles as a misplaced form of racism (Rudon 1997). Many Creoles were offended by Hyde's division of Creoles into "Royal Creoles"—the Courtneys, Browns, Fullers, and others—and "Roots Creoles"—Creoles from the ghettos of Belize City. Even American blacks who have recently arrived in Belize find *Amandala*'s position on black issues in the United States to reflect a 1960s time lag that no longer applies to present-day American blacks, much less to Belizean Creoles or Garifuna (Edmondson, 1997, 2).

The influence of transnational ideas of ethnicity in Belize can be found in a number of areas of social and political life. First, there is an increase in the rhetoric of ethnicity in Belize and its use by Belizeans to describe themselves. Such rhetoric can be heard both in the streets and in private conversation; it has existed for some time, making it hard to measure just how much it has increased over time. However, in the last few years, Belizean politicians have become more vocal about expressing social issues in terms of ethnicity. Furthermore, newspapers regularly feature articles, letters, and op-ed pieces expressing concern about ethnic divisiveness and negative racial stereotypes among Belizeans. Many of these writings are responses to *Amandala*'s openly Afrocentric position—a position that most Belizeans do not share.

A record of this increased ethnic consciousness is being written by both Belizean and American researchers (Palacio 1996 and Haug and Haug 1994 for Creoles; Howard 1975 for Maya; Ropp 1995 for Chinese; Cardenas 1991 for East Indians; Palacio 1994 for Garifuna; Haug and Haug 1994 and Sutherland 1996 for interethnic relations). It may be too soon to know how ethnic divisiveness will develop, but certain events stand out as markers of its increase. First, Belize, as one of the last British colonies to gain independence, has become a nation in which the idea of a specifically Belizean national (as opposed to colonial) identity has taken shape only since the early 1980s. Consciousness of Belizean identity, of course, is not new and was a feature of Belize before independence. What does represent a more recent change is the convergence of the postindependence political development of Belize and things Belizean with the end of the Cold War global emphasis on ethnicity as identity.

For example, in an article titled "Is There Any Future for Africanness in Belize?" Joseph Palacio argues that in Belize, cultural identity has been more important than skin color: "The Belize case introduces the concept of cultural segmentation as overriding identity among peoples sharing black skin colour. Or, in other words, two persons may be black but they relate primarily to their distinct ethnic culture and not their colour" (1996, 36). Palacio goes on to say that this is a "problem" because it has led to a rejection of Africa, even though the foundation of Belizean culture, was African, and what is needed is a renewed identification with Africa, a revitalization of African elements in Belizean culture, and a privileged status for immigrants of African descent:

Very few people pay tribute to the fact that it was the desire of persons of African ancestry for freedom that became a founding stone for what would eventually become the nation state of Belize. . . . With such a significant lead, how has Africanness eroded within a period of a little more than two hundred years? . . .

What the Garifuna and Creole have not fully realized is that they are products of a British colonial system that inflicted on them the original sin of hating blackness and the source of that blackness, mother Africa. . . .

At the community level the responsibility lies for all peoples of African ancestry to heal the cultural divide that has separated them. The principal actors are the Garifuna and the Creole. The aim would be to identify and retrieve the common African elements that they share in language, food, traditional medicine, religious beliefs, aesthetic culture, abiding sense of kinship, etc. Closely related would be to extend to Africans and West Indians some sort of preferred immigrant status that Latinos have taken for granted during the past three decades. (1996, 34, 35, 44)

One of the difficulties of appealing to primordialism in race issues in a multicultural society is deciding which identity to consider primary. Thus, in spite of calls for Creole/Garifuna unity as African brothers, the Garifuna, as often as not, are concerned with their indigenous roots and identity more than with their African ancestry (Kerns 1983; Foster 1986). According to Godsman Ellis, the founder of the Garifuna Cultural Council, the Garifuna see themselves as an oppressed indigenous group and have joined the Consejo de Indígenas de Centro America and the Funda Indígena (an accord for funding development of indigenous people in Latin America) rather than the Creole Council or Evan Hyde's "Black Power" group, The United Black Association for Development. Furthermore, the Garifuna (primarily located in Dandriga and Punta Gorda) have not forgotten their not-too-distant treatment by Creoles as social and political inferiors, an attitude fueled by the British, who portrayed the Garifuna as cannibals and kept the two black groups separated by making it necessary for the Garifuna to obtain permits to travel from Dandriga to Belize City. It is not surprising that the Garifuna have thus developed a strong cultural resurgence and political action movement to elevate their status as an indigenous, rather than an African, people. Cultural pride among the Garifuna has been heightened by the Garifuna Cultural Council, as manifested in the resurgence of Punta Rock, Garifuna dances, Settlement Day celebrations on November 19, and the effort to revive traditions such as language (Carib/Arawak), rituals, foods, and crafts, most of which are based on indigenous identity (Haug and Haug 1994, 8). The entire Garifuna nation from Nicaragua, Honduras, and Belize has become linked on the Internet, and they jointly celebrated their bicentennial on April 12, 1997, marking 200 years since leaving St. Vincent.

This recent resurgence of ethnic and cultural identity issues has spilled over into the politics of the two political parties (UDP and PUP) that alternately hold power in Belize. In contrast with the colonial period, in which power was controlled by the British government and the British-appointed local elites, mostly Creoles, today the two Belizean political parties compete for votes partly (but increasingly) by appealing to specific ethnic groups. Many politicians are concerned about the ethnicization of the parties, conscious of the inherent dangers in the increase of such cleavages.

DEMOGRAPHIC CHANGES

Another factor influencing the increase in ethnic identity issues is the change in demographics in Belize since the late 1980s. A real demographic shift showed up in the 1990 census, with Afro-Belizeans dropping from 48 to 36 percent of the population, while the mestizo population increased from 33 to 44 percent (Woods, Perry, and Steagall 1995). An article in *The Houston Chronicle*, "Belize Finds Melting Pot May Be Coming to a Boil—Creole Population Faces Uneasy Changes" (Gunson 1996), highlights the Creoles' fears about what they call the "latinization" of Belize and the increasing emigration of Creoles to the United States in large numbers. Recent calls for Creoles to link their interests with their "Garifuna African brothers" is a response to these changes.

With a small national population, the slightest change in demographics has an important impact on the political balance between ethnic groups. During the 1980s, when civil wars in El Salvador and Guatemala, and political unrest in Nicaragua and Honduras, were at their peak, the flow of Central American refugees into Belize gave the country one of the highest rates of immigration relative to current population of any country in the world (Ropp 1995). More important, the relative position of the two largest ethnic groups, Spanish (mestizo) and Creole, shifted. With the mestizo population now larger than the Creole nationwide (although Belize district and most civil service jobs are still predominantly occupied by Creoles), the political ties to Central America are stronger than ever and the issues that most concern the Spanish-speaking population must be addressed politically. These include the teaching of Spanish in the schools and a strong reaction against the push by Creoles, who want Creole taught in the schools (Gillett 1996). Although Belize has been a member of CARICOM for some time, it did not join the OAS until August 15, 1995, a move that has been linked directly to establishing closer strategic ties with Central America (World Wide Web, Belize Information Service).

A local television program titled "The Mestization of Belize," made by Great Belize Productions, illustrates the ethnic tension. In this documentary, the editor of *Amandala*, a newspaper that explicitly promotes black pride and consciousness, calls mestization "a prob-

lem" that will result in Belize's losing its "character." When ques-
tioned about this "racist" point of view, he responds that if promoting his race is racism, then he has to live with that label, but he
wants the government to "do something" about keeping blacks in
Belize in order to counter the immigration of Central Americans. In
this same program, other Creoles disagree. A representative from
SPEAR argues that since this shift was inevitable, the government
should have seen it coming and prepared people for the psychologi-
cal change. The late Topsy Harriat, director of the Department of
Archaeology in Belize at the time, and also a Creole, pointed out
that this had happened before, during the Caste Wars, when some
7,000 mestizos became Belizeans, overwhelming the 3,000 Creoles;
but Belize still kept its character. The program illustrates the threat
that recent migrations pose for the previously predominant Belize
district Creoles.

As mentioned earlier, another factor in the increased ethnic tension is the influx of tourists (from the United States and Europe)
and returning émigrés (primarily from the United States), both of
whom bring their own experiences with race and ideas of the primordial nature of ethnicity as identity to bear on the Belizean
ethnoscape.

Ethnic issues in Belize are highly complex and multicultural.
There is a push for greater identity with Africa by a small but vocal
intelligentsia; there is a national demographic shift from a predominance of Creoles to a predominance of mestizos; there are contested language issues; and the Garifuna are enjoying a revival in
cultural pride after a long history of cultural repression. In addition, the Maya are entangled in a conflict with ethnic dimensions.
An interesting development is the appearance of an umbrella organization—the Belize National Ethnic Organization (BENIC)—for
ethnic groups that includes the Garifuna Cultural Council, the
Toledo Cultural Council, and the Alcalde Cultural Council, the last
two both Maya organizations. BENIC represents 18 percent of the
population of Belize. The Maya consciousness movement is illus-
trative of the way that ethnicity, cloaked in primordial language,
comes to turn on more concrete issues concerned with historical
structures of inequality.

MAYA CONSCIOUSNESS

In the south of Belize there is a strong resurgence of Maya consciousness, a resurgence that is tied directly to issues of land
rights, indigenous people's rights, and identity. The Maya have
lived in the Maya Mountains in the Toledo district of Belize since

the peak of the Maya civilization. Although there have been fluctuations in population density over time—with the highest population just before the arrival of the Europeans and the lowest just
after—this area has always been an area of Maya residence. By the
1880s, Maya population density had increased again. In a search
for work on banana plantations and in response to repressive legislation against the Maya in Guatemala, there was a surge in Maya
migration into the Toledo region at that time. It was during that period of migration that the main Mopan village of San Antonio was
formed. However, soon after the arrival of those Maya, the banana
plantations failed, and they were forced to turn to subsistence
farming (Howard 1975, 2). To this day, remnants of that migration
of Kekchi and Mopan Maya live in very isolated villages in the Maya
Mountains.

The issue of whether the Maya have continuously occupied the
Toledo district is now a very hotly contested argument between
the Maya and the state. Today, these Maya are claiming the land
they live on as theirs, although it is former Crown land now
owned by the state. They base this claim on their continuous oc-
cupation of the land as indigenous people and seek to create a
Maya homeland. The reaction of the state to a Maya homeland
was so negative that the Maya have shifted the argument away
from a claim on a homeland and toward the issue of control of
land traditionally used by the Maya. In pursuing these land
claims, they have taken their case all the way to the Supreme
Court of Belize.

Their case was sparked when, in 1995, the government of Belize,
anxious for a source of foreign currency to pay off their $200 mil-
lion foreign debt, sold land rights for logging mahogany to a Southeast Asian company. The Maya became aware of the logging
contracts when Malaysian loggers arrived in the Columbia Forest
Reserve, which is one of the most important biodiversity areas of
Central America and is land traditionally occupied by Maya. The
Maya immediately protested, referring to the development of a
"massive industrial export-oriented logging industry in Toledo" as
an "environmental nightmare" (*The Reporter* 1996, 4).

The Maya are not one united group but consist of several factions
based on language, region, and culture. Three Maya organizations
are particularly active in opposing the logging—the Toledo Maya
Cultural Council (Mopan, who represent one-third of the Maya), The
Kekchi Cultural Council (who represent two-thirds of the Maya),
and the Alcalde Association (a combination of both Mopan and
Kekchi). Although historically they have been at odds with each
other, resistance to logging concessions has united these three

groups and spurred them into political action. Initially their aim was to pressure the government to suspend all logging licenses and allow the Maya to undertake sustainable logging themselves (and put the profits back into the local community). Now they are seeking recognition as an indigenous group with land rights.

The emergence of the Maya into mainstream Belizean politics is very recent but extremely successful. They have been aided by a global indigenous rights movement that has provided them with moral justifications and legal representation, and they have also been helped by environmentalists who see the Maya as stewards of the land through whom the environmental cause against logging can be fought.

Just how fledgling their emergence onto the national and international arena is came home to me during the SPEAR conference on civil society in October 1996. The Kekchi Cultural Council sent representatives, one of whom spoke only Kekchi, forcing other Belizeans at the conference to find an English/Kekchi translator. A Spanish/Kekchi translator was suggested, but this was no help, since the other Kekchi there did not speak Spanish. The Mopan were represented by two women leaders from San Antonio. On the first night, while I was relaxing in the hotel pool, they approached me. "Can *anybody* swim here?" one of them asked me. "Anyone," I replied. They stared for a while in disbelief, then slowly descended into the pool in their bright yellow and orange dresses, and floated in the water. Maya, particularly Maya women, are entering the mainstream for the first time.

Ideoscapes from Europe and North America have always influenced Belize. Today such ideas include an assumption of the primordial nature of ethnicity and a cultural view that race is a primary focus of identity over all other sources. These ideoscapes have had an impact on Belizean ideas that previously had operated mostly, but not entirely, on assumptions of hybridity, creolization, and *mestizaje*, with language and culture as the key identifying features of Belizeans. This new emphasis on a primordial idea of ethnicity has begun to infiltrate the political arena, particularly as Belize has shifted from approximately equal numbers of mestizos and Creoles to an increase of mestizos by almost 15 percent by 1991. Finally, post-Cold War media images of ethnicity and ethnic conflict (e.g., Bosnia and Rwanda) have reinforced these essentialist views.

BORN BELIZEAN

The formation of ethnic consciousness in relation to global ideas of ethnicity has contributed to the fragmentation of ethnic relationships among all the groups who had in common their hybrid Belizean identity and their diaspora history. Belizean Maya and Garifuna are now encouraged to identify with all Native Americans; Garifuna and Creole, with all African-Americans; and Spanish, not only with Central Americans but also with Hispanics and Latinos internationally (Campbell 1996; Palacio 1990, 1994, 1996; Haug and Haug 1994).

The globalization of Belize has brought the nation and people into more and more contact with the outside world and given them more familiarity with global ethnic categories and movements. The nation of Belize is developing a modern form late in the history of nationalism, just as the nation-state elsewhere is being eroded by globalization. Belize never defined itself as anything but a multicultural mosaic of peoples, but now that designation is being redefined in the light of primordial ethnic movements to be a series of fragmented ethnic groups. These modern ethnic movements subscribe to the primordialist idea that particular groups are the outgrowth of natural affinities of race, language, or kinship, and share a common sentimental or affective bond. Furthermore, they link rights and entitlements to these primordial identities. As such ideas creep into Belizean politics, defining it more and more as a kind of deterritorialized identity politics, the ethnic fragmentation so virulent and obvious on the international scene begins to show its face in Belize. Creole, "Spanish," Garifuna, and Maya ethnicities, once regarded as "cool" ethnicities, can easily become "hot" when energized by local issues that summon up transnational loyalties to primordially defined groups.

The tourist discovery of Belize, the transforming presence of expatriates, and the influx of Central Americans since independence (and, recently, of Chinese) that have resulted in a demographic shift in Belize are all part of the ethnoscape of this small, diverse country. These elements have led to a national debate about authenticity, about who is an authentic Belizean. The notion of privileging those who are "born Belizean" (as opposed to naturalized Belizean) has a strong nationalistic sentiment with economic implications behind it. For example, there is a rule in San Pedro that only "born Belizeans" can become tour guides, a rule that the resident, naturalized Belizean community resents. The "born Belizean" rhetoric has led to some strange ambiguities—for example, Belizean émigrés who, though born in Belize, have spent their entire adult life in the United States and have returned for their retirement thoroughly Americanized. Or the increasing numbers of Chinese with "economic" passports who are denied residency. There is an acrimonious debate about the rights of citizenship for these naturalized Belizean citizens who have come from the United States, Britain, Canada, Central America, Hong Kong, and Taiwan, a debate that will merge with the one on ethnicity and national identity.

A street in Belize City.

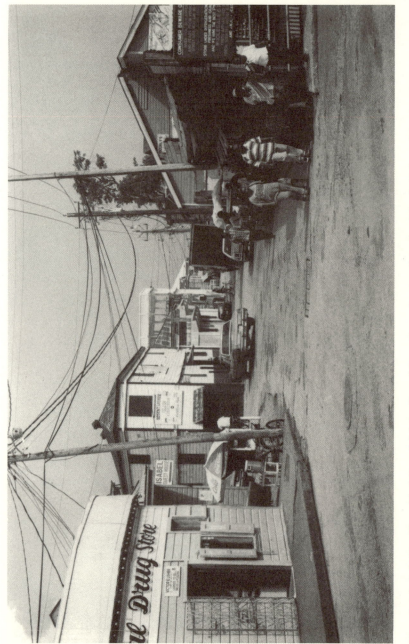

The triangle in Belize City with (left to right) the Central Drug Store, the site of the first Mom's Cafe, and the site of the burned down Minerva Hotel.

The Paslow Building that houses the Post Office, the Belize Family Court, and the Lands Office.

The new USAID-funded Water Taxi Express Terminal on Haulover Creek with a boat from Caye Caulker waiting for passengers. The Paslow Building is behind on the far left.

The back street of Caye Caulker. The bakery is located in one of the early cement buildings.

A wooden rain barrel. The water is funneled from the tin roof.

The Hawksworth Bridge over the Macal River in Cayo. A noisy one way bridge that at one time had the only traffic light in Belize. There are now three traffic lights in the country.

The women's craft shop at Maya Center just outside the gates of the Cockscomb Jaguar Wildlife Sanctuary.

The Hoy House at Bacalar Chico circa 1942. Father Hickey, who started the cooperative movement in Belize, is standing in front. Brother John Jacobi, who started the Boy Scout movement, is next to his Boy Scout troop. Seventy-five people living in the Bacalar Chico area came to be married and brought their children to be baptized by Father Hickey. There were 2 marriages and 25 baptisms that day. Only the young women, girls, and boys were photographed on the porch. The men stayed behind the house drinking, and the older women and babies were inside cooking. William Knight Hoy from Devonshire, England, purchased the whole of Bacalar Chico and later sold portions to the Huesner and Valencia families. Courtesy of Alfonso Franco, Hoy's grandson.

A shop in Cowpen made from scrap wood and tin. Guatemalen and Honduran women talk with the author.

The new Central Bank of Belize being built at the site of the colonial prison.

The Light Chop to Choppy Cafe on the road to San Ignacio in Cayo.

7

The Tourists Are Coming

"Did you see all those tourists?" a tan, long-haired Californian asked me. "This place is overrun by gringos. It is really spoiling the place for the rest of us." Having lived in San Pedro for less than a year, she had already learned to set herself up as a "resident," as opposed to a "tourist." Supported by a small trust fund from her parents, she filled her days in San Pedro snorkeling, drinking, smoking marijuana, and throwing pots at a local "art gallery" that sells kitsch to tourists at inflated prices. She apparently had quickly adopted the attitude of many of the resident foreigners, mostly Americans and Canadians, that all other foreigners are "gringos" or tourists. In spite of her self-designation as resident, she had almost no contact with the San Pedranos. She did not know what they do, who their families are, what they think, or how they feel about her and her resident friends. She was part of a wave who settled in Belize during the 1980s, if only for short periods of time, drove up prices, bought up the prime real estate, and demanded American goods and services. It struck me as somewhat odd that she was now soliciting my complicity in her disgust for the tourists who come for a week or two of sun, sea, sand, and sex.

I have said that Belize skipped modernism and went straight to postmodernism, meaning that it never developed an industrial/manufacturing-based economy before moving rapidly into the information/technology age. This leapfrogging of modernity made Belize desirable to people from a postindustrial society who were seeking to escape modernism. Tourism blossomed precisely because the country had not developed and was unnoticed in the world market economy. Belize suddenly became a desirable tourist destination only in the mid-1980s, when the country was featured on a *60 Minutes* segment as one of the last pieces of undiscovered paradise where one could retreat to a simple lifestyle unspoiled by civilization. The first Belize guidebooks appeared in the early 1990s. Today virtually all the main guidebook series (Insight Guide, Rough Guide, Sierra Club, The Lonely Planet, Frommers, Inside Guides, etc.) feature Belize, as do many off-beat independent guides (Ritz, Mallan, Pariser, Glassman, Bradbury). The introduction to the *Adventure Guide to Belize* is instructive because it encapsulated early on the direction tourism has taken in Belize.

Caribbean yet Central American, Belize encompasses a cultural potpourri. Among its bountiful treasures are the hemisphere's longest coral reef, hundreds of sandy offshore islands, 250 varieties of wild orchids, 500 species of birds, cats and other wildlife and innumerable Maya ruins— many still unexplored. . . . Both the relatively small population and the nation's physical isolation have made the construction of roads a formidable task, and many parts of the nation remain inaccessible today. If you're looking for a large resort with a pristine white beach and attendants holding out white towels and catering to your every need, then Belize is not the place for you. Belize is for the adventurous traveler—one who doesn't mind trading a modicum of discomfort for a maximum amount of experience. (Pariser 1992, 1)

Pariser's message—come to Belize for an ethnic potpourri, nature, and adventure, but do not come to find a replica of your comfortable world at home—has had enormous appeal. This image of Belize is still being touted by travel agents. A 1996 ad urged the traveler to "enjoy the unspoiled world of 'Make Belize' " (*Minneapolis Star Tribune*, February 14, 1996, 6). As television programs regularly began to feature Belize, major U.S. airlines (Continental, American, and Delta in 1998) included Belize on their Central American routes, providing competition for Taca, the Central-American airline and long-term provider of service to Belize.

Today tourism in Belize is booming. There are now more tourists coming to Belize each year than there are Belizeans living there. The estimated number of visitors in 1993 was 260,056, about 55,000 more visitors than the total population of Belize, and tourism is the fastest growing industry in Belize. It represents 17.81 percent of Belize's GDP, or $50 million per year (out of a national GDP of $414 million). With its natural resources of forests and coastline and its multicultural, English-speaking population friendly to the United States, Belize is an important tourist destination for the alternative tourist and the ecotourist, as well as the recreational "sun-sea-sand-sex" tourist. This recent "discovery" of Belize by foreigners as a tourist mecca and destination for the "authentic" experience could happen only because in the past, Belize was undeveloped, underpopulated, and unknown.

Dean MacCannell (1973, 589) has described tourism as the quest of modern, postindustrial humans for authenticity in other cultures. He also argues that the term "tourist" is increasingly used as a derisive label for someone who seems content with obviously unauthentic experiences (MacCannell 1976, 94). Yet, among tourists and tourism promoters, there are a number of places, Belize being one, that are advertised specifically as destinations for the "authentic" experience.

In *The Loss of the Creature*, Walker Percy describes travelers who seek the authentic experience as those who try to recover the feelings of "first" discovery by leaving the beaten path (1981, 48). He tells the story of two travelers who, when they think they have found the authentic experience, immediately wish that an anthropologist friend had been with them. Percy remarks that they longed for their anthropologist friend not to share their experience, but to certify their experience as genuine (1981, 53). Perhaps the tan, long-haired Californian spoke to me in hopes that I would certify her position as genuine resident by condemning the inauthentic tourists.

EARLY TOURISM

In the early 1970s Belize was a complete unknown in the tourist industry. The first travelers to Belize were offbeat individuals with a sense of adventure and a desire to experience a back-to-nature, back-to-basics, simple life. Belize attracted people seeking to escape the "ills" of postindustrial society: pollution, traffic, and angst. In Belize these travelers could be transported to a world where they were in touch only with the fundamentals of survival. Those foreigners who moved to Belize and stayed, spent most of their time in subsistence activities: finding food and a place to live, and struggling with the rudimentary communications to the outside world, isolated from the telephone, the news, and television. They felt renewed and revitalized by contact with life in its "simplest" form.

Some of them came because they had illnesses they attributed to "civilization" and American life, diseases that baffled American doctors who were also caught up in the maelstrom of modernity. These victims of civilization were cured when they came to Belize and took up a basic lifestyle remote from their former lives. I personally know of many such cures. One woman, for example, found that she was allergic to virtually everything produced by "civilization"—paint, most foods, all chemicals, car exhaust. With everything around her making her sick and unable to eat, she became so emaciated that doctors gave her only a few weeks to live. When she arrived on Caye Caulker, she had to be carried off the boat. She lay in a tent on the beach, ate only food gathered from the island, and breathed the fresh sea air coming in on the trade winds. Gradually, she gained weight and thrived. Her story still goes the rounds of the expatriates in Belize. "You better Belize it," they say.

Being an explorer manqué like many of my British anthropology colleagues, I, too, was susceptible to the Belize of the authentic adventure and conveyed my enthusiasm to my students at the English university where I was teaching. Accompanied by an eager group of students, we set off for August Pine Ridge in the summer of 1972 to carry out fieldwork. We found thatched marl cottages built on the edge of the village for our shelter, collected rainwater to drink, and hired a cook to provide meals of rice and beans, tortillas, and tomatoes. The cottages shared one outhouse, a thatched encirclement around a hole in the ground. A large bull snake took up residence in the roof of the thatch, causing no end of consternation among the students. Our houses had mahogany bed frames built by the Mennonites and hammocks woven by the local Mayans. Much to the dismay of the English students, who were averse to insects, we had scorpions, spiders, and colonies of gecko lizards who scurried about their business all night long.

One young man, Colin, was not altogether sure that he wanted to become an anthropologist. But I assured him he had nothing to worry about in the bush. Belize was perfectly safe I told him. Nevertheless, he was nervous about being so far from civilization, sure he would get sick. Just in case, he brought a medicine kit larger than his suitcase, well stocked with antibiotic pills and creams, laxatives, sulfa drugs for diarrhea, bandages of all kinds, antihistamines for insect bites, and antiseptics to wash his potential wounds. He kept his passport close to his chest at all times and his suitcase packed just in case he needed to leave suddenly if a revolution broke out. Every time he went into the village, he carried a flashlight in case he got caught out in the dark, his canteen in case of drought, an umbrella in case of tropical rain, and a stick to ward off rabid dogs with infectious sores. He was a nervous fellow. The villagers stared at him.

Colin was particularly anxious about insects. The second night we were there, it rained torrents, and the scorpions, who had retreated to the warmth and security of the thick thatch, seemed to lose their hold during the night and dropped like ripe fruit to the ground. The first landed on Colin's chest as he dozed. His scream was heard throughout the village. The next morning we found him wide awake in bed, black circles under his eyes, his umbrella protecting his head, scanning the ceiling with his flashlight like an airport searchlight. He left that day, giving up all dreams of becoming an anthropologist.

The next year I went to Caye Caulker, a place that was not yet a tourist destination, and met the handful of Americans and Canadians resident there, a rugged, self-reliant group of iconoclasts some of whom were married to locals. Early tourism on Caye Caulker was sparse, and the few accommodations that sprang up were airless, boxed-in spaces under someone's house. The tourists who trickled in were, on the whole, a raggle-taggle bunch of eccentric adventurers. These foreigners were oddities, often casualties of modern society. One, an engineer from Cape Canaveral, who had finally buckled under the stress of the race for space, came to Caye Caulker with bleeding ulcers and an emotional breakdown. For six months he sat quietly in a Mennonite mahogany rocking chair and ate papaya, then returned to the United States a new man. Caye Caulker cures for modernism were a common feature of these early visitors.

Caye Caulker was the ultimate undiscovered island of an anthropologist's dream—two and a half hours from Houston, Texas, but light-years away from the rest of the world. As it turned out, it was also the ultimate hippie's dream island, and just at the time I began to do fieldwork on Caye Caulker, the island became known on the word-of-mouth backpackers' trail that runs through Central America as a hippie paradise because of its laid-back demeanor and lack of modern communications. I viewed these travelers as modern-day pirates. People arrived with a "story" and a "past," and usually some scheme for making a fortune. One year, a man arrived wearing nothing but green hospital "scrub" shirts and pants. Almost never sober, he wandered around the island, announcing to all that he was a Freemason and an anthropologist, a psychologist and a professor of art, as well as a stone mason. We later dubbed him the "stoned Freemason." There was also a group referred to as "the Texans," a crowd of time-warp hippies who came every year to whoop it up on beer and marijuana and relive the sixties over and over. One of them was called "Shark Bait" because his friends once dragged him, in a drug-induced stupor, along the reef to attract sharks. He was so proud of his experience that he had a picture of a naked woman riding a shark tattooed on his arm with "Shark Bait" written underneath.

Both American hippies and European antiestablishment youth (sometimes referred to as "Euro-trash" by the Americans) swarmed to Caye Caulker to smoke pot and hang out with the Rasta boys from Belize City. No one seemed to bother them or care what they did, even when they took coconuts off the trees and ate them as if they belonged to no one and made bonfires from palmetto sticks brought from the mainland by the islanders for making lobster traps. The easy tolerance of the village prevailed.

In contrast to Caye Caulker, San Pedro, a little fishing village 12 miles north of the island, had a number of American businessmen, from such unlikely places as Michigan and Louisiana, who were developing plans for turning the village into a place where sport-fishermen and reef divers could find some of the amenities of home among the local fishermen. Their goal was to establish nature recreational tourism (sportfishing, wind surfing, sailing, snorkeling, diving) as well as some hunting-and-gathering tourism (hunting deer and peccary, shell collecting, archaeological ruins). These entrepreneurs, along with a few farsighted locals, bought up land on the island, built hotels and restaurants, and set up an area that was far more palatable to them than the enormous government-sponsored tourist complexes of Cancún and Cozumel just to the north, and with an even richer reef life (Dachary and Burne 1991, 144). To them, Belize had certain advantages over Cancún. It was small and still had a local flavor, it had respect for the British laws that had been established, and English was widely spoken. The tolerance that the population had developed among themselves, a tolerance that the entrepreneurs felt Mexico lacked, spilled over into tolerance for foreigners. The land speculation and development of hotel resorts that these fishermen-businessmen developed in the 1970s reached a fever pitch in the late 1980s as land prices and resort development put all but the back mangrove swamps out of the financial reach of most of the local inhabitants of San Pedro. Now the precious reef outside San Pedro is straining to stay alive, and the larger fish and conch are pretty much gone from the waters behind the reef. San Pedro now faces multiple problems, such as a critical water shortage and inadequate sanitation, due to the sudden increase in population.

Today San Pedro has a sophisticated tourist industry. Hotels can be booked by fax or E-mail, accounts are computerized, and businesses are financed by international banks. People use checks (instead of cash), give receipts, have computerized bookkeeping records, and pay taxes. A measure of San Pedro's cosmopolitan tourism is the arrival of people who don't "know" or care where they are, as if spaces are interchangeable. I struck up a conversation with one of these tourists on a day trip to Caye Caulker from San Pedro. She had arrived by boat at a beach at one end of the island, had done some sunbathing, and had had a drink. She did not know where she was ("some island," she thought), but it didn't matter, because she kept her eye on her tour guide, who would tell her when it was time to get back on the boat.

In San Pedro the tourism business has priced itself so high that tourists have moved to other, less expensive parts of the country. The tourists who are willing to pay San Pedro's high prices may find that their tour guide knows less about Belize than the tourist who reads one of the many new guidebooks. These tourists, unlike those on Caye Caulker, are not looking for an authentic experience, but they expect to receive certain comforts and services (running water, air conditioning, and good food) in exchange for the high prices they pay. Food for the tourists in San Pedro is expensive with restaurants often having a 900 percent markup. For example, the ingredients for an eggs-and-bacon breakfast cost U.S.$.75, but the tourist will pay U.S.$7.50 to eat it.

Given these conditions, it was inevitable that San Pedro would experience a tourism slump. In 1996, its share of the Belize tourist market eroded considerably, affecting the number of tourists in Belize overall (18 percent fewer in the second quarter of 1996). According to Bruce Collins, editor of the San Pedro Sun, the tourist industry in San Pedro responded to the drop in number of tourists by raising its prices even more (10 percent in March 1997). With San Pedro's reputation for being expensive while supplying a "mediocre to poor tourism product," the rise in prices may lead to an even bigger drop in tourism.

In the low months of October and November 1996, there was so little income from tourism in San Pedro that the same money circulated around the island again and again. One San Pedrano mentioned that she had had the same $20 bill pass through her hands twice in one week: she paid a bill with it, the person she paid then paid a bill, and she got the $20 back when someone else paid a debt to her.

Because of tourism, San Pedro has grown beyond its capacity to provide housing, water, and sewers. Residents no longer able to afford to live in San Pedro are moving to San Pablo, a newly created town in the swampy backland. Water is being supplied by barge and a desalination plant has begun operating. Wells are contaminated with sewage due to uncontrolled placement of septic tanks. The best land on the coastline has filled with tourist resorts from the tip of the caye in the south to Robles in the north. Land prices have skyrocketed with speculation. All the way to the border of

Mexico at Bacalar Chico, the last of the coastline is being divided into lots that sell for U.S.$55,000 each. The Caribbean coast is already, to a large extent, mainly in the hands of non-Belizean resort owners.

What has happened to San Pedro is an illustration of a fairly common life cycle of tourism (Butler 1980). There is an initial exploration of a newly "discovered" area; then increased involvement of tourists in that area; then development of tourist projects on a large scale, primarily through foreign rather than local investment, with land, food, and housing prices becoming so expensive locals cannot afford to live there. The adventurous individuals move on, and tourism consolidates into a regular pattern of intensive recreational sun-sea-sand-sex activities until the prices become so high and the experience so "inauthentic" that there follows a period of stagnation or decline. There is a direct correlation between the number of tourists and these phases of tourism over time. (See Figure 7.1.)

Figure 7.1
Phases of Tourism Development

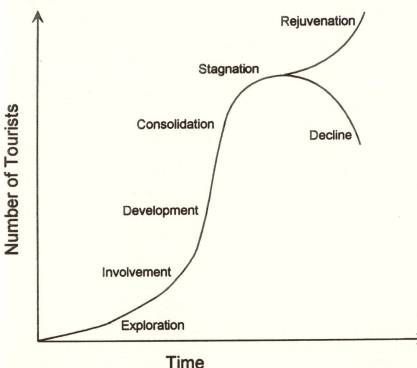

Today there is a tourism boom in the south of the country in and around Placencia, where the tourism life cycle experienced in San Pedro is already well under way. Land that sold for U.S.$5 an acre in 1990 is now selling for U.S.$500 an acre in 1997. The next boom will almost certainly move south to the last remote and undeveloped area of Belize, the Toledo district and the Columbia Forest Reserve.

ECOTOURISM

Belize may be the only country where the Minister of Tourism is simultaneously the Minister of the Environment (Pariser 1992, 41), thus making official the link between tourism and the environment. The government of Belize has designated tourism its second priority after agriculture. The government's policy is to try to reserve the less capital-intensive tourist development businesses for Belizeans, while encouraging foreign investors to develop projects that require greater amounts of capital.

If the 1970s in Belize can be characterized by adventure tourism and the 1980s by recreational tourism, then the 1990s should be known as the decade of ecotourism. Ecotourism is touted as the most enlightened, nondestructive form of tourism, a panacea for tourism itself, and an antidote to mass tourism. It represents the sensitive, authentic, yet sustainable experience of today's cosmopolitan traveler. Belize has become one of the world's foremost ecological tourist destinations.

Ecotourism is firmly lodged in a global ethical debate about the necessity and urgency of "saving" the environment from destruction by humans. This debate argues that humans are the problem (they destroy the environment), and that the plants, animals, and ecosystem are the innocent victims of human malfeasance. Most environmentalists believe that the environment should have priority over the human condition; therefore, it is a debate that privileges the environment. This debate is the basis of the push for ecotourism that is a marketing tool for that perspective. Ecotourism is hailed as a benevolent form of tourism because it makes the preservation of the environment the tourist's top priority. This includes an expectation that the ecotourist will give donations and pay fees for the "privilege" of seeing the preserved nature. One of the paradoxes of ecotourism is that although it is framed as an ethical issue, it is still calculated in terms of the money it brings in. For ecotourism to work, it must be profitable.

In the interior of Belize, ecotourism became the battle cry. The Cayo district, near the border of Guatemala, is a beautiful area of broadleaf-forested mountains topped with a ridge of pines above the broadleaf line. The sides of the mountains have a tropical rain forest with waterfalls and myriad tropical birds and animals. The tops of the mountains have pine forests reminiscent of Germany, with sandy red soil and fresh air. In this region a curious medley of environmentalists organized both an environmental movement and ecotourist resorts. This mixture included archaeologists, biologists, members of religious cults, survivalists from Oregon and Idaho, and the straggling hippies and Euro-trash found on Caye Caulker. They share romantic, New Age spiritual views of life that include an abhorrence of technology and civilization, and a self-righteous, sometimes militant, environmentalism.

Environmentalists from Europe and the United States arrived in Belize in the early 1980s and established a foothold in an astonishingly short time. They immediately convinced transnational environmental groups that Belize was a small, unspoiled place where these groups could invest a relatively modest amount of money with the biggest impact on the preservation of the environment. One of the first environmental projects was the Belize Zoo. Started in 1983 by Sharon Matola, a former circus entertainer, this modest project to save some animals who had been used in a movie was turned into a national zoo with support from the World Wildlife Fund, Conservation International, the Inter-American Foundation, and Wildlife Preservation Trust International. Nongovernmental organizations (NGOs) such as the World Wildlife Fund, the Belize Audubon Society (BAS), and Wildlife Conservation International have been instrumental in developing ecotourism in the interior of Belize. They have lobbied the government, written the environmental laws, and dedicated themselves to turning large tracts of land into preserves and parks with environmental protection. They have been very successful in establishing close working relationships with government agencies by funding and administering government parks and reserves (Harborne et al. 1994). The BAS, for example, has responsibility for administering and gathering fees from seven parks and reserves. The Programme for Belize, founded in 1988 with land given by Coca-Cola, Inc., is an example of an experiment to integrate environmental and tourism issues (Wilkinson 1992, 388). Funded by many environmental NGOs, it controls a Mayan site called La Milpa and all ecotours in the area, and is also involved in ecology-based tropical-forest industries selling products to tourists.

Environmental NGOs have also been very successful in preventing the development of tourism to which they have ecological objections. For example, a proposal was made by Glenn Godfrey, who at the time was Minister of the Environment and Tourism, to turn the entire back portion of Ambergris Caye into a reserve, with the oceanfront allocated to major resorts (Dachary and Burne 1991, 144–145). Various environmental groups were instrumental in halting the plan. When the government changed hands in the next election, these groups lobbied the new UDP government to pass a law to establish the Bacalar Chico Reserve (allowing no large hotels), prepared the documents to set up the reserve, and funded the salaries of those who manage the reserve. Even more interesting are the roles of two powerful environmental NGOs: the BAS, which now controls many of the reserves, and the ecocapitalist Programme for Belize and its private reserve, the Rio Bravo Conservation Area. Activities of both groups are a part of virtually every ecotourist's itinerary.

NGO MANAGEMENT OF RESERVES

Formed in 1973 as an independent NGO but affiliated with the National Audubon Society of the United States, the BAS became the first Belizean member of the International Union for the Conservation of Nature and Natural Resources, the world's largest environmental organization, which is based in Switzerland. From the beginning of the entrance of environmentalists into Belize, Switzerland was held up as a model. A European "farmer resident" in Belize once exhorted Belizeans in the local newspaper:

When you don't take care of this land today you are a traitor against God and your children. . . . Don't cut down the rainforest. Don't shoot the wildlife. . . . You can make your country the Switzerland of Central America. You have a wonderful land with parts of intact rainforest, wide varieties of tropical flora and fauna, wonderful islands with the largest living barrier reef. You have low mountain regions. You have an evergreen country with friendly hospitable people. You have all those good conditions which were the basis for the European Swiss to develop a touristic country. (*Amandala* June 2, 1996a, 19–20)

Since 1984, the BAS has been handed responsibility for the management of protected areas under the National Parks System Act. At the request of the government, BAS has financed, developed, and operated theses areas. A 1996 Memorandum of Agreement with the government of Belize gave BAS control of seven preserves (Shipstern and Tapir Mountain nature reserves, Crooked Tree and Cockscomb Basin wildlife sanctuaries, Half Moon Caye Natural Monument, Blue Hole and Guanacaste national parks), altogether a total of 150,000 acres. This may be the first example of a country handing over the management of a large number of its protected areas to an NGO. BAS collects fees for entrance into the reserves and retains a percentage of the fees for management costs. It, like other NGOs, can apply for financial support from the Protected Area Conservation Trust, which controls the U.S.$7.50 departure tax and other in-country fees that go toward environmental activities.

BAS's activities have other connections to ecotourism. They are also supported by Rainforest Rescue, Ltd., the commercial for-profit arm of BAS that sells T-shirts (in white, jungle green, and desert spray) with a jaguar logo; rain forest habanero pepper sauce, rain forest honey (in coconut, passion fruit, mango, banana, and cho flavors); tropical fruit jam; trail mix; herbal teas made from provision bark, cacao beans, and cinnamon sticks; banana peanut butter; herbal soap; rain forest jewelry; documentary films such as *Belize Adventure* and *Path of the Rain God*; and books such as *Rainforest Remedies: One Hundred Healing Herbs of Belize*, by Rosita Arvigo and Michael Balick, and *A Belizean Rain Forest: The Community Baboon Sanctuary*, by Robert Horwich and Jonathon Lyon. Only 6 percent of the proceeds of these purchases go to the BAS, although the ecotourists who buy them believe they are contributing much more to environmentalism.

COMBINING CONSERVATION WITH TROPICAL FOREST INDUSTRY

The Rio Bravo Conservation Area came into being as the result of a land scandal involving the huge holdings of Barry Bowen's Belize Estate and Produce Company, two Houston businessmen, and Coca-Cola Foods, as well as several government ministers whose private law firm profited from the sale ("Is Belize up for Sale?" 1985). The sale of 700,000 acres in northwestern Belize, a bit more than 12 percent of all land in Belize, for U.S.$6 million (less than $9 an acre), was for a suspiciously low price. The *Dallas Morning News* estimated at the time that the land was worth between U.S.$150 and $200 million. When protests over this sale reached a fever pitch, the Coca-Cola Company gave 90,000 acres of the land to the Rio Bravo Conservation Area.

The Rio Bravo Conservation Area is a private reserve owned by Programme for Belize. Funded initially by the Massachusetts Audubon Society, Coca-Cola Foods, USAID, the Nature Conservancy, the MacArthur Foundation, and Perkin-Elmer, the Programme is now self-funded through ecotourism projects and forestry resources. The reserve comes under environmental laws through an agreement with the Belize government that can be renegotiated at any time. The link between Programme for Belize and important government and financial institutions is fixed in the board of directors: the U.S. ambassador to Belize, a manager of the Belize sugar industry, the governor of the Central Bank of Belize, the financial secretary of the Ministry of Finance, the permanent secretary of the Ministry of Natural Resources, an adviser to the Deputy Prime Minister, and the vice president of BAS, thus covering all the important international and national players in Belize. I was assured by Roger Wilson, the technical director of Programme for Belize and a board member, that all board members act as private citizens in their role on the board.

With 229,000 acres of land, Programme for Belize controls one of the largest pieces of land in Belize. On it is situated one of the most important Maya sites in Belize, La Milpa. With more than 24 courtyards and over 85 structures, it is one of the largest public spaces in the Maya world. In the nineteenth century, the Maya mounted attacks from La Milpa against the loggers in mahogany camps that were established in the region. Discovered in 1938 by Sir Eric Thompson, it was completely looted in the 1970s. The Rio Bravo Conservation Area, once heavily populated by the Maya, has more than 60 Maya sites besides La Milpa.

According to Roger Wilson, the objective of the Programme is "conservation of biodiversity and sustainable use of its resources." Its desire is to be financially viable and socially sustainable, with all research serving "our social ends rather than being project driven." Currently, it is studying chicle production, which has proven not to be commercially viable in a sustainable way. It has had more success with sustainable production of thatch and house plants, and carbon offsets (the practice of exchanging CO^2 emissions in, e.g., the U.S. for investment in forest reserves in Belize), which brought in over U.S.$1 million in 1996. Hoping to pay for itself with sustainable development projects, it admits to mixed results so far. On the other hand, the proceeds do pay the salaries of employees such as Wilson and the director, Joy Grant.

Advocates of an ecology-based tropical forest industry sometimes come into conflict with more purist environmentalists. When the Rainforest Action Network, based in San Francisco, called for a boycott of mahogany products by American consumers, Dr. Nick Brokaw of the Manomet Observatory for Conservation Sciences in Massachusetts, whose work has been in the Rio Bravo Conservation Area, argued against it. "A boycott is a bad idea. We should be buying tropical timber so that it remains valuable. If there's no market for the wood, the forests will be mowed down and the land turned to agriculture. Biologists and foresters must work together to restore a strong economic incentive for conserving the forest" (Line 1996, B6).

Today a large portion of Belize consists of nature reserves adjacent to major ecotourist resort developments. Mountain Pine Ridge Forest Reserve surrounds resorts such as Mountain Equestrian Trails, Hidden Valley Inn, and Francis Ford Coppola's Blancaneux Lodge; the Hol Chan Marine Park, on the reef, is located next to Caye Caulker and San Pedro. Places such as Community Baboon Sanctuary at Bermudian Landing (funded by World Wide Fund for Nature) and Crooked Tree Wildlife Sanctuary (funded by the Belize Audubon Society) are engaged in ecotourist resort development. Resort owners are closely involved in the establishment of government reserves and serve on environmental committees to protect the reserves. Francis Ford Coppola, who established Blancaneux Lodge initially for his own "R and R," has been involved in media productions to educate Belizeans about the environment. A wealthy Belizean, Barry Bowen, owns the popular ecotourist Chan Chich Lodge adjacent to the Rio Bravo Conservation Area. According to Richard and Sally Price, a considerable amount of the forests of Belize and the Caribbean coastline are owned by foreigners (Price and Price 1995, 100). These foreigners benefit from the nature reserves that they have helped establish near their land.

TOURISM AS DEVELOPMENT

It is hard to know whether tourism is a good or a bad development in a country. In Belize the tourism industry involves Belizeans as employees but the money for development comes from foreigners, and therefore the large resorts are controlled by foreigners. While it is clear that tourism brings in valuable foreign exchange and provides jobs in the service sector that are much needed in a poor country, it is also true that tourism creates an economy dependent on the hyperrealist perceptions of the tourist and the fashions of the industry (ecotourism being the latest fashion), and that it can overwhelm the local culture, driving it in directions that make it accessible only to the most wealthy. Whether tourism is a valuable way for countries to develop their resources or a destructive postmodern imperialism depends on who you ask.

In spite of the vastly different assessments of the benefits and drawbacks of tourism development, several things are clear. Tourism is now the largest item in world trade, with a growth of 6 percent per annum since the 1960s (Woods et al. 1994, 2). In Belize it is second only to agriculture and is rapidly becoming the number one source of income. Globally, tourism represents perhaps the largest movement of human populations outside of wartime, and in Belize, tourists outnumber the nation's population. Almost every community in the world is influenced by tourism, and many Third World countries have opted for tourism as a central development strategy. The same trends we see in international tourism can be found in Belize, where tourism has grown in influence and is part of the development strategy of both the Belize government and the USAID programs.

Given the political economy of international tourism as it plays out in Belize, it clearly is already a major force in the development of the country. Although there are aspects of neocolonialism in Belize's tourism, in that most investment in tourism comes from outside, nevertheless a number of Belizeans have been able to take advantage of the business opportunities that tourism affords. Although Belize has the same seasonal fluctuations, boom and bust periods, and dubious foreign exchange advantages that tourism brings elsewhere, it has been able to garner some of the advantages of tourist development: the building of an infrastructure that will benefit the local population, preservation of the environment through the activities of international environmental NGOs, influx of capital investment in the country, and increased awareness of international news, global concerns, and the place of Belize in the world economy.

This brief history of tourism is simultaneously a partial history of the globalization of Belize, that is, of Belize's entry into the global economy and its connection with the different global "scapes." Tourists have arrived in large numbers during the period in which Belize has been formed as a nation. In a small nation with few skilled people, these tourists, resort developers, and environmentalists have influenced the government and people through the ideas they have transplanted into Belize and through their actions. They have set up nature reserves, built tourist resorts, created offshore investment opportunities, bought land, and built houses for retirement or vacation. Because their numbers have been large relative to the population of Belize, their impact has been significant.

TOURIST SPACES

With tourism fast becoming the world's largest industry and the number of known visitors reaching over half a billion people and growing steadily, tourism today represents the single largest movement of people around the globe. Given its economic and social importance, it is curious that the study of tourism has not been given the serious social science attention its trade importance warrants. Anthropologists still regard the study of tourism as somewhat frivolous and suffer as well from a slight embarrassment at being tourists ourselves, given our claims to authority on the authentic experience, as Walker Percy noted. Nevertheless, tourism raises many fascinating questions for geographers, economists, and anthropologists, one being the different uses of social and natural space that tourism creates.

Tourism operates basically in three tourist spaces: a *core* or space where tourism is generated, a national or international *gateway* through which tourists pass, and a pleasure *periphery* where tourists act out tourist behavior (Zurick 1992). (See Figure 7.2.) The activities of these three areas are quite different. The *core* area, where tourism is generated, is where people work and live ordinary lives. The ways in which tourism is generated have much to tell us about the culture of the core area. The *gateway* is the area associated with the transition of people into tourists and is associated with stress, liminality, and a change in behavior. The *periphery* is a ludic space where tourists engage in leisure activities. According to this spatial model, tourism originates out of the metropole from a condition of affluence and is constructed from excess in consumption patterns. It has often been called a form of "leisure imperialism" because of the relatively unequal power distribution between tourists and hosts (Nash 1989).

According to Malcolm Crick (1989, 327), tourism is also a form of migration and a desire to opt out of ordinary social reality; to embrace freedom and fun (hence avoiding duty and structure) and, therefore, hedonism (drugs, sex, nude swimming); to turn toward relaxation and conspicuous spending; and often to search for a reproduction of a colonial past. The local-tourist relationship therefore is based on a paradox. The tourist is at play, with considerable economic assets but poor cultural information, whereas the local is

Figure 7.2
Tourist Spaces

Core Area   ———Gateway———>   Pleasure
                                         Periphery

(Generates Tourism)   (Tourist Spaces)

at work, lacks money, but has cultural capital. The local becomes a kind of cultural broker for the tourist.

Another approach to understanding tourism space is to look at the kinds of tourist spaces that are created or suppressed by tourism. I have already mentioned the *ludic* space, created at the pleasure periphery of a metropolis, where aimless, playful behavior is encouraged. There are also *liminal* spaces created by tourism, spaces where the normal moral codes of conduct are compromised. These liminal spaces are often referred to as a kind of sun-sea-sand-sex tourism in which tourists engage in behavior they would be embarrassed to enact at home. Hence the acute embarrassment of tourism among cosmopolitans from the core.

Yet a third kind of space is a *hyperreal* space. It is hyperreal because destinations themselves "create" the environment tourists are already seeking. Hyperreality occurs in all kinds of host-guest spaces. It might take the form of reenactment of a colonialist past with wildlife safaris, lodges full of stuffed animals, and a trekking atmosphere, or it might be a cultural journey to a past indigenous civilization (e.g., La Ruta Maya). The Fort George Hotel in Belize City recently underwent extensive renovation to create just such a hyperreality for its high-paying guests. The furniture is distinctly East India Trading Company—heavy mahogany with coffee tables made from tea shipping crates and cushions covered in mock African animal skins. The jet-black doorman is dressed in white colonial shorts, khaki knee socks, and a pith helmet, complete with a spear on top. Afternoon tea is served at 3:30 P.M., in traditional English colonial fashion, for the largely American clientele. Hyperreal space is not confined to tourists but may also include the scientist or archaeologist who sees the environment as a "place to collect data" independent of humans living in the area, their social rules, or any necessity for cultural sensitivity.

Belize's success as a tourist destination is, in part, attributable to its having all three tourist spaces. It has the ludic space of getting away from the metropolis; it has the liminal space of abandonment of moral codes of sexuality; it has the hyperreal spaces of colonialism and "real" Maya villages, while offering the "authentic" experience.

8

Tour Guides and Rastas

I waited inside the small, air-conditioned Island Air office for the one-engine Cessna to arrive from Belize City and take me to the international airport. One by one, a few other tourists arrived and threw their luggage on the cart outside the office before coming inside, out of the piercing sunlight and heat. One of the Island's Rastas walked up, carrying a large backpack, followed by a young German woman sweating in tight, dark-brown nylon shirt and pants. He tossed her bag effortlessly on the cart, his dark muscles gleaming with sweat, his short dreads hanging down in front of his face. He was gorgeous, muscular, trim, and manly—and he knew it. They sat on the steps rather than coming inside with the others. She leaned against his body and held onto his arm muscles, looking intently into his eyes. He looked into the distance with a distracted air, picked at his teeth, and sighed. This was another "job" for him but, to give him credit, he carried it through to the end with the farewell kiss when the plane arrived and the promises to see each other sometime in the future. I knew him well. He made a good living from women tourists—gave them bang for their buck, showing them a good time, providing any drugs they requested, and sending them on their way with stories to tell their friends back home about their fling on Caye Caulker. She sat next to me on the plane and complained of the heat. I smiled and asked her if she had had a good time on Caye Caulker. "Oh, yes." She laughed happily. "I'll never forget it."

TOURISTS AND LOCALS

Tourist-local interactions on Caye Caulker can take many forms, but the most common are those with tour guides seeking to take tourists out to the reef or to visit other cayes. In the early days of tourism, getting to the reef required finding a group of like-minded tourists who want to snorkel and rustling up a young local who was not busy fishing and was willing to go. Today the tour guide business is highly competitive. There has been an enormous increase in numbers of tourists, creating a huge demand for tour guides, but there has also been a big increase in the numbers of men who work exclusively in tourism. They stand in the sand lanes or in small booths on the sides of the lanes in the morning and hustle tourists as they walk by.

What are you doing today? Wanna go to the reef? You'll have a good time if you come with us. Come see the natural wonders of the reef. We got some girls [or boys] going on our trip. Why don't you join us? Don't go out with that guy. He doesn't know the reef. I hear he harasses people.

The tour guides have an easy, teasing style of talk and can be very creative with language. Hustling is so much a part of the tourist industry in Belize that one tour operation in San Pedro has named itself Hustler Tours. To the tourists on Caye Caulker, the tour guides seem relaxed, carefree, and easygoing, consistent with the laid-back image of Caye Caulker promoted by the guidebooks. The tour guide's life is attractive: chatting it up with tourists, taking groups out to the reef, swimming and drinking with them, and hanging out in the evenings. The tourist, who is not working and is at play, enjoys the relaxed style of the tour guide who appears to be doing little work, earning a good living while enjoying himself.

Being a tour guide, however, calls for personal skills and political acumen not always apparent to the tourists. Competition for tourists is very stiff, not only on Caye Caulker but throughout the tourist industry in Belize. Those who work in the tourist industry must be aggressive, outgoing, and competitive; able to talk to tourists and know what preconceptions they have, what attracts and interests them; and above all, the tour guide must know how to entertain the tourists. Personal skills in salesmanship, hustling, and partying are essential to the job, as are a colossal patience for answering the same questions day after day and maintaining an appearance of enthusiasm. Not all Belizeans have these skills or want to work in the tourist business even if it provides a good income.

In the last few years the Belize Tourism Industry Association (BTIA) has tried to organize and professionalize tourism with guidelines for hotel operators, tour guides, and tourist-related enterprises. Since 1994, tour guides have been licensed by the National Tour Guide Committee, composed of members from various tour guide associations, the Belize Tourist Board, the BTIA, and the Ministry of Tourism. On Caye Caulker, for example, they must attend seminars on reef ecology, boat safety, and a behavior code for tour guide interactions with tourists (no sexual harassment) in order to qualify for their licenses. Licenses for tour guides, being a recent requirement, have resulted in intense competition between islanders who have not been certified as tour guides, but who may have great experience in taking out tourists and may be very knowledgeable about the area, and tour guides who may be licensed, but are not from the area and may have less knowledge about dive sites and reef ecology. This competition is exacerbated when the unlicensed islander is a respectable family man and the licensed tour guide is a Rasta from Belize City. Tourists, who often are unable to read the cultural cues, may shun a respectable tour guide entrepreneur who approaches them in the street with a hustle, finding the Rastas more "authentic" Belizeans.

RASTAS

The Rastas, who are mostly from Belize City, have found a niche on Caye Caulker, where they are reluctantly tolerated by the community. When they first came to Caye Caulker, they lived in trees in the middle of the island, surrounded by bush and mosquitoes, but today a group of them live in the village at the swampy back part of the island where the poorest people live. There the Rastas have built leaky, makeshift driftwood or *teciste* houses covered with written psalms and symbols such as the Star of David, the Tao, and the red/green/yellow of the Ethiopian flag.

Ras Creek is an example of a tour guide who projects the Rasta image in order to be attractive to young American and European tourists who are enamored with the images of exotic, dark-skinned, dreadlocked Rastas whose reputation as the hedonists of the Caribbean circulates in American and European bohemian circles. Ras Creek has a rickety boat with a small motor that he has painted in bright greens and reds and has topped with a palm thatch roof. His dreadlocks—dark at the roots and sun-bleached blonde at the tips—his philosophy of oneness with the animal world, and his engaging, outgoing personality have led to his being cited in the "hippie" guidebook *The Rough Guide* as one of the best snorkeling tour guides on Caye Caulker.

Rastafarian ideas from Jamaica became influential with Creoles and other Belizeans through the music of Bob Marley and the fascination of European and American tourists with reggae, ganja, and Rastafarian philosophy. A few Belizeans, mostly Creoles, are attracted to the Rastafarian philosophy and life, smoke ganja, and expound the ideas. Ras Milan, perhaps the most versed Rasta on Caye Caulker, explained:

There are many people in all this world, but very few think enough to see the truth. They do not see Babylon, the oppressor. They do not see the presence of Ja [God] in every little thing. They do not see Ja in the trees, the rum, the sea, the reef, the clouds, the houses, . . . every person. They cannot feel salvation and they just add to the suffering of the poor and the weak. But I see, I pay attention. I know, for I am Rasta, follower of Haile Selassie, Ras Tafari, King of Kings, Lord of Lords, the Lion of Judah, cousin to King David, I and I. (personal communication, C. Croom)

Many of them learned about Rastafarianism while living and working in the United States, although some of the influence has come directly from Jamaica through the small number of Jamaican immigrants to Belize. Ras Milan, for example, learned most of his information about Rasta from books he photocopied at the University of Chicago Library while visiting that city with an American friend. He also made a copy of the Old Testament and quoted certain passages, particularly the Psalms, which provide biblical justification for the Rasta movement. Psalm 87 is quoted by a number of Rastas on Caye Caulker as the psalm that predicts and justifies the movement and explains Haile Selassie and the role of reggae music.

His foundation is in the holy mountains. The Lord loves the gates of Zion more than all the other dwelling places of Jacob. Glorious things are spoken of you, o city of God. Selah. I shall mention Rahab and Babylon among those who know me; behold, Philista and Tyre with Ethiopia: "This one was born there." But of Zion it shall be said, "This one and that one were born in her," and the Most High Himself will establish her. The Lord shall count when he registers the peoples, "This one was born there." Selah. Then those who sing and those who play the flutes shall say, "all my springs of joy are in you."

The Caye Caulker Rasta interpretation of this passage takes Zion to be Ethiopia and "city of God" to refer to Addis Ababa. People born in Zion ("this one and that one were born in her")—that is, all black people—are singled out for distinction, and "the Most High Himself" is Haile Selassie. The Lord knows who was "born in Zion," and "those who sing and play the flutes" will sing praise to Zion. The latter reference is thought to portend reggae music.

According to Ras Milan, Ras Tafari is the Lion of Judah, who is Haile Selassie, King of Kings, Lord of Lords, direct descendant of King David by blood, and hence a relative of Jesus. But Ras Tafari (Rasta) is also Ja (God), who is in everyone and everything, and is also Jesus, and Buddha, and Shiva, and you and me. Haile Selassie had a lot of writings that the Rastafarian movement has used, along with the Bible, to provide the skeleton for a religion distinct from Christianity and Judaism, yet borrowing from both. Ras Milan recounted that Haile Selassie wrote about the value of sport (nurtures teamwork) and health (vital to the good life), and about recognizing the need for material goods but not being dominated by them. Selassie was against the use of alcohol and eating pork, but does not mention marijuana.

Rastafarian ideas, at least on Caye Caulker, are a syncretism of Taoism, Judaism, Christianity, Islam, and Afrocentrism. The yin-yang symbol, sometimes found as background to the Lion of Judah on houses and necklaces, is a reminder that Ja recognizes both good and evil as necessary, integral parts of existence. The Rasta origin myth is based on the belief that Ethiopia was the original homeland of all human beings; thus the ritual use of red, yellow, and green, the colors of the Ethiopian flag. Rastafarianism also claims a connection to Zion, the Jewish people, as evidenced by Bob Marley's song in which he urges Rastas to be strong, like iron, like the lion (of Judah). Like Hasidic Jews, Rastafarians have strict standards of cultural purity, that is, that everyone black is originally from Ethiopia and should bond together for strength and solidarity against a world that persecutes for them for being black and for smoking pot. African solidarity against Babylon, the oppressive system that persecutes Ja's children and ganja, is a necessity. The reference to a buffalo soldier (in the song by Bob Marley) is to a Ja person (closer to God, smoking ganja) who will one day help overthrow Babylon, because "when smoking de herb, it makes one think about life and what is wrong wid life." Not only is marijuana used as a symbol of being antiestablishment, it is also used as a sacrament (because the good spirit of the herb brings one closer to Ja). Apparently, there is a certain time of every month when herb is stronger, and a Rasta will go off into the bush by himself, smoke, and meditate (personal correspondence, C. Croom).

However, Rastafarian ideas and Rastas would not have found an economic niche in Belize except for the tourist industry. Young white tourists from Europe and the United States seem to have an endless fascination with the exotic dreadlocked Rastas and reggae music—especially the words and music of Bob Marley, who is constantly quoted on Caye Caulker—and the association with a pot-smoking, laid-back lifestyle. While the tourists, especially white tourist women, find the Rastas romantic and exotic, the locals view them as pot-smoking deadbeats who do not want to work and would rather con the tourists by charging high prices for ganja and their artwork. At worst, but all too frequently, a Rasta will get a group of tourists stoned in order to rob them when they fall asleep. The islanders often claim that Rastas are fakes who wear dreadlocks and sell pot in order to obtain money and sex from the tourists. This view is shared by some of the guidebook writers. The *Adventure Guide to Belize* describes the situation thus:

The island has been plagued by Rastaphonians. Coming from as far away as Roatan in Honduras, most of these dreadlocks-with-attitudes are thoroughly obnoxious, and their presence is resented by locals. Many of the men supplement their income by playing gigolo to naive visiting foreign women and selling drugs, including crack. (Pariser 1992, 141–142)

Even Ras Creek, who has gained some respect by working as a tour guide and owning a house and boat, has disdain for most Caye Caulker Rastas.

Some guys, dey just play dread, man. You gotta be careful of them, they are con artists. They grow the dreads, they talk like Rasta and go to bars, hang around, waiting for tourist women who don't know what's going on. Dread have nothing to do with Rasta. Anybody can be Rasta. Rasta just has to do with respect for every living thing. You just have to have respect and know that Babylon is made of people who don't respect. (personal communication, C. Croom)

Part of the attraction, for tourists, of the Rasta hustle is the antimaterialist, money-is-the-root-of-all-evil philosophy. The tactic is to start talking about how money is bad and evil, and how some wicked people do nothing but spend their entire lives hunting money. Once the tourist—feeling guilty that she has more money than the Rasta—agrees with the premise that money is bad, and that the less money we have, the happier we will be, it is easier to ask the tourist to be generous with her money for a meal, a joint, or cigarettes.

A Rasta on Caye Caulker often claims that he lives a natural life, drinking coconut water, eating only one meal a day (consisting of conch from the ocean and breadfruit from the trees), and sleeping in a tree in the bush. Some actually do sleep in trees, but the islanders take a less romantic view and claim that they are just too lazy to build a house. Roland, for example, believes that materialism is a disease and people who have material things get into a cycle of wanting (the Buddhist idea of samsara). He argues for the immediate satisfaction of physical needs and personal fulfillment, a kind of hedonistic approach very much in vogue among American youth and reminiscent of Bob Marley's "One Love." One day when I was cycling to the grocery store, Roland stood bare-chested in my path, his hand on his heart,

"Would you like to try de herbs? It makes you feel good inside."

"Which herbs? Marijuana?" I asked. But he was cautious.

"Natural herbs from de jungle. Makes you feel good inside."

PART III

Globalization in the Margins

9

The New Missionaries

Tourists visiting Cockscomb Jaguar Preserve are encouraged to read the book *Jaguar* (1986) by Alan Rabinowitz of the New York Zoological Society. The book tells the story of the author's two-year study of the jaguar at Cockscomb, an "amazing story," according to the jacket, "of heroism, tragedy and triumph" that ended in the establishment of the world's first jaguar preserve. In his book Rabinowitz describes his relationship with the Maya people living at Cockscomb, how they helped him find and capture the jaguars to study, how they tried to understand his mission, and how they learned to accept his presence, although he admits he never really warmed to them. He listens to their stories of the Duende, a legendary folk figure thought to guard plants and animals, and claims to have seen one himself, and he discovers archaeological sites, remnants of their ancient civilization. But in the end, these experiences are only episodes in his personal journey of discovery, and he concludes that the Maya must be moved off the land in order to "save" the jaguar and set up the Cockscomb preserve. Ironically, according to his book, all of the jaguars he captured and tagged, died or were killed during his stay there.

On December 2, 1984, the Cockscomb Basin was made a national preserve, and by the end of that month all the Indian families had been moved from their homes (Rabinowitz 1986, 359). Today these same Maya sit forlornly on the edge of the park, where they were moved, selling trinkets to tourists. Although it is a depressing sight, a tourist returning from Belize nevertheless described his trip to Cockscomb as the most wonderful time of his life and kindly suggested visitors take "children's clothing to the Popp family at the gate" (June 12, 1997, Bz-Culture@psg.com). Environmental groups also advertise the Cockscomb Preserve as an example of ecotourism successfully replacing formerly "destructive ways of making a living." *EarthWatch*, for example, reported:

> Part of the plans for the Cockscomb reserve for jaguars in Belize, in fact, involved relocating Maya residents to a new site, Maya Center, six kilometers from their original village. Despite initial resentment, the local population gradually began to see potential economic benefits from ecotourism after a local school teacher was hired as sanctuary director. (*EarthWatch* 1996, 33–34)

The sacrifice that the Maya community made for the park—giving up their homes, their land, and their traditional subsistence farming in return for one job as sanctuary director—seems not to worry the transnational environmental consciousness.

In 1985 the Bermudian Landing Community Baboon Sanctuary, a 20-mile stretch along the Belize River, became a sanctuary for black howler monkeys (called baboons in Belize). The howler monkeys were the subjects of a study by biologists, who suggested a preserve to local residents. After the experience of the locals at the Cockscomb Jaguar Preserve, there was an effort to pay more attention to the fate of the local residents. Touted as a successful example of community involvement in the establishment of a reserve, this sanctuary now provides howler monkeys for the Cockscomb Basin Wildlife Sanctuary and Shipstern Nature Reserve (a private reserve), where the population of monkeys was wiped out by habitat destruction resulting from hurricanes. But the income it produces for local residents who act as guides is negligible, and they still live in poverty with no prospects of development.

In Belize today, the new globalized Belize of the twenty-first century, the missionaries of the past, the Christian evangelists from North American sects, have been replaced by the new missionaries, the environmentalists. Armed not with Bibles but with ecological fervor, they have obtained 40 percent of the landmass in Belize and reserved it for animals, fish, and Mayan archaeological sites.

Environmentalists in Belize, as elsewhere, belong to a number of transnational organizations with complex systems of finance, recruitment, coordination, communication, and reproduction. The classic example of these transnational organizations is the multinational corporation. Other examples include networks of Christian philanthropy, bureaucracies concerned with refugee issues, the Olympic movement, "green" movements, fundamentalist reli-

gious movements such as the Muslim Brotherhood, and a proliferation of nongovernmental organizations (NGOs) organized around
issues of environment, health, arts, and development. Most of
these transnational social formations are designed explicitly to
counter or monitor the activities of the nation-state (Appadurai
1996, 167–168). I mentioned in Chapter 7 that environmentalism
is part of a global ethical debate that privileges the environment
over humans. The debate takes as its premise that people are de-
stroyers of the environment (with exceptions sometimes allowed for
indigenous people and women), and both the ecosystem and animals are the victims. This debate is now raging in Belize.

At the time of independence in Belize (1981), a primary issue facing the new government was how to distribute to Belizeans the
Crown lands acquired from the British government. This priority of
the newly independent government was preempted by the priorities of the environmentalists, who established the Law for Protected Areas in the same year. A large part of the Crown land has
now been put into reserves, its use by Belizeans restricted or prohibited. Environmental NGOs have placed themselves within government ministries and created their own units under those
ministries to finance and implement the environmental agenda.
Environmentalists view their actions as the result of a savvy strategy to influence a fledgling government to set aside Belize's natural
resources.

In 1995, *Caribbean and World Magazine*, an award-winning journal with headquarters in London, voted Belize the winner of the
Caribbean Ecoregion of the Year. According to Belize Online, a web
site for tourists wanting to visit Belize, Belize is the country with
the greatest percentage of its landmass dedicated to natural reserves, conservation refuges, parks, and wildlife preserves in the
world. (See Figure 9.1.) Belize has the world's first and only preserves dedicated to a specific animal—the jaguar, the howler monkey and the jabiru stork. In December 1996, the Belize Barrier
Reef was declared a World Heritage Site by the World Heritage
Commission of the United Nations. With seven national preserves
on the barrier reef and more being proposed, the reef is under constant international scrutiny.

The fame of Belize as an ecoregion has been accomplished in a
very short time. By 1993 Belize had over 6,000 square kilometers
of protected reserves and conservation areas, and the number of
protected areas was growing astronomically. By its tenth anniver-
sary as a nation, a staggering one-third of the country had been
put into nature reserves. The number of reserves is now estimated
to be over 40 percent of the land. The goal, according to John How-

Figure 9.1
Protected Areas in Belize

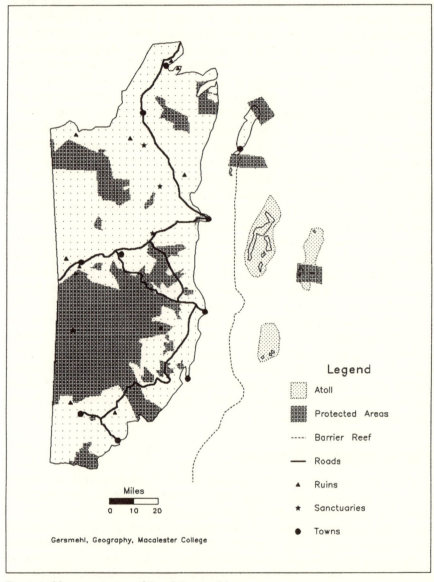

Legend

Atoll

Protected Areas

Barrier Reef

Roads

▲ Ruins

★ Sanctuaries

● Towns

Miles

0   10   20

Gersmehl, Geography, Macalester College

Reprinted by permission of Carol Gersmehl.

ell of the Natural History Museum in Belmopan, is to reach at least 50 percent of the landmass of the country.

As of 1997, there are ten government-established protected areas in Belize, a number of private reserves, and many, many more in the planning stages. Their management falls under one of three government departments: the Forest Department deals with protected forest areas such as Mountain Pine Ridge Forest Reserve, a pine forest similar to the Black Forest in Germany; and the Columbia Forest Reserve and Chiquibul Forest Reserve, both broadleaf forests in the Maya Mountains. In 1983 the Fisheries Department was charged with establishing protected areas for marine life, and the Archaeology Department with overseeing ancient monuments and antiquities. The government-established parks include Half Moon Caye Natural Monument (created in 1982), Crooked Tree Wildlife Sanctuary (1984), Cockscomb Basin Wildlife Sanctuary (1984), Community Baboon Sanctuary (1985), Blue Hole National Park (1986), Chiquibul National Park and the Hol Chan Marine Reserve (1987), Guanacaste National Park (1990), Bladen Reserve (1995), and Bacalar Chico National Park (1996).

The first reserves were established to "save" a specific species. Half Moon Caye Natural Monument was designated in 1982 for the protection of the red-footed booby. In 1984 Crooked Tree Wildlife Sanctuary was established to save the extremely rare jabiru stork. Described on-line as a world-class birdwatching destination and home to several hundred bird species, it is a favorite place for the many birdwatchers who come to Belize. With funding from several environmental organizations, today it is maintained by the Belize Audubon Society. In 1986 Belize created the Cockscomb Jaguar Preserve, the world's only jaguar preserve, consisting of 155 square miles of forest, funded by Wildlife Conservation International and the Belize Audubon Society.

ENVIRONMENTAL SUCCESS

The environmental progress that Belize has made in just a few years is, in fact, quite staggering. There is no question that the transnational environmental movement can consider Belize one of its major success stories. An underpopulated country with only the mere beginnings of development and a revenue-poor government looking for sources of financial backing, Belize was the ideal target for the movement. The establishment and management of an extensive system of reserves was only the beginning. The pace of environmental action continues to this day. Some recent examples of successful environmental action include the following:

1. In September 1996 Belize joined the Central American Commission on Environment and Development to develop plans to implement the Meso-America Biological Corridor Project. The aim of the project is to see environmental laws enacted into the constitutions of all Latin American countries from Mexico to Argentina. Formed in 1990, Belize's Ministry of Tourism and the Environment has worked with the Commission since its inception and signed the Alliance for Sustainable Development and the Concausa Declaration, an agreement between the United States and Central American countries to protect the environment. The conference in 1996 was held in Belize and the next week the Minister of Tourism and the Environment went to Nicaragua to help Nicaragua draft environmental legislation (*The Reporter* 1996, 4).

2. The citrus industry, in cooperation with the Department of the Environment, the Ministry of Trade and Industry and the United Nations Development Project, has formed a task force to deal with the environmental impact of acidic waste from citrus processing on water (resulting in fish kills). The task force is seeking foreign investors to fund a project that would use citrus peels as a base for cattle feed (*San Pedro Sun* 1996, 7).

3. USAID has funded an ecotourism and nature conservancy program at the La Milpa Field Station on the Rio Bravo Conservation Area. Twenty-eight representatives from ten Latin American and Caribbean countries attended the six-day conference at Programme for Belize to learn how to develop a market plan to incorporate ecotourism into their countries (*The Belize Times* 1996a, 15).

4. In September 1995 the Belize Marine Research Center was established at Calabash Caye, which is part of the Turneffe Atoll. The center, constructed by Coral Caye Conservation (an NGO from England, funded by the European Union) is being run in collaboration with University College Belize and the government of Belize. Its purpose is to train Belizeans in management of coastal reserves. The center recently (August, 1997) received a grant of Bz$60,000 from the Texaco Foundation (*Coral Caye Conservation Newsletter* 1996).

5. In Belize today marine turtles are steadily increasing in numbers for the first time. Marine turtles, the green turtle, the hawksbill and the loggerhead have been eaten as a delicacy since the days of the baymen, and by 1830 they were exported to Europe for their meat as well as the shells. Promoted by the Belize Audubon Society, Belize passed the first turtle restriction law in 1977 and a turtle preservation act in 1982. Belize and the Cayman Islands are the only two Caribbean countries to have turtle protection laws (*The Reporter* 1996f, 4).

6. Belize has the best chance of genetic diversity in the manatee population and the largest group for one area. In January 1997 the Coastal Zone Management Project (funded by the United Nations Development Project) identified 232 manatee in a nine-hour period. Placencia Lagoon

has the largest groups (usually they are solitary) and the largest numbers in one lagoon (100 manatee). There are twenty-four manatee between Hicks Caye and Southern Drowned Caye (*The Reporter* 1997a).

The "conservation community" in Belize views itself as a powerful and influential lobby, highly effective in creating and implementing government policies. It is also well organized politically, having recently formed an umbrella organization called BACONGO that serves as a lobby for, among other things, obtaining funds from the Protected Areas Conservation Trust, which is well funded by the exit tax paid by tourists. Some members own large tourist businesses and have even set up their own private reserves; others work for the environmental NGOs. They are influential in that they have direct access to government ministers and legislators, to the United States Embassy, to the international press, and to the tourists themselves. They actively pursue their interests by going directly to the press, the U.S. government, and the tourists to pressure the Belize government. For example, they have publicized logging activities in Toledo district in the mainstream press (e.g., the *New York Times, The Economist* [1993], and *U.S. News & World Report* [March 10, 1997]) and organized a campaign of faxes, letters, and E-mail to government offices from "would-be" tourists who had decided to go elsewhere on their vacations because of the government's stance on the logging in the Columbia Forest Reserve (Bz-Culture group, March 12, 1997, Marguerite Bevis).

How has the environmental movement been so successful in establishing the environment as one of the nation's highest priorities? How has it been able to convince the government to reserve nearly half the country's land for environmental purposes? How has it come to control the management of the reserves? How has Belize, stagnating in obscurity for so many years, come to be recognized as the top ecoregion of the area? To explore these questions, I want to detail the history of the latest reserve, the Bacalar Chico National Park, and the Coastal Zone Management Group.

THE COASTAL ZONE

A more detailed history of the environmental "management" of the coastal zone illustrates the environmental issues prevalent in Belize today. The coastal area of Belize supports the country's two major industries—tourism and fisheries. Tourism is now the number one industry, and fishery products constitute the fourth most important export commodity (after sugarcane, citrus, and bananas). Each of these industries is a valuable source of foreign exchange and provides employment for a large number of coastal inhabitants (4,500). Subsistence fishing is also a very important source of protein in the diet. Linked to the coastal zone are the coastal plains and watershed that support the sugarcane, citrus, and banana industries (UNDP 1993, 2–3). In short, the coastal zone supports the most important sectors of the Belizean economy.

The environmental urgency and fervor bearing on Belize's coastal zone stems not from its economic importance, which is considerable, but from its global ecological position. Coral reefs are among the most diverse ecosystems on earth and the variety of reef formations in Belize is unparalleled in the Caribbean (UNDP 1993, 2). The Belize coastline contains the second longest, and the longest living, barrier reef in the world. The Belize Barrier Reef stretches approximately 220 kilometers from the Mexican border in the north to the Sapodilla Cayes in the south. The barrier reef and the three offshore atolls have formed on a series of fault blocks, lying in submarine "steps" off the coast of Belize. The international environmental community views the Belize Barrier Reef with its seven preserves as important enough to hand over to Belize the presidency of the Central American Environment and Development Commission on July 31, 1997.

In general, tropical seas are very poor in nutrients, but the reef ecosystem has evolved mechanisms over thousands of years to recycle its nutrients. Coral reefs are made from coral polyps, which secrete a hard skeleton of calcium carbonate. In Belize, over 60 species of hard coral and 36 species of soft coral have been identified. This diversity is second only to Jamaica, where more coral species have been identified because research has been more extensive (Raines et al. 1997). The coral reef is also home to many species of invertebrates (e.g., shrimp and sea urchins), noncommercial fish (e.g., triggerfish, parrot fish, and butterfly fish) and commercial fish (e.g., snapper, grouper, and jack). Thus, from the basis of the tiny coral polyp, a complex ecosystem has evolved that rivals the tropical rain forest in its diversity.

In the northern part of the country, the barrier reef, about a mile east of Caye Caulker, does not lie in the lee of one of the offshore atolls but is exposed to the full wave action of the open ocean. Thus, the reef is characterized by slow-growing, narrow, discontinuous communities composed of elkhorn, star, lettuce, fire, and brain corals. Several cuts, or channels, in the reef provide interesting dive sites where the fish life is diverse and coral formations flourish. In a sense, the reef at Caye Caulker is an atypical part of the Belize Barrier Reef due to its being on migratory routes of fish and lobsters. The shallow waters and sandy coral bottom are ideal feeding grounds for lobsters, making these lobster beds the best in the nation. These specialized flats are found nowhere else in Belize except South Water Caye.

These reefs are extremely important to the economy and well-being of the cayes. The fishing industry is based on reef species, the spiny lobster being the primary product. A vibrant tourism industry is based on diving, snorkeling, and recreational fishing. The reef provides a physical barrier against the force of the sea, dissipating the wave energy and thus protecting the island from erosion. This is particularly important in reducing storm surge during hurricanes. One of the environmental concerns today is the rise in tropical storm activity, allegedly due to global warming, that will have a major effect on mangroves, cayes, and coastal areas.

COASTAL ZONE RESERVES

The first attempt to preserve the coastal and marine ecosystem in Belize was the establishment in 1987 of the Hol Chan Marine Reserve on the southern tip of Ambergris Caye. According to the environmentalists who set it up in conjunction with the fishermen and tour guides of San Pedro, it has been moderately successful in protecting that particular swath of reef to coast. In addition, it has been a boon to the tourist industry by providing a segment of the reef where marine life is once again abundant after being depleted for many years (Carter et al. 1994, 220–221). However, it is clear that the establishment of the park was supported locally only when it became obvious to the people of San Pedro that some protection of the reef would be needed if their livelihood were to be sustained (Carter et al. 1994, 225)—and even then, only after months of discussion. The hope of the environmentalists was that the Hol Chan Marine Reserve would be a model for future marine reserves, a role it has certainly played (Carter et al. 1994, 230).

In order to implement the various plans for establishing and managing reserves, the NGOs needed an organization sanctioned by the government that could ostensibly be in charge. Thus, the Fisheries Department, established to promote and manage Belize's fishing industry, in 1990 became the holding tank for a newly established unit called Coastal Zone Management Unit (CZMU). CZMU was the brainchild of NGOs such as Wildlife Conservation International, World Wide Fund for Nature, World Conservation Union, Coral Caye Conservation, and the Belize Audubon Society. Funding for CZMU has come from grants through NGOs such as these.

Who are the NGOs and why did they come to Belize? Many of them are recognizable global organizations based in England or the United States; others are smaller operations such as an English NGO, Coral Caye Conservation (CCC), that came to Belize to carry out the research needed before proposing environmental plans for the preservation of coastal areas. Founded in 1988 by Peter Raines, Coral Caye Conservation is a nonprofit organization that uses paying volunteers (charging them approximately U.S.$2,000 each) to help fund their projects. Raines is a biologist who, after concluding that academic research was useless, decided to take an active role in reef preservation. An athletic, attractive man and an accomplished diver who worked for a while as a builder to earn the money to establish CCC, Raines found that his academic background nevertheless proved useful in writing grants to obtain funding from European governmental sources. In 1989, he began to work on management plans to present to the Fisheries Department's Coastal Zone Management Unit. In addition to diving and mapping South Water Caye, the Sapodilla Cayes, and Calabash Caye, CCC set up a "research center" at Calabash Caye to teach diving to students from University College Belize as part of their training in becoming park rangers.

In 1994, CCC started work on the Bacalar Chico project. It conducted a study of marine resources, wrote a management plan for a reserve, and decided how to restrict use of and access to the new reserve. Such decisions taken at the research and planning stage set the stage for considerable power over use of park resources by one NGO. Then, with a grant from the European Union, CCC funded CZMU to send rangers out to enforce the new rules. Because the Bacalar Chico Reserve included coastal areas and interior land, the Forestry Department and the Fisheries Department competed for control of the park and its funding. With grant funding coming to an end, the government will take over the management of the reserve, but no one is sure how it will be paid for unless hefty user fees are established.

According to Raines, CCC's work has added 15 species to the list of corals in Belize, including the blue cross coral discovered at Bacalar Chico. In a study in which it assessed its own data, CCC concluded that its research, while not a scientific contribution to reef ecology, does provide sufficient data for coastal zone management purposes. At the end of 1998, CCC will leave Belize and move on to other adventures—the Red Sea, Sulawesi, New Guinea, and the Philippines.

What is the importance of the management plans that NGOs such as CCC present to the government? First, the plans are the basis of decisions for setting up laws to restrict and prevent use of resources in particular areas, thus giving the NGO considerable power to determine resource use. This power is even greater when the NGO provides the financing to establish, manage, and police the reserves. In a small, weak country such as Belize, this process amounts to almost total NGO control of decisions on reserve resources.

Although the first reserves in Belize created in this way were in place before anyone living in the area was consulted, local people are now more aware of the implications of the reserves for their lives and immediately take an interest when a reserve is proposed. In the case of Bacalar Chico, local interest was very high the minute the proposed reserve was announced. The first proposal included the possibility of resort hotels and land for a new village of locals. Set forth under the PUP government, this proposal was protested both by environmental groups, who objected to the building of hotels, and tourist interests in San Pedro, who objected to the building of hotels they would not own. Rumors abounded that government ministers were going to take large pieces of land for themselves and profit from selling it to resort owners from the United States. There was no lobby speaking in favor of the proposal to set up a new village and give land to the landless poor. The San Pedro tourist interests wanted in on the profits, but they lost to the environmentalists, who, through their considerable influence with the UDP government, successfully established the park with no major tourist development allowed.

ENVIRONMENTAL TENSIONS

Virtually everyone, myself included, agrees that there is a need to preserve the complex and delicate reef system and that tourist resort development does pose a threat to this ecosystem. This threat can easily be seen in areas where mangroves are being cut down and destructive seawalls are being built, as well as in the huge garbage dumps on the island. There are even incidents of deliberate damage to the reef by resort developers who dynamite inlets in the reef (e.g., at Hatchet Caye) for boat access to their resorts. The environmental movement has been very successful at combating these offenses.

Under pressure from environmentalists, Belize has established an extensive network of seven marine protected areas: Blue Hole, Sapodilla Caye, Laughing Bird Caye, South Water Caye, Glover's Reef, Half Moon Caye, and Bacalar Chico. A large portion of fringing reef is within the boundaries of the Half Moon Caye Natural Monument, located on Lighthouse Reef atoll. The Hol Chan Marine

Reserve, at the south end of Ambergris Caye, and the Bacalar Chico Preserve protect a good portion of the northern barrier reef, sea grass beds, and mangroves. Eight more coastal reserves are in the process of being studied. (See Figure 9.2.) If these reserves are established, a large portion of the entire reef will be in reserves.

In Belize, because of lack of government funds, NGOs have become the managers of most of the preserves (the Belize Audubon Society manages seven), giving them a position of considerable power and decision-making in the distribution of resources in Belize.

Today there are indications that the days of NGO hegemony may be on the wane. Although the World Bank and U.N. Development Programme support the Coastal Zone Management Project to develop management plans for coastal zone areas, develop policies on dredging and mangroves, and map the coastal areas as well as monitor them, the funding for this project runs out in March 1998, at which time the Belize government is supposed to take over these functions. Whether it has the financial capacity or the political will to do so remains to be seen.

All of this preservation activity, while admirable, has raised a pressing question in Belize today. What about the people living in the now preserved areas, where their traditional subsistence activities have become criminal acts? The environmentalists view the problem as an issue of public relations with the local population. The solution, they suggest, is to involve local people in the planning process rather than having the plan come directly from the NGOs through the government. The argument they make is that the success of marine conservation is dependent on an awareness among the general public of the need to protect marine resources, and that the most important group in which to instill a conservation ethic is the fishermen. Up to now, this tactic has had a great deal of success. The fishermen, for some time, have accepted prohibitions on eating manatee or turtle, and on killing crocodiles (even though crocodiles come ashore to eat puppies on Caye Caulker). They generally follow the lobster season and size rules, and are fined when they do not. However, in the new reserves, commercial lobster traps and fishing will be prohibited, and criminalized in some areas.

Of course, even with all these regulations, fishermen and other Belizeans must somehow continue to make their living from the sea. When areas are under strict no-use regulation, they are told to become tour guides for sportfishing and snorkeling. Ecotourism is touted as the solution; fishing is labeled the problem.

Figure 9.2
Proposed Coastal Reserves in Belize

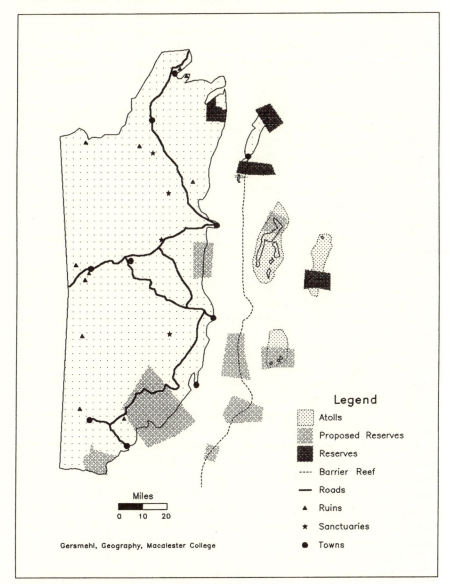

Legend

Atolls
Proposed Reserves
Reserves
---- Barrier Reef
— Roads
▲ Ruins
★ Sanctuaries
● Towns

Miles
0   10   20

Gersmehl, Geography, Macalester College

Reprinted by permission of Carol Gersmehl.

THE BACALAR CHICO NATIONAL PARK

The Bacalar Chico National Park is one of the latest reserves on the coast. Established in June 1996, it comprises a 15,000-acre marine reserve and 12,000 acres of land habitat in the northern part of Ambergris Caye. Touted in the literature as a model of government/NGO collaboration in conservation projects (Harborne et al. 1994), it has been funded by the European Community through three NGOs: Coral Caye Conservation, International Tropical Conservation Foundation, and the World Conservation Union. These groups have also worked with CZMU to develop a countrywide management strategy for the entire coastline of Belize. The headquarters of the park are situated on a Maya site, San Juan, and on the Bacalar Chico coast. The headquarters building has space for a marine biologist, a terrestrial biologist, and two marine rangers. A visitors center is being built. Negotiations are under way to establish a similar reserve on the Mexican side of the border, on the Yucatan Peninsula. Once a favorite fishing site for fishermen from Sarteneja, Corozal, and Mexico, Bacalar Chico is now off limits to them, and a traditional activity has become a criminal offense.

I have been visiting the Bacalar Chico area since the early 1980s. Ambergris Caye is really a peninsula off the southeast tip of Mexico east of the Bay of Chetumal. It is the largest of the Belizean cayes, 28 miles long, and separated from the Yucatan mainland of Mexico by a narrow canal. Bacalar Chico is the piece of land that lies just below the canal, 6 miles south of the Mexican village of Xcalak and 25 miles from the village of San Pedro, on the south of the caye. It is a remote piece of coast between the outposts of each country, and is accessible only by boat. Getting to Bacalar Chico from San Pedro is not easy because halfway up the coast, the barrier reef rises out of the sea and crawls onto the land. Reef Point looks like the surface of the moon, shielding whelks and shellfish in its tidal pools and acting as a spawning ground, on the windward side, for thousands of Nassau grouper.

One of the last wild, untouched coastlines, it is separated from Mexico by the Bacalar Chico canal, which was made by the Maya before the Spaniards arrived. The canal is so narrow you can touch Mexico and Belize on opposite sides of the boat, and so shallow the bottom is visible the whole way. It is a magical place, but also very remote. So remote that once, when I was stranded at the Pinkerton site at San Juan because of motor failure, I waited 48 hours for a boat to appear and rescue my 2 children, my husband, my then 78-year-old mother, my Belizean brother, and me. We ate Mexican cookies, the kind with pink marshmallow sprinkled with coconut on top, and collected water from the huge, abandoned rainwater tank that Pinkerton had built. Pinkerton was a man from Louisiana who bought up the entire back area of northern Ambergris Caye and built a house at San Juan, where it is alleged he looted the major Maya site under his house. He was also thought to be a gun smuggler, and kept armed guards on his dock who would not let fishermen stop there to collect freshwater. This won him no friends among the Sarteneja fishermen crossing the Bay of Chetumal, and eventually he was arrested and forced to leave the country. The land was taken over by the Belize government.

Archaeologists excavated the area many years later and found enough green obsidian, burial mounds, and polychrome pots to conclude that it was a major transshipment point for Maya traders coming from the Yucatan in seagoing vessels, transferring goods to river craft, and continuing to Guatemala by river. The archaeological evidence points to a successful and wealthy society with trade goods from the entire Maya world (Guderjan 1993, 31). Although Bacalar Chico was heavily populated in Maya times, by the 1850s there was only a small town composed basically of three families— the Blakes, the Huesners, and the Hoys—who came from the town of Bacalar during the Caste Wars of Yucatan and stayed until the 1931 hurricane destroyed the entire town, obliterating even the graveyard. After the hurricane it remained virtually unpopulated for many years. In 1982 my mother bought land on the windward side, where she built a house.

Only four people lived on the five-mile stretch of coast that is now in the park. Francisco, a Mexican of Mayan descent, tilled a *canuco*, an area of fertile black dirt brought in by the Mayas, on land owned by the Huesner family. Chanai, a Belizean from Sarlineja, and his wife and 15-year-old daughter, Rosita, harvested coconuts on the land owned by the Franco family. The fishermen who periodically came down the coast to Bacalar nicknamed Francisco "Paisano" because he was a man of the land, not the sea. Francisco was familiar with the world of plants and animals, as his Mayan ancestors had been, and his *canuco* flourished with melons, bananas, plantains, limes, squash, tomatoes, and the Mayan staples, corn and beans. What he did not eat, he harvested and sold in Xcalak. He built a house entirely from objects the tide had brought in—rope, pieces of wood, and parts of ships fashioned into a Rube Goldberg structure. A long gangplank led to his driftwood outhouse over the sea. Inside the house he had papered the walls with Mexican comic books for reading material. He combed the beach daily for goodies from the sea. A huge rope from a ship was made into two Maya-style hammocks; hand-blown bottles from

Portugal became ashtrays; various unmatched shoes became his footwear; he cooked with pots and pans washed up on the shore; and we barbecued barracuda on metal racks from old refrigerators. The most jarring bits of flotsam were the numerous mangled and decapitated dolls on the beach, testament to childhoods long gone. The bale of marijuana he found one day was shoved back into the sea.

Slowly, over the years, people began to take notice of Bacalar Chico. Tour guides from San Pedro began to bring more and more tourists, hunters, and sportfishermen to the area. Archaeologists arrived, excavated behind his house, and angered the local fishermen by refusing to buy their fresh fish, sending instead to San Pedro for frozen hamburger meat. Every day they lit fires to drive away the mosquitos, and through carelessness in putting out a fire, Paisano's *canuco* was burned down, destroying his only source of cash. Soon after, the cocaine drops began. People from San Pedro and Mexico came to the remote coast to collect the drugs, and suddenly Paisano was no longer the only inhabitant of Bacalar Chico. One day a machete-chopped body was floating under the dock, and empty cocaine bags were found buried in the bush.

All this land is now part of the new national park. Delighted that the area, which is wild and beautiful, would be preserved in its present "pristine" state (apart from the tons of plastic that float up on the beach from all over the world), I decided to visit Bacalar Chico, a hair-raising trip by boat through the reef even in good weather. The park rangers from the CZMU had set up headquarters complete with electric generators, ham radios, chemical toilets, and an unsightly garbage pit full of cans and bottles, marked by a sign that said "Western Civilization." The U.S. student who had erected the sign did not see the irony in the fact that they had brought the garbage there. Suspicious at my sudden arrival, one ranger began to question me on my feelings about hotel development versus conservation in the area, making it clear that their belief system, environmentalism, gave them rights to the use of land that were bestowed by a higher spiritual power than by any individual ownership.

The similarity of their position to that of the Christian missionaries of the nineteenth century struck me. If God is your beacon, you do not have to question why you are there or what you are doing to people; in fact, it is the people there who must justify their existence to you. I asked myself, If the ecological fervor of these environmentalists seems sanctimonious to me, how must people feel when their livelihood is suddenly taken away because an area has been declared a reserve, or they are evicted because they might disturb the animals? I began to understand on a more personal level why many Belizeans I had talked with felt invaded by environmentalism.

For whom are all the reserves in Belize? Are they are being established for Belizeans, for the good of the natural environment (a higher power than any mere human), for the resort owners, for the tourists, for the drug dealers who need remote, unpopulated areas—for whom? The old adage "follow the money" came to mind. While I have no reason to doubt the sincerity of these new missionaries any more than that of the old ones, I still wonder who benefits from the environmental project. Is it the people in the First World who have already destroyed much of their natural resources; the people who are in a financial position to establish tourist resorts; the international corporations, such as the Malaysian logging interests; the tourists; the government officials; the NGOs and the people who work for them? Some of these questions may never be answered, but they need to be asked nevertheless.

LIKE BABOONS WITHOUT A SANCTUARY

When the parks and reserves in Belize were created, the local communities were unaware of the events until after the fact. Frequently informed only after a reserve was established, local residents were then told they no longer had access to or rights to use local resources. The "don't touch" attitude of the environmentalists is a view of humans as intruders on otherwise pristine environments, even when current evidence indicates that people have played an important role in the evolution of virtually all of the region's terrestrial ecosystems (Salas 1993, 3). Local residents found their ability to make a living restricted in the best of cases and were displaced from their homes and forcibly moved to other areas in the worst of cases. In all cases, the protected areas were originally established with little or no regard for local people, few of whom could benefit from increased tourism in the preserve. These benefits have gone mostly to the few who could develop a tourism business or resort adjacent to the reserve. In effect, local people were excluded from consideration when the parks were established, and local management of the parks focused on enforcing park rules on local people, rules that made traditional land use a criminal activity.

The first stanza of Adalbert Tucker's poem "Like Baboons Without a Sanctuary" captures these circumstances:

In the name of the Jaguar,
please reserve some land for me.
With the blessing of the butterfly,
leave an acre for me.
The same is true of my friend the hiccatee;
How come I am the problem,
only recently,
speaking environmentally
and forgetting humanity?
In the name of the jaguar
and in the name of the baboon,
leave an acre of sanctuary
for Belizean man and Belizean woman
and another one for Belizean children.
We are like baboons without sanctuary
on the edge of marginality's marginality.
(Read at the SPEAR conference, October 1996)

In some cases, people who had been living in areas made into reserves were forcibly evicted. In 1992, a village of 190 Mayans was moved from the Chiquibul National Park to a small hamlet outside the park, called Red Bank. The villagers did not consent to the move, and the people in Red Bank did not know they were coming. Tensions developed when the Mayans wanted to keep their village structure and their alcalde, but the Belizeans in Red Bank wanted them to assimilate and come under their own chairman's rules. At the time of the move, the Mayans were forced to live in tents in very unsanitary, muddy conditions that led to chronic diarrhea and pneumonia.

In other instances, people have been allowed to live near the parks, but without access to the resources they had formerly enjoyed—for instance, those Maya who were moved from Cockscomb. Local people/park relations have been poor if not outright hostile. Recognition is now growing that the successful long-term management of protected areas depends on the cooperation and support of local people (Wells et al. 1992). Recognition that local people will thwart conservation efforts if they are excluded has led to a new approach, integrated conservation development projects that try to combine environmental protection with local social and economic development (Salas 1993, 7–8). However, these rural development efforts are being undertaken by environmentalists who have little experience with development at the community level. With a primary goal of conserving biological diversity, it is questionable whether these projects will succeed where more experienced development projects, with the sole goal of reducing poverty, have failed. Salas, who worked with the Belize Audubon Society on local involvement, has concluded that working with people is difficult and time-consuming, particularly if local people want participation in decision-making (Salas 1993, 12).

The Belize Audubon Society, which has had a major role in setting up many reserves, has considerable experience and success in highlighting environmental concerns, implementing education and awareness programs, lobbying for legislation, mobilizing funds, and managing protected areas (Salas 1993, 5). However, it has no experience in sustainable development and limited experience in working with rural people.

Because of the accusation that reserves are set up by "tree huggers who only want to lock away resources," there are signs that recent reserves will include the people who use the natural resources in the making of the management plan. The Center for Environmental Studies (another NGO), in collaboration with the Fisheries Department, has proposed a Port Honduras Marine Reserve at Punta Hicacos (from Monkey River to Three Snake Caye), just north of Punta Gorda, with a primary goal of including community involvement in the management planning.

According to Evan Cayetano, who has been developing the plan, the Port Honduras project would be the first reserve to allow sustainable use of the "flora and fauna for the folks." Fisheries does allow some use of marine resources for subsistence fishing. This will be particularly important in an area that is rich in scale fish and shellfish. There are only 130 Belizean fishermen in the area, but there are about 2,000 Guatemalan and Honduran fishermen. Local dissatisfaction with the Fisheries Department centers around the prohibition of net fishing and killing of manatee for Belizeans, who then watch a crew from Honduras, with legal Belizean licenses issued by Fisheries, continue to fish with nets and sell the fish in Honduras.

The plan calls for establishing three zones: a no-touch zone of natural resource values; a low-scale zone for tourism, where only sightseeing would be allowed, with protection of ecosystem as primary; and a zone where sustainable fishing by local residents is allowed. Even here killing of manatee would be prohibited and net fishing would be banned. For tourists, fly-fishing would be encouraged as an alternative to commercial fishing.

To manage these zones there will be a board composed of people from the Forestry Department (for the mangroves), a representative from the Ministry of Economic Development, local stakeholders (fishermen, schools, tourism businesses), NGOs (planning and donor agencies), Fisheries management staff, and natural and social scientists approved by Fisheries and Forestry. When this plan was shown to the community, there were objections from fishermen who felt the zoning plan was too restrictive of fishing and wanted to redraw the maps to allow a larger fishing zone. The response of the Center for Environmental Studies was to initiate an "education phase" for the community to phase in protection of the environment. According to the Center, the people of "Monkey River are 'ready' for this plan, but the people of Punta Negra [consisting of one family of 50], who traditionally fish with nets, are not 'ready' for it."

Efforts to increase community participation often are only superficial attempts to look participatory when decisions have already been made. One such effort was the public meeting held on Caye Caulker over the proposed reserve there. Roger Few, a doctoral student at Leicester University, described the meeting:

The idea of the meeting was to get community participation. But participation meant that people were told what was going to happen. They could respond, but there would be no obligation to change decisions that had already been made. The decisions were basically top down. People felt broad support for the reserve but wanted more information on the different uses of different areas. Many people on Caye Caulker did not know that there was planning for a reserve.

The issues raised at the meeting showed that the community had a very different perception of the reserve from the planners. The people there thought the reserve was to keep out foreign fishermen, that it was meant only for tourists, and they had disbelief in the data on fish stocks that were presented to them. There was a sense of disempowerment, that the government was going to do what it wanted no matter what anyone in the community said.

The planners, on the other hand, were pushing tourism as the answer to everything. Fishermen, in particular, were being ignored, and they felt that since they were to be the most affected by the reserve they should be consulted. There was an over-emphasis on the prospects for increased tourism which left the fishermen who were unable or unwilling to switch to tourism, without either a voice or a way to make a living.

There was much misinformation due to information not being presented in a way that was intelligible to the fishermen. The meeting was run by the planners, and debate was not really encouraged. Planners were not flexible in the decisions already taken, and they did not take into account or respect local knowledge of the areas being talked about. (Speech to the Interdisciplinary Conference on Belize, Belize City, March 6–7, 1997)

Even after Few's report, the CZMU decided to bring a master plan for Caye Caulker to the village council and planned to set up a reserve, regardless of community support and without solving the problems raised by the community.

An example of community management arising from the grass roots, rather than a management plan being presented to a community for approval, is the Five Blues Lakes plan developed and proposed by the people of St. Margaret village, where the Five Blue Lakes are located. The reaction of the government has been obstructive, making it very difficult for this approach to succeed. For example, the Belize government has only recently allowed fees to be collected from tourists by the local park board, so that income from the park can be put into maintenance of facilities. The government has been very reluctant to give locals access to the income from tourist dollars. The influential NGOs have no interest in the park because the plan does not come from them. There is also internal tension between the Creoles, who are the historical residents of the area and want to develop it as a tourist draw, and the new Central American immigrants, who want to build houses and plant crops there (personal communications, Charlie Houghton, Peace Corps; Augusto Palacio, St. Margaret village).

ECOCOLONIALISM

Military rhetoric is often combined with New Age religiosity in the new ecocolonialism much as it was with Christianity in the old colonialism. The opening of the Maritime Museum at the marine terminal in Belize City in the fall of 1996 illustrates this New Age religiosity. The first visual image at the entrance to the museum is a quote in large letters from Chief Seattle: "All things are connected, like the blood which unites one family." Chief Seattle, a mythological figure among New Age Americans, is often quoted by environmentalists to authenticate their position that the world is one ecological priority, that native American peoples were stewards of the land and have a lesson in ecology for all of us, one that can provide an antidote to the "brutalizing" philosophy behind Western civilization.

Chief Seattle is an interesting pawn in the environmental game. His words in a famous letter he is alleged to have written were picked up by the environmental movement, quoted and praised in films, songs, radio, television programs, and serious environmental literature. Chief Seattle's "letter" was actually written to represent a generic Indian for a film script by Ted Perry, a professor at the University of Texas (Kaiser 1987; DeGregori 1997). How this particular "quote" was chosen to set the tone for the Maritime Museum and what the words have to do with Belize's maritime life— or, for that matter, with Belize itself—remain a mystery. The quote sits in a strange vacuum, imported from a foreign environmental movement that uses North American Indians as models of stewardship of the land—whether they were or not—plunked down without any apparent connection to the local context or any meaning for the people of Belize.

The environmental movement, so rapidly exported to Belize, has since the early 1980s not only sequestered 40 percent of the landmass of Belize into preserves but also has appointed itself the "manager" of this land. By creating and financing jobs in government offices responsible for the preserves, individuals in environmental NGOs have taken on the planning and management of this land. Management of land in Belize refers primarily to keeping local people from using the land to make a living, except for a few people who can do so under strictly controlled conditions of ecotourism. These "managers" control the land in the name of a higher good, Nature, operating with the logic that what is good for nature is good for all of us. The colonialists of the past, of course, operated in the name of the higher good of God, king, and country. To control access to the land for a higher good, it is necessary to criminalize traditional subsistence activities of the locals. Hunting is criminalized as poaching, and slash-and-burn agriculture is criminalized as a "destructive way of making a living" that contributes to air pollution and global warming. The consequences of this criminalization are only just being felt in Belize. On July 20, 1997, two men were arrested for fishing in a river in the Hill Bank Forest Reserve. When forest rangers from the Programme for Belize cut the fishing line, the two men allegedly fired at them and were arrested for attempted murder, aggravated assault, and use of deadly means of harm (*Amandala*, 1997e).

The almost total disregard for the interests of the people of Belize, unless those interests coincide with environmental priorities, has not gone unnoticed. Objections to these tactics have forced environmentalists at least to pay lip service to a conservation approach that includes people's lives and livelihood in the equation. But sensitivity to the issue of peoples' interests is not high. In some cases there is use of military language, with the saving of the environment as the prize and the people of the country as the enemy to be conquered. In other cases, environmental fervor has a religious tone, with the environmental mission likened to a moral imperative that places the environment over the interests of people. People are, after all, the ones who destroy the environment and from whom it needs protection. As Janet Gibson, director of the CZMP, told me, "I believe people do not have a right even to go to some areas." This lack of right would, however, extend to environmental protectors such as CZMP personnel.

A good example of a more subtle disregard for people is the 1993 U.N. Development Programme project report on coastal zone management for Belize. While the report notes that 37 percent of the population of Belize live and make their living in the coastal zone, and a large part of the economy is dependent on coastal areas, it outlines the need for preservation of the coast and reef by establishing reserves, managing existing use of resources, and in general decreasing the use of the area by the local population and tourists. The report focuses on sustainable development (in this case, development limited to what the environment can sustain), but not once does it make any suggestion about how the 37 percent of the population living in these areas will make a living if the UNDP proposals are implemented.

This new form of "ecocolonialism" is not restricted to Belize. In Africa, Westerners viewing rhinoceroses and elephants from afar have no idea of the cost to local people when they forgo the development of their lands, and suffer losses of crops, houses, and lives to the elephants and their preservation. Like Belizeans, Africans are asked to give up very substantial needs in order to ensure that wildlife prospers (Wells 1997). There is criticism in Africa of these absolutist preservation approaches by some of the new "entrepreneurial" conservationists in Africa, who argue for giving local people access to limited use of wildlife and preservation areas, and finding ways to make those uses profitable so that locals have a vested interest in maintaining the reserves.

Ecocolonialism in Belize was illuminated to me in a talk by John Howell, of the Natural History Museum in Belmopan. His talk in 1997 at an international conference in Belize City described the environmental movement as a war needing trickery, military strategies, and armies. Director of the Las Cuevas Project in the Maya Mountains and a former British commissioner who worked for years in Africa, Howell recounted that he left Africa when it "got too violent" in the national parks, with poachers and game wardens killing each other. In Africa "poachers" are people whose traditional livelihood—hunting game, for example—has become criminalized by environmental laws, and game wardens are people whose livelihood has become treating local people as criminals. In Belize, he found that the enemy was local people defined as "Guatemalan invaders," that is, Mayans who fled violence in Guatemala to try to make a living from traditional milpas.

According to Howell, "a whopping 40 percent of the country is in reserves, with half of that in forest reserves and the other half in parks." He figures that "more than half of the country can fall into our grasp," and hopes to make Belize a model for "other dependent countries" The following paraphrase of his talk is from my notes, and therefore is my version of his message to the audience:

To get this much land [50 percent] we need strategies. First, you have to have legislation. Belize has excellent environmental legislation which goes way back before people realized it was coming in and could object.

The second strategy is to make reserves. Thirty percent of Belize is in forest reserves, but chunks of this have gone to national parks [Chiqubul and Bladen]. Our tactics in those days was to make large forest reserves and then get to parks later. I made the largest reserve in Nigeria by going out with porters and a gun. Today we need corridors to stop the taking away of forests. We have reached the boundaries. And we need documents, a management plan to use as a weapon.

Stage three is to put in an infrastructure so we can patrol the reserves. In the last five years 15,000 Guatemalans are inching across the border at Chiquibul. They have the big Guatemalan army behind them. We have only 1,000 young, new Belize Defense Force. When the Guatemalans come in, we will shoot them. In the last five to ten years we have got the infrastructure to win, but the wave of people is reaching the boundaries. The forests are becoming occupied. The next ten years will be a battle. We have to take on the government, oil companies, shipping lines. We need a national forum to control the government. The spoil of war is land. The main threat is Guatemala. We need to keep Canadians and Americans doing research along the border to send a message to Guatemala.

Howell's military approach to environmentalism is hardly only a rhetorical style. On February 21–22, 1997, the Belize Defense Force was ordered to a village around the high jungle of Hiccatte Creek in Toledo district near the Guatemalan border. There they set about destroying the crops, the only livelihood of the people of a Maya Kekchi village. Acting on information from environmentalists in the region, the government claimed that the people were Guatemalan squatters, but the Catholic Church, which has a school there, countered that many of the residents were Belizeans, others were married to Belizeans, and many of the children were born in Belize. Since this is an area with no visible border or checkpoint and no telephone, and no one had any papers, the testimony of the schoolteachers and the environmentalists in the area was the only information available on the people living in the village. In any case, no one asked them who they were. The village's source of food was destroyed, leaving the children facing hunger.

Adalbert Tucker, of the Belize River Valley Association, a grassroots organization concerned with reducing poverty in the Belize River valley and securing land for the landless poor, pinpointed the issue: "Thirty percent of our people live on Crown land. I have never seen a baboon who applied for land, but the baboon now has land, and *we* are the visitors on his land. The jaguar, too, tells us to walk softly on his land."

10

The Sea Lottery

Walking up and down the coastline of Bacalar Chico on Ambergris Caye one day, I looked out to sea and saw large bundles of lumber bobbing over the reef. I ran to Paisano, greatly excited. We got into the dory and paddled out to find lumber, enormous quantities of lumber, crashing on the reef in huge bundles that broke upon impact. Then we saw the packages emerging from the bundles of wood, wrapped in black plastic and duct tape, outpacing the lumber in the race for the shoreline. We gathered lumber all that evening, the next day, and the next—exhausting work but satisfying. All along the coastline from Xcalak down to San Pedro, lumber came floating in from the sea. The Honduran ship that lost its cargo at sea, for what reason we never knew, provided us with enough lumber to build a small house on the land. It also provided those willing to take the risk with a ready source of quick cash. A sea lottery.

The history of Belize is abundant with pirates, booty from Spanish galleons, contraband, and trade from the sea. The profitable days of Prohibition in the United States, which many older Belizeans remember fondly as good times for the business of rumrunning, are now relegated to history, much like the English pirates of the eighteenth century. But today contraband still thrives through foreign goods brought in without paying duty and the "sea lottery." The sea lottery—the cocaine drops in the ocean along the entire coast of Belize—has catapulted some local men into instant riches. Crime, gangs, the drug trade, and killings are now part of daily life in Belize. Today's piracy also continues in financial scams, money laundering, contraband goods, and even the pirated TV stations.

According to an editorial in *The Reporter*, contraband is a Belizean way of life.

From the earliest days the settlers in the Bay of Honduras have shown a propensity for bootlegging and contraband. During the days of Prohibition in the United States Belizeans smuggled whiskey. During the dark days of World War II they smuggled gasoline to lurking German U-boats off the coast of Honduras. Today the product of choice is cocaine, but these proponents of get-rich-quick activity are not averse to big ticket items such as late model cars and mini vans. Apart from cocaine and shiny new automobiles, however, the big money is in everyday consumer items imported into this country with invoices which list the goods well below cost price. But in Belize the practice is so widespread it is generally accepted as the smart way of doing business. (1996b, 2)

The editor of *The Reporter* was not the first to notice the importance of smuggling to the Belize economy. At the height of Prohibition, Aldous Huxley wrote about Belize, "when Prohibition is abolished, the last of its [Belize's] profitable enterprises—the re-export of alcohol by rum-runners, who use Belize as their base of operations—will have gone the way of its commerce in logwood, mahogany and chicle" (Huxley 1934, 32).

Huxley was wrong. Rum was not the last of Belize's profitable enterprises. On the Mexican/Orange Walk border, warehouses are full of two-liter Coca-Cola bottles awaiting boats to take them to Belize. Paths have been cut through the bush for the boats to come in, and villagers across the border at Douglan, Botes, and San Victor carry cases of two-liter Coke bottles through the bush on their shoulders for approximately three miles (*Amandala*, 1997d). Immense profits allegedly are being made from contraband Coca-Cola.

THE BLACK MARKET IN GOODS AND MONEY

In the center of Belize City is a small shop, run by an East Indian, that sells tobacco, newspapers, lightbulbs, and other household necessities. Above the shop he and his family live in an apartment that could just as easily be in Calcutta as in Belize. He took me to his apartment to change money, giving me Bz$2.05 on the U.S. dollar instead of the Bz$1.98 I could get at the bank. We chatted about his family and relatives in India, and then he called his son to accompany me to the bank. The boy and I emerged into the hot sunlight, and because I was carrying a large amount of cash, I was sure everyone was staring at me. Never mind, the boy

took me quietly to the nearby Belize Bank, where the armed doorman smiled politely and opened the door for me. I stepped into the
cool darkness. The teller smiled and asked me, "How much do you
want to deposit? Don't worry, I go to the Indian, too."

In Belize there is a thriving black market in both currency and
imported goods, and each black market is run by a particular ethnic group. The black market in money tends to be monopolized by
East Indian merchants and importers, while the black market in
goods from Mexico is run by mestizos. East Indians deal in the
purchase of dollars on the black market because they have a system by which they work with importers who are family members
(e.g., in Miami or England) who send undervalued invoices (so that
customs duty is less when the goods enter Belize); then they pay
their relatives in the U.S. dollars they have obtained on the black
market. This is a method of avoiding import duties that depends
on the development of long-term, informal ties to international
suppliers, since both sides have to agree on the arrangement. The
suppliers must trust that when they underinvoice and receive the
official dollars approved by the Bank of Belize from their pur-
chasers, they will also receive the rest in black market currency in
an informal way (Wiegand 1994).

The mestizo black market trade is based on a simple transaction:
smuggling Mexican goods across the border and selling them to
Belizean merchants and hotel owners at a profit (but for less than
the goods cost in Belize). This can be a very profitable business, for
there is an enormous difference in prices between Belize and Mexico. For example, a dinner with wine for two in Corozal, Belize, that
costs U.S.$40 can be purchased for U.S.$17 just across the border
in Chetumal.

The contraband in Mexican goods is built around the social
structure of border villages where villagers who share a common
mestizo culture and language, and who have social and familial
ties in Mexico, cooperate in the smuggling of goods from Mexico or
Guatemala to Belizean merchants. This and the black market in
money have two aspects in common. Their ethnicity is an important factor in making it possible for them to function smoothly.
And the Creole-dominated Customs Department can expect little
cooperation from the mestizo villagers or the East Indian merchants (Wiegand 1994).

There has also been for a long time a thriving black market in
stolen and contraband automobiles in Belize. In the 1970s cars
from the United States that might have been destined for junking
could be sold for a good price in Belize. The "Texans" who visited
Caye Caulker frequently during the 1970s made their living by

driving down automobiles as "tourists" and selling them the day they arrived. As Belize became more affluent and roads got better, good automobiles were in demand and the contraband market in stolen cars took off. In June 1996, a Belize City civil servant, a Taiwanese, and an American "businessman" were charged for evasion of customs duties by bringing into Belize stolen vehicles worth U.S.$200,000. The car in question, a Jeep Cherokee, was thought to be one of 60 cars brought into Belize without payment of customs duty. In this case the American stole the car and drove it to Belize; the civil servant allowed it to be brought into the country without duty; and the Taiwanese bought it. Because of American Embassy pressure on Belize not to provide a ready market for stolen vehicles, 1996 was a big year for the confiscation of cars by customs and police officials. Six cars were seized by officials during the first two weeks of June in connection with the scam (*The Reporter on-line*, June 6, 1996). All of these cases have gone to court; the first conviction was won May 1997.

There also has been a thriving contraband business in stolen Maya art and pots for some time. The most famous case was the Crystal Skull, taken from the Maya site of Lubantuun in Toledo district by the British adventurer Mitchell-Hedges around 1926. The treasure is now in the possession of Mitchell-Hedges's daughter, who indicates the skull will be returned to Belize after her death (Foster 1989, 70). Any Maya site is subject to theft. La Milpa, in the Rio Bravo Conservation Area, was thoroughly looted after it was discovered. Artifacts from lesser sites are found in many houses in Belize and in the possession of archaeologists in the United States. The protection of cultural property by the Archaeology Department in Belmopan has been very haphazard at best. Deals between U.S. archaeologists and Archaeology Department employees to divide some of the best artifacts among themselves have not gone unnoticed.

Contraband, black market currency, and theft flourish partly because the police in Belize are understaffed, undereducated, and underpaid. Furthermore, they are regularly accused of corruption and brutality, though they are rarely disciplined or suspended, so the opportunity for rot in the system is plentiful. Because of the blatant corruption, Dean Barrow, in his role as Minister of Internal Security, recently disciplined three policemen for corruption and traveled around the country visiting police forces in order "to increase the morale of the police force." In one of the few cases in San Pedro in which a policeman was charged with brutality to a prisoner, it was another policeman who made the charge; he did so because when he objected to the slapping of the prisoner, the first policeman swore at him. There are signs that the days of corrupt and abusive police may be numbered. The new police chief, Ornel Brooks, who took office in November 1996, by July 1997 had charged 22 police officers, including 3 senior officers, with corruption.

THE INTERNATIONAL DRUG TRADE

The traffic in contraband goods, automobiles, Maya artifacts, and money pales in comparison with the arrival of the international drug trade in Belize. In the 1970s local milpas included a few marijuana plants, whose leaves, when smoked, were useful for enduring the tedious daily weeding and fending off mosquitoes. By the 1980s demand for marijuana and the high prices it brought on the market made marijuana production for export very attractive. It was known as "Belize Breeze" when it became commercial, and Belize was for a short time a major exporter of marijuana to the United States. However, the United States declared a war on drugs and threatened to cut off aid to Belize unless the government agreed to aerial spraying with the herbicide paraquat. In 1982 aerial spraying of marijuana fields proved highly effective, but it was stopped, primarily by cabinet ministers who were heavily involved in the drug trade and environmentalists who were worried about the toxic effects of paraquat on plants and animals (*Africa* 1985). In 1984 the Belize Defense Force destroyed approximately 20 percent of the marijuana crop, about 1 million plants, by hacking it down with machetes; but this was an arduous task and not considered effective enough. The next year, despite the protest of environmental groups, fields were sprayed to render the crop useless. Today export production of marijuana is greatly reduced.

Unfortunately, by the 1990s the use of the Belize coastline as a conduit for cocaine from South America was common. At first, remote airstrips in the Orange Walk district and on the cayes, and even stretches of the Northern Highway, were used to refuel planes and to transfer shipments of drugs to trucks that would move through Mexico to the United States. Then "wet drops" of bags of cocaine from airplanes, to be picked up by boats, began to float ashore.

Tales abound of locals with boats finding a three-foot-by-three-foot-by-three-foot cube bale of cocaine—half floating, half sinking—wrapped entirely in duct tape. For example, on February 9, 1997, the San Pedro police and personnel from the Hol Chan Marine Reserve were informed of the presence of sacks of cocaine from a wet drop that had washed up on the beach at the home of an American biologist who lives in the Basil Jones area (13 miles north of San Pedro). A search of Rocky Point and later of the Bacalar Chico area yielded 5 sacks containing 99 packages of cocaine with a total weight of about 250 pounds. The next day, another search turned up 17 more packages weighing almost 40 pounds (*San Pedro Sun* 1997).

The government regularly stumbles on large shipments of cocaine. In the past few years, there have been several major busts with street values of millions of dollars and confiscation of large amounts of cocaine, accompanied by the arrests of numerous individuals. Although there are weekly trials, convictions are rare, and when they do occur, jail sentences are not usually completed. There has never been a successful conviction of a major drug dealer in Belize.

DRUGS ON CAYE CAULKER

"Drugs have *always* been on Caye Caulker, and so have some people who are frequent users," Juni Saldivar explained. "The sea lottery, on the other hand, is only a very recent phenomenon which has become more common in the last five years. There must be satellites or something following those packages, because there are guys with cellular phones on the island who go out to sea the minute they get the call that the stuff is there." Last year a major wet drop came ashore at Caye Caulker, and today tales of its consequences abound. For example, according to one resident:

There were seven men who each found a bag of cocaine. Of the seven, six immediately sold the drugs for about U.S.$1 million each. But today their lives are ruined, and they live on the street and have nothing. One man was a proverbially jolly, fat man with a house of his own and a wife and kids. He led a normal life until he found the bale of cocaine in the ocean. He sold it and became rich overnight, snorted a lot of it, and lost his wife and kids. He now has no home, and lives on the streets. He is extremely thin from not eating and doing coke. Of the seven men, only one leads the same life as before because he cut open the bag he found and kicked it into the ocean, where it sank. He went on with his life.

According to local legend, another man found a bale while bringing a group of tourists from the mainland. Three policemen were on board. They all took it to the police station, where the sergeant locked it in a jail cell and slept outside the cell, guarding it all night. All night long, residents could see the local coke addicts circling the jail. In the morning the cocaine was gone. One of the local coke addicts said he saw a man who is "in the business" loading it onto a skiff from the back door of the police station, helped by the sergeant. People do not have much respect for the police, and it is stories like this that fuel their contempt.

CONTRABAND FROM THE SEA

The Caribbean islands have acquired a new significance as a major drug trafficking route between the cocaine producers of South America and consumers in the United States. The Caribbean islands are near-perfect conduits for drug shipments and money laundering, with their numerous unpoliced islets and duty-free ports, and a multitude of secretive Swiss-style banks. Drug trafficking is on the upswing in this region after slacking off for nearly a decade. The U.S. State Department describes the Caribbean as a "significant drug transit zone" and has warned that "drug traffickers have penetrated the highest levels of society and government institutions in Antigua, Trinidad and Tobago, St. Kitts and Nevis, Aruba, Jamaica and the Dominican Republic." Puerto Rico is described as an "island under siege," from which drugs can be shipped anywhere in the mainland United States without passing through customs. Drug smugglers have targeted the Caribbean again after law enforcement efforts in Florida and Mexico—both key transit sites for drugs headed to the United States—made those routes more difficult (*The Reporter* 1996h). The United States and Belize signed an agreement on February 9, 1989, to cooperate in eradicating illicit drug crops and to take strong measures against drug trafficking.

Belize has also joined other Caribbean nations in a treaty with the United States to work in conjunction with Drug Enforcement Agency (DEA) authorities in catching boats suspected of carrying drugs. This controversial treaty, which allows U.S. authorities to board vessels registered in Belize or other Caribbean countries to search for contraband drugs, is the subject of a heated debate. Fishermen in Grenada, for example, were shocked that their government had signed an agreement allowing U.S. vessels to pursue suspected drug traffickers into a Caribbean nation's territorial waters. One fisherman, an admitted smuggler of liquor, cigarettes, and appliances, was worried his contraband trade would become riskier now that U.S. vessels could pursue him if they suspected drug smuggling. Jamaica and Barbados have refused to sign the treaty, citing issues of sovereignty. Belize reputedly felt compelled to sign by implied U.S. threats to oppose loans from international monetary institutions.

The Belize Defense Force has acquired two new Belizean-built patrol boats for its Maritime Wing as a gift from the British High

Commissioner. There is some optimism that these patrol boats will enhance drug interdiction efforts and aid Customs and Fisheries in their patrols. The boats, *Ocean Sentinel* and *Reef Sniper*, are equipped with radar, electronic spotlights, bullhorns, and sophisticated radios. The Maritime Wing now has 10 seaworthy craft and 7 skiffs.

The United States has also shown an interest in helping Belize combat drugs with an aid package of $224,000 to law enforcement agencies. This assistance was extended after the murder of a DEA agent in Orange Walk district (*The Reporter* 1996e). There is a great deal of anger in the American government at the inability of Belize to produce even one successful conviction for drug smuggling, even when the accused are caught red-handed. In April 1996 dogs from the counternarcotics Canine Unit visited Belize to help with training. "At the port of Belize the dogs were unable to perform, as the smell of drugs was so strong in the warehouse they suffered from sensory overload" (Farah 1997, A27).

In June 1996, the United States put Belize on the list of major drug-trafficking countries (*The Reporter* 1996c). Gerhard Gallucci, the U.S. Embassy's Deputy Chief of Mission, is quoted as saying, "Belize is essentially uncontrolled territory. It is possible for drug traffickers to work with almost complete impunity. The increased traffic involves hundreds and hundreds of kilos of cocaine, and now there is evidence that local Belizeans are actively cooperating with these people" (*The Reporter* 1996c). Gallucci was referring to the arrest of a number of family members of government ministers in Orange Walk district in connection with drug trafficking in 1993 and in 1996, leading to a suspicion that at least two ministers from that district were closely involved in the drug trade.

Because of the increased evidence of cocaine trafficking and indications of high-level government involvement in that trafficking, on February 28, 1997, the U.S. government declared Belize a "major drug transit country" (*Amandala* 1997b), and Belize was officially "decertified."

Richard Gelbard, Assistant Secretary of State for International Narcotics and Law Enforcement Affairs, was quoted in *The Reporter* as saying:

Belize's geographic position and ineffectual law enforcement and corruption allowed U.S. bound drugs easy access via Belize. This year, largely due to high-level corruption in their government, Belize did little to stop the drugs moving through its country. Drug related arrests, drug seizures and the eradication of marijuana dropped sharply in 1996, while the government made no progress in completing extradition and multilateral assistance treaties. Its counter narcotics performance clearly fell short of the standards. (*The Reporter* 1997b)

The reaction in Belize was hypernationalistic, with accusations of hypocrisy against the United States. The news media, the government of Belize, and even organizations critical of the government, such as SPEAR, expressed outrage at the decertification. However, two weeks after decertification, Belize seemed to be stepping up its efforts. In a joint Belizean-U.S. raid, the police "Dragon Unit" intercepted 1.3 tons of cocaine (worth U.S.$33 million) from a boat at South Water Caye. The boat's crew included four Colombians (*Amandala* 1997c). In May they seized another Colombian skiff carrying 1.5 tons of cocaine with a street value of $26 million and arrested more Colombians, Mexicans, and Belizeans from Sarteneja. Since 1994, three major drug busts have involved men from Sarteneja. But, as in the past, the Belizeans somehow managed to get bail, or avoid trial altogether, allowing the local cartel to keep on trafficking. At the CARICOM summit with President Clinton later in May 1997, Dean Barrow brought attention to Belize's efforts to stamp out drug trafficking, and Belize was given a national security waiver to allow continuation of U.S. aid. This led to a report in the *Washington Post* that a State Department report prepared by the Bureau for International Narcotics and Law Enforcement Affairs had concluded that there had been a "significant increase in the detected activities of Colombian drug-trafficking organizations in Belize. . . . Belizean traffickers are also working with Mexican groups to move Colombian cocaine north to the United States." This report also concluded that the ability of the Belizean government to combat drug trafficking, "was severely undermined by deeply entrenched corruption, which reaches into the senior levels of the government. . . . Politics, incompetence, and corruption have accompanied undermanned and poorly equipped police investigative efforts" (Farah 1997, A27).

Although no one knows how much cocaine and heroin passes through Belize, the amount has increased noticeably. The State Department report notes that the chances of prosecuting drug cases are virtually nil. The arrest in 1996 of the son-in-law of Minister of Home Affairs Elito Urbina for running an illegal airstrip where an aircraft tracked by the U.S. Drug Enforcement Agency was found to be carrying 286 kilos (849 pounds) of cocaine ended with "no convictions . . . in this case, however, owing to mismanaged investigations and the destruction of files in a mysterious police car fire" (Farah 1997, A27).

The government of Belize has recognized that drugs have become a problem within the population and a major source of crime, particularly the murders of gang members in Belize City. The National Drug Control Plan was created in January 1996 with the help of the United Nations International Drug Control Program (*The Reporter* 1996l). There is also Pride Belize Foundation, an NGO that works on drug prevention and education, which has received over $2.5 million from USAID over 11 years. However, with the closing of the USAID office in Belize in June 1997, this sole source of funding was terminated (Pride Belize Foundation home page).

The talk of government ministers and their involvement in the drug trade also has escalated. The scandals in the 1980s of several government ministers making money from marijuana trade is similar to the talk today of cocaine cartel connections between government ministers and the routing of cocaine through Belize. No conviction has ever been obtained.

In spite of the obviously devastating effects of involvement in the drug trade, people still pick up bales of cocaine dropped during the night and sell them for instant riches. The village of Xcalak was inundated with cocaine after a Colombian plane jettisoned numerous bags of cocaine wrapped in plastic, a float light on each, just outside the reef. In the next few days one man was macheted to death and found floating down the coastline, and another had disappeared. The villagers claimed that it was a fight over the cocaine haul. Black plastic bags were found buried in the bush. There is even more of this activity in the south, in Placencia and Dandriga.

CRIME

Crime on Caye Caulker in the 1970s consisted of stealing a chicken or some clothes off a clothesline. For the most part such petty crime was ignored or tolerated, since most people knew who had done it and did not care to make a fuss. When larger items, such as boat motors, began to be stolen, the whole community was outraged, and usually the motors were found. On Caye Caulker the worst theft was theft from lobster traps. This occurred quite frequently but was perpetrated by a very few, known to all the fishermen, who sometimes took justice into their own hands. Each lobster fisherman laid his traps on the seabed in a pattern known only to him, with a way to spot the traps through triangulation with a point on the mainland. They would also take circuitous routes out to their traps so as to foil a thief who might be following them. These measures deterred theft to a large extent, though not completely, and each season saw its share of fistfights and threats to local thieves. When tourists began to arrive on Caye Caulker in larger numbers, theft of money, cameras, and snorkeling equipment from them became common. Still, the island had only had one murder (due to a family feud), and the first rape (acknowledged as rape) that I was aware of took place in 1984, committed by a man from Belize City.

Today there is a great deal more crime, much of it linked to the arrival of crack (also called primo, rock, or snow). Freebasing—smoking rock cocaine in a homemade water pipe—has created a new class of drug addict. Those who freebase are often on the streets all night, every night, in the same clothes, living from hit to hit. The few crack addicts on Caye Caulker are known by everyone, including the tourists and the police. They are responsible for most of the thefts and are periodically arrested, serve time in Hattieville jail, and return to the island to continue their downward spiral. Crack is the scourge of the young men on the island. Several have been in rehabilitation in Punta Gorda, but so far they keep lapsing. One crack addict is now serving two years in Hattieville jail for trying to break into the local Chinese restaurant. According to his brother, "The authorities have tried for years to arrest him on drug charges with no success. The attempted robbery was a chance to throw the book at him." In San Pedro, where crime has become an even more serious problem than on Caye Caulker, the murder of two prominent American residents by a crack addict in February 1994 shocked the town.

The police force in Belize has a poor reputation for effectiveness in dealing with crime, and even less training in doing so. Some of the police are so uneducated that they cannot read and write with ease. After a recent spate of thefts at hotels in San Pedro, tourists who were robbed requested a police report so they could file a claim with their insurance company when they returned to the United States. They were unable to obtain the reports because the police could not write them. A literacy level sufficient to write a report also is lacking in some police on Caye Caulker, who have to ask the employee at the Belize Telecommunications office to write out a fax to send to the Police Headquarters in Belize City.

To cope with rising crime, several towns in Belize have enlisted the help of civilian crime committees. In San Pedro, members of the Civilian Crime Committee help the police by acting as civilian constables on a part-time basis. This group has proved to be even more unreliable than the police. After drinking together all day on a Sunday, they have been known to set out on an arrest spree in the evening, targeting young people and teenagers for harassment. Accusations by tourists of drugs being planted on them and of physical abuse have plagued the civilian constables. The Civilian Crime Committee and the civilian constables soon split into two factions, divided along lines of born San Pedranos and naturalized Belizeans, with the San Pedranos being far outnumbered and unhappy about it.

The theft of Orlando Carasco's boat in the fall of 1996 provides an example of the impotence of the law. Two men from Belize City, well known to everyone on the island, took Orlando's boat, loaded it with lumber in Belize City, and went to the Turneffe Islands to build a fishing camp. They were caught by the coast guard with the boat, which was returned to Caye Caulker a few days later; missing were the two motors, worth about Bz$12,000. Orlando went to Belize City to find his motors and got into an argument with the father of the two men. The argument quickly escalated into a feud involving myriad family members on both sides, some of whom are known to be tough characters and well armed. As the feud escalated into warfare, the law seemed powerless to act. Generally speaking, islanders on Caye Caulker do not go to the police for help with crime. They view the policemen on the island as ineffective at best, and corrupt at worst. The many instances on Caye Caulker of police collaboration with drug dealers, and the disappearances of cocaine while in police possession, have done nothing to improve their reputation.

As I mentioned earlier, there are signs that the Belize government intends to take action to clean up the police force. In July 1997, Minister of National Security Dean Barrow and Police Commissioner Ornel Brooks completed an investigation of 22 junior and senior police officers for alleged drug trafficking as part of the government's commitment to wage war on corruption in the police force (Bz-Culture@psg.com, July 23, 1997).

11

Bananas and Banks

The economy of Belize was founded on trade in the eighteenth century, continued to operate through trade in the nineteenth century, and today is still fundamentally based on trade. The modern economy of the twentieth century, based on the production of manufactured goods, never came to pass in Belize. Belize skipped twentieth-century modernity and went straight to a postmodern, textbook case of a small export/import economy.

Overall, Belizeans enjoy a relatively high standard of living. According to the United Nations Human Development Index, Belize is among the top one-third of all 174 countries evaluated (including industrialized First World countries) and ninth among the 24 independent countries of Central America and the Caribbean. It is one of the least densely populated areas of the world, and has a relatively positive employment picture. The real GDP, according to Steagall, Perry, and Woods (1997), is Bz$3,373 per year per person; 10 percent of the population is unemployed and 5 percent is underemployed. Most of Belize's economy (63 percent of the workforce) is devoted to subsistence, but Belize is not a low-wage, low-skill society. Literacy is said to be very high, and therefore it is appropriate to bring in technological industries. In terms of globalization, this can be an important advantage. In addition, people are educated in English and speak more than one language, and many have traveled considerably (a very large percentage have lived in the United States) and have a fairly cosmopolitan outlook.

The Belize economy is still primarily an agricultural export economy. Sugar, bananas, and citrus (as well as sawn wood and seafood products) are primary products, accounting for 21 percent of GNP (gross national product) and 23 percent of employment in Belize (*Belize: Recent Economic Developments* 1996, 5). The manufacturing and domestic production sector accounts for 26 percent of GNP and 18 percent of employment. It includes agro-based processing (e.g., sugar and citrus); production of basic consumer goods (e.g., beer and matches); some textile assembly (which has fallen considerably due to competition in the region); supply of electricity and water; and construction. The services sector is the largest employer, accounting for 53 percent of GNP and 59 percent of total employment in 1995.

Imports are very high, making the economy dependent on world prices. Exports to the same few markets with protected pricing (on bananas to Europe and on other products to CARICOM) make it possible for domestic producers to survive. Belize still has an economy like the other Latin American economies in the 1960s, one that is very dependent on world market conditions. It is very sensitive to government policies and is influenced by NAFTA, CARICOM, OAS, and other regional arrangements. OAS membership does not provide any tax advantage to Belize, but it means Belize can vote with the other OAS countries and gives Belize recognition in Central America as a country separate from Guatemala. There is some indication that Prime Minister Esquivel views NAFTA and GATT (General Agreement on Tariffs and Trade) with alarm—NAFTA because it is diverting investment from Belize to Mexico, and GATT because it is "threatening our banana industry and accelerating the implementation of international free trade" (Independence Day speech, September 1996).

BANANAS

The British, fanatical mapmakers that they are, have given Belize some of the best land-use maps of any country. Like the rest of the Mosquito Coast all the way down to Panama, Belize has a difficult climate, frequent hurricanes, and poor soil. About 84 percent of the land is not suitable for traditional agriculture, including logging, and 44 percent has no known use whatsoever. Only 16 percent of the soil is suitable for agriculture. Large-scale agricultural projects, such as rice and cacao, have been tried in Belize, but they have not been commercially successful because the land is not able to sustain these crops.

Agricultural exports are the largest source of foreign currency, with tourism a close second. The history of any one of the traditional plantation crops—citrus, sugar, and bananas—would illustrate the import substitution policy of the country and the social and cultural role of export agriculture in the nation. I write about bananas because they have become a flash point in the current economy of Belize and are tied to other recent issues, such as ethnicity, the formation of labor unions, the corruption of the government, and the control of land by foreigners.

Although banana plantations have a long and sordid history in Central America, bananas are a relatively recent crop in Belize. They were first exported from small farms in southern Belize between the 1880s and 1920, at which time the farms were devastated by the banana fungus (*Fusarium cubense*), and several severe hurricanes, and production collapsed. In 1971 the government tried to revive the banana industry at Cowpen, but its efforts proved unprofitable, and the farms were sold in 1985 to 29 private farmers. Most of these farmers went bankrupt or sold out, leaving nine growers in control of 88 percent of the nation's banana farms (Moberg 1996b, 316). Even with preferential access to European Union (EU) banana markets, the high cost of production (approximately U.S.$6.00 per box) and the low international market price (U.S.$2.80 per box) have made banana production a very risky venture in Belize. Exacerbating this situation is the fact that Belizean bananas are sold exclusively through Fyffes, Ltd., a European company headquartered in Ireland. Fyffes has not become involved in production but acts only as a buyer, thus leaving the risks of production to the farmers while keeping a monopoly on the crop prices. Most growers in Belize attribute the low wages and poor living conditions of banana workers to the high costs of production and the low prices paid by Fyffes (Moberg 1996b, 316).

The situation of the banana workers has a decidedly ethnic dimension. Of the 1,380 field workers employed on the nation's banana farms in 1993, 34 percent were Guatemalan, 32 percent were Hondurans, and 25 percent were Salvadorans. Only 7 percent of the workers are Belizeans, of whom less than half were ethnic Creoles or Garifuna, and the rest were Maya (Moberg 1996b, 316). There is an economic hierarchy among the ethnic groups, with the Belizeans being paid the most (on average U.S.$92 per two-week pay period), Hondurans the next highest paid (U.S.$82), then Guatemalans (U.S.$74), and the Salvadorans (U.S.$63) (Moberg 1996b, 324). The historical enmity that has existed among members of these Central American nations is reproduced in the banana industry by the employers through the way they have organized work on banana farms. This rivalry and traditional enmity have worked to the employers' advantage most of the time by creating a fragmented and mutually suspicious workforce. However, in spite of this fragmentation, the workforce is predominantly mestizo and the management is exclusively Afro-Belizean, and it is this division that has proved to be the most significant, not only in the formation of the union but also in the everyday forms of resistance (theft and sabotage) by the workforce, a resistance that has proven costly to banana growers (Moberg 1996b, 325). The Afro-Belizean/mestizo ethnic divisiveness being played out in Toledo district is only one example of the power struggles between the two groups in the national arena.

Whatever the reason—low prices or a fragile, easily exploited workforce—it is clear that living conditions for banana workers are extremely poor. Cowpen, for example, is a small hamlet of makeshift thatched houses, a few miles off the Southern Highway, where most of the banana workers in Belize live. Water comes from a few wells, and only a few houses have latrines. Chickens eat the garbage thrown in the backyards. There is no bus service to Cowpen, no health clinic, and only one elementary school. Most of the people living there are recent immigrants from Central America who do not speak English and are illiterate, a situation making them very vulnerable to exploitation as a labor force. Conditions in Cowpen were described by an American student who visited there.

The conditions that I observed in Cowpen were shocking. Stopping at a home ready to collapse, Ms. Funez (the president of the labor union) quietly converses with a young mother. Two of her children have pneumonia and her husband was deported after the union's strike several months ago. They have no income and cannot afford any medication. The two women walk to the back of the house. A plastic tarp hangs from the ceiling to protect against the daily aerial spraying of insecticide. A pool of urine has not permeated into the ground that serves as the kitchen floor. Workers report continuous illness (hepatitis, malaria, diarrhea, pneumonia, lice, and skin diseases), especially among children under five.

Everyone who lives in Cowpen is sprayed aerially several times a week. Cowpen is below the water line, so with the spraying and the use of the fields as latrines, the water appears to be contaminated. A water supply evaluation undertaken by Fyffes in 1993 indicated that in general the water supply was satisfactory in terms of sanitation, disinfection, and distance traveled to get water. Although the plantations are irrigated with fresh water, people are not allowed to bathe with the irrigation water and instead bathe in and drink the run-off water that has had contact with both the chemicals and waste. Thus, no surprise that there is high incidence of disease.

Many of these problems could be resolved if the workers and their families could move out of the spray zone and above the water line, but this is a highly contested issue. The union wants to move the workers to Bella Vista, where they could build their own homes and operate their own stores, but the company wants the workers to move to Fyffes Village (called San Juan), where the cement homes have already been constructed, where there is a curfew, and workers cannot operate their own stores. This is the most essential debate in the banana industry right now. (personal communication, Cecily Vix)

According to Mark Moberg (personal communication), the issue of where workers live was a major factor leading to the foundation of Banderas Unidas in 1995 and is an issue that is yet to be resolved.

The housing and health conditions in Cowpen are some of the worst in Belize, but such conditions seem to be prevalent in the banana industry in Central America. In Costa Rica, as in Belize, banana plantations are completely dependent on highly toxic chemicals that contaminate the homes of workers and water sources. Banana workers are subject to frequent accidents and allergic, pulmonary, and cancerous ailments caused by constant exposure to pesticides, such as benomyl, paraquat, and clorothalonil. In Costa Rica, there was a notorious case in which an estimated 10,000 banana workers became sterile due to exposure to a very toxic nematicide, dibromochloropropane (DBCP) (Wheat 1996). But in contrast to Belize, the banana workers in the rest of Central America have some access to health care. In Costa Rica, as in Belize, workers are fired for union activity and other political reasons (Foro Emaus, Bz-Culture@psg.com, May 1, 1997).

Because of these conditions, unrest and constant migration of banana workers takes place throughout Central America, and Belize is no exception. The situation in Belize has led to considerable unrest among banana workers, who in 1995 tried to unionize to improve wages and working conditions. On May 17, the only Belizean-born member of the executive committee of the newly formed United Banana Banners Workers Union (UBBWU), also known as Banderas Unidas, was elected president. The union sought to negotiate with the Banana Growers Association (BGA), which represents the banana farms. They raised numerous issues—wages, housing conditions, the practice of seizing work permits and passports of immigrant workers, and management abuse of workers. The union president, Marciana Funez, was then arrested and charged with possession of 40 grams of marijuana, which she claimed was retaliation for her refusal to accept a $50,000 bribe to resign as head of the union (*Amandala* 1995; Vix 1996, 11). In June 1995, 600 members of the Banderas Unidas decided to strike. The BGA responded by calling in the Belize Defense Force and deporting 125 immigrant workers, firing and replacing

400 workers, and canceling 200 work permits (Vix 1996, 11). The BGA has consistently refused to recognize the union and its claims to represent a significant number of the banana workers.

In spite of the labor unrest in the banana belt and the troubles in the industry, the BGA announced that it had exceeded its 1996 quota of bananas shipped to Europe at the preferential price of U.S.$10.60 per box, and had to ship the rest of the crop at the open market price of $2.80 per box.

In May, Marciana Funez, the president of the union, went to Ireland, where Fyffes is headquartered, and was able to develop interest there in the Belize situation. In August 1996, the UBBWU accused the BGA of firing 89 union members, and the next week a supervisor claimed to have found a note from "the organized movement of campesinos from Guatemala, Salvador and Belize" threatening to "take up arms if the union was denied" (*Amandala* 1996b). After this crisis, an Irish group of NGOs called Banana Watch, in discussions with Fyffes, was able to get Fyffes to agree to negotiate with any union showing the support of 40 percent of the workers on any of the farms that Fyffes manages in Belize. Previously they had agreed to union recognition only if the union could prove that it had 40 percent of all banana workers (*Belize Times* 1996; *The Reporter* 1996k). Whatever transpires with the recognition of the union, as of August 1997, conditions in Cowpen had not improved and only a few workers appeared to be living in the official Fyffes village of San Juan.

THE BRITISH SYSTEM IN THE MARGINS

The banana export industry is only an example of some of the problems looming on the horizon for the Belize economy. One of the more serious is the deficit in balance of trade that has been increasing since the early 1970s. From 1979 to 1992 the ratio of imports to exports increased every year, with the result that the national debt has soared to U.S.$200 million (U.S.$1,000 per person). Currently 35 percent of the proceeds of all Belizean exports go to paying the Chase Manhattan Bank, which owns the debt. Chase Manhattan bought the debt for 30 cents on the dollar. The International Monetary Fund negotiated the loans and their structural adjustment requirements. The structural adjustments that the UDP government has made since coming to power include the imposition of a 15 percent value-added tax (VAT) on all items sold, lower wages for civil servants, and firing over 600 civil servants.

Because Belize relies heavily on imports from the United States, prices there strongly affect prices in Belize, with domestic policy having only a small impact on prices. In addition, Belize is the Caribbean country where an employer gets the least work for the wages paid. Furthermore, Creoles, who were for the most part an urban culture with a trade rather than agricultural background, have not engaged significantly in agricultural work. Only 16 percent of the land in Belize, is arable; it is worked primarily by Central American immigrants in export agriculture and the Mennonites in domestic agriculture.

According to Dr. Carla Barnett, an economist formerly with the Belize Bank, the structure of the Belize economy has stayed basically the same since independence in 1981. The 1980s was a period of strong growth (about 10 percent a year between 1987 and 1990), and by 1986 this economic growth had created new areas of activity. Sugar, citrus, and particularly banana exports expanded, partly because all three enjoy preferential access to U.S. and EU markets. However, the United States and the United Kingdon are also the source of most imports into Belize. Between 1986 and 1990, growth was 15 to 16 percent, but imports also continued to rise. Tate & Lyle, an English company, sold its interests in sugar production and manufacturing in Orange Walk district, and began to limit its involvement in Belize sugar to marketing. In the Stann Creek area, the banana industry went through a major consolidation from small to large plots, fueled by migrant and immigrant labor.

By the early 1990s, the economy had weakened considerably. The government increased foreign commercial borrowing to finance its investment projects; at the same time growth dropped to about 5 percent. This drop was due mainly to slower growth in the agricultural sector owing to unfavorable weather conditions and weaker prices for citrus concentrates and sugar. In 1993, when the UDP entered office and applied for loans, the IMF suggested structural adjustments in the economy that included a reduction in the size of the government. A number of civil servants in Belize City were fired and the government negotiated new trade agreements through USAID. Unemployment rose to 14 percent (*Belize: Recent Economic Developments* 1996, 1).

Recent trends in the economy include a boom in the number of tourist arrivals, with tourism gradually moving from the recreational tourism of the cayes to the ecotourism of the interior. But tourism growth did not filter though the system, and between 1991 and 1995 the economy slowed, particularly in construction, and growth dropped to 4 or 5 percent. The construction of large hotels ground to a halt. Growth in tourism was about 22 percent a year in 1992 and 1993 but dropped considerably from 1994 to 1996.

The country showed a decline in tourism dollars coming into the country, and some regions experienced low hotel occupancy rates. Most of the increases in arrivals are European rather than American tourists. The extremely high VAT (15 percent) had a devastating effect on tourism in 1996 and 1997 by raising the already high prices of hotel rooms and services.

The government shifted from operating on a surplus to a deficit by 1993, and it began to look for ways to bring in foreign exchange. There was also increased borrowing by the government and a return to the kind of retrenchment and refinancing that was experienced in the early 1980s. Belize seems to have settled into a regular cycle of high growth and increased debt, followed by retrenchment.

In March 1995, a number of measures were introduced to reduce the fiscal imbalance. Government wages were frozen, the Economic Citizenship Program (sale of passports) was reinstituted, and, in November, domestic excise taxes and import duties were raised. The government also reduced the number of government employees by 860 (9 percent of total government employment). In spite of all these measures, the deficit remained at about 5 percent of GNP (*Belize: Recent Economic Developments* 1996, 2).

A number of structural changes took place as well. In the early 1990s, Belize pursued an active privatization policy: the Banana Control Board in 1991, the telephone company in 1992, and the electricity company (partially) in 1993. In April 1996, in line with the CARICOM free trade agreement, import tariff rates were reduced and stamp duties on imports, export taxes, and gross receipts tax were eliminated. The VAT was instituted to compensate for the loss of revenue (*Belize: Recent Economic Developments* 1996, 3).

Assad Shoman, a Belizean author and historian, suggests that the present Westminster system provides a meaningless choice between two parties (PUP and UDP)—meaningless because all economic decisions are coming from outside the country and because there is a weak civil society to influence government policies. Shoman is not alone in noticing that access to the government is in the hands of a very few local elites who control both information and speech. According to Shoman, this has been the case throughout the history of Belize, leading many Belizeans to have an idealized vision of the British Crown because in the past, when injustices perpetuated by local elites became unbearable, people could petition the Crown, and England often responded by preventing the local elites from too much abuse. The postcolonial experience in a fundamental sense was not a move to democracy but a transfer of power from England to local elites. Belize has kept the paternalistic system where each individual supports politicians and a political party in order to obtain favors when they/it are in power. Ordinary Belizeans who need permits and papers from the government, or want to run businesses, must depend on these favors simply to operate.

For the local elites, the stakes are higher. Government tax concessions are the economic plums that government ministers can hand out to their supporters and friends. For example, under the PUP, Barry Bowen, who owns the Coca-Cola and Belikin Beer monopolies, obtained duty-free import concessions and a tax holiday to set up a milk factory. When the UDP came into power, they canceled his contract and began negotiating with a Mexican brewery to break Bowen's beer monopoly and provide a less expensive beer for the Belize market. Belikin Beer is very expensive—a case costs $U.S.21.50 wholesale with an additional 15 percent VAT, and retails at $U.S.1.85 per beer; a Mexican beer sells for $U.S.1.00 per beer. Mexico, of course, is eager to enter the CARICOM market through Belize and bring Mexican beer into Belize legally for the first time.

Another recent trend in the economy is the building of big hotels and resorts. In San Pedro, this construction has ground to a halt, but not before foreigners had obtained almost complete ownership of the seafront. This has created a great deal of resentment among locals, who find the land far too expensive to purchase. Their concerns are supported by data from the *Wall Street Journal* (Paik 13, 1997), which reported that since 1991, developed property in Belize had appreciated about 10 percent per year, and land prices had increased nearly 20 percent per year. Today, the rhetoric in San Pedro is "Small is beautiful."

Although people in San Pedro who were involved in tourism made a lot of money between 1986 and 1994, they also developed a lifestyle they are now having trouble sustaining. Many in the tourist business have such high debt that they can no longer obtain credit and are on the brink of foreclosure. In 1995 and 1996, tourism had dropped so much that people were beginning to hit a brick wall in their debt. The proprietor of one of the biggest hotels in San Pedro had to borrow his payroll from a local moneylender for two pay periods in a row. At the beginning of the 1996 high season, he was not making enough to meet the payroll, much less pay his bills.

REMITTANCES AS INCOME

There is a perception in Belize that jobs are easy to find in the United States. This perception was increased after 1981, when TV came to Belize and instant visions of the United States were available. Partly as a consequence of this, emigration to the United States, primarily by the Creole population, has steadily increased. Between 1980 and 1991 there were 41,000 legal emigrants from Belize (35,000 went to the United States); it is estimated that there are probably three illegal emigrants for every legal emigrant (Steagall et al. 1997). Steagall et al. calculate that legal remittances (money sent through the post office) account for between 4.3 and 10.8 percent of per capita income. These remittance calculations exclude gifts and illegal transfers of money. Such unofficial remittances are probably high, because cash sent by a relative brings a better rate of exchange than the official rate through the post office. The data indicate that real transfers declined from 1984 to 1992, which means that there was less remittance and an increase in the permanence of Creoles in the United States.

Officially there are 54,000 Belizeans in the United States (in real terms, the number is three times greater), concentrated in New York City, Los Angeles, Houston, Chicago, New Orleans, and Miami. There is also increased illegal immigration to the United States. The younger generation of Belizeans are going with less commitment to their relatives back home. They are a less educated group and earn less, but have higher costs living in the United States. More and more of them are involved in illegal activities, making it more difficult for them to send money home (Steagall et al., 1997).

Cash remittances from the United States are a main source of income for many Caribbean and Central American countries. For example, in El Salvador it is estimated that cash remittances from the United States are the single largest source of income, accounting for 12 percent of GNP (Rohter 1997, 1). In Belize remittances are a main source of livelihood for Creoles in the Belize district due to the long-established trend of Creoles and Garifuna predominating among emigrants to the United States (Stegall et al. 1997, 38–40). Although these remittances from abroad are a significant part of the economy, they do not show up in the economic figures because they are not put into investments and savings, as the government would like, but are used for consumption. Factors that affect remittances are the number of migrants, length of stay, levels of earnings, and differences in exchange rates.

Because of the regular flow of dollars into Belize through remittances and tourists, and because the Belize dollar is directly tied to the American dollar in foreign exchange, a dual monetary system has emerged where U.S. dollars and Belize dollars are used in any transaction in Belize. Every shop, restaurant, and business takes U.S. dollars and gives change in both U.S. and Belize dollars. The Belize dollar, which is pegged to the U.S. dollar at 2:1, is inflated in value and under strain. However, the inflated value of the Belize dollar encourages remittances to be sent to Belize and encourages Belizeans with pensions to move back to Belize. The IMF has suggested that Belize needs to unlink the Belize dollar from the American dollar. When this happens, probably after the next election, the Belize dollar will fall in value.

BUYING CITIZENSHIP

The Belize government has an economic citizenship investment program made possible through an amendment to the Belizean Constitution. The amendment makes provision for the granting of citizenship to persons (and their spouses and dependent children) who make a substantial contribution to the economy of Belize. According to one advertisement on the Internet (Belize Passports Consultants and Co.):

Some individuals are interested in citizenship in order to establish legal domicile in order to protect assets and income from burdensome taxation in their countries of origin, judgements, creditors or litigants. Others need a second legal passport to ease travel . . . difficult or impossible under their current citizenship. Other applicants face persecution on religious, ethnic or political grounds in their countries of origin and desire to migrate to a democratic and peace-loving country such as Belize. (www. belize.com/citzdoc.html)

Americans living in Belize are taking out Belizean citizenship (in 1995, about 150 Americans in San Pedro took out Belizean citizenship) while keeping their American citizenship. There are certain advantages in becoming a citizen. Residency restrictions are removed, leaving a citizen free to do any job or work in the country. Americans are getting Belizean citizenship as a protection against the "anti-gringo" sentiment in the tourism industry. In San Pedro, for example, only Belizean-born citizens can be licensed as tour guides, a rule that has caused resentment between Belizean citizens of American birth and born Belizeans. On the other hand, although the hotels pay to train Belizeans as middle-level managers, often the Belizean service workers do not take these managers as seriously as they do the foreign-born managers. In addition, Belizeans who are trained in the tourism business are sometimes ridiculed by other Belizeans as Uncle Toms who have sold out to the foreigners.

In spite of these tensions, citizenship gives Americans and other foreigners the ability to vote and influence the government in a country where the number of voters is small. In addition, there are tax advantages. For example, the exchange tax on a piece of land when it is sold is 10 percent for a foreigner, 8 percent for a resident, and 5 percent for a citizen.

The Chinese have also been purchasing citizenship, buying land, and investing heavily in the country. In the case of Hong Kong Chinese, Belizean citizenship is a hedge against the return of Hong Kong to China that took place in June 1997. But many Chinese are also obtaining citizenship merely as a stepping-stone to make it easier to enter the United States as legal immigrants. The U.S. government is aware of this ruse and has tightened up its visa process in Belize City. The cost of citizenship until 1997 was U.S.$25,000 per person; now it has risen to $50,000, all of which goes to the Belize government. Belizean citizenship was advertised in Europe by the Ministry of Finance in *The International Times* of Brussels for the first time in 1996, under the heading "Help Us Build a New Nation" (*San Pedro Sun*, December 28, 1996, 10). The Belize Passport Consultants and Co. maintains offices in the United Arab Emirates, the United States, Canada, England, Cyprus, Australia, Russia, Taiwan, and Singapore.

Because of the economic citizenship program, there is a move by the Belize government to treat citizenship as a separate issue from a right to residency or the right to vote. Chinese who have bought passports, and therefore citizenships, are sometimes delayed as much as two years in getting residency papers, thus making it impossible for them to stay in Belize. Recently the government decided to reregister voters in the country because of all the illegal aliens registered to vote and others with citizenship but not residency. Voting registration will be available only to those who have been resident in Belize in the two months prior to registration, thus disenfranchising Belizeans abroad. Voting, residency, citizenship, and passports are treated as separate issues, each of which is fraught with tension as the government tries to sort out its citizenship issues.

BANKS AND OTHER DUBIOUS FINANSCAPES

Legitimate banking in Belize is a very small operation. The Central Bank was established in 1982 and has been an active player in setting interest rate ceilings and monetary stability. It prints Belize dollars and allows exchange for U.S. dollars through the bank to keep up with the demand for U.S. dollars. Belize has several commercial banks, but they are undercapitalized (with a capital of U.S.$25 million), and inflation outpaces interest rates. There are 21 active credit unions and 14 insurance companies.

Caye Caulker got its first bank, a branch of the Atlantic Bank, in 1994. Within two weeks of opening, it was robbed, but as usual everyone knew who did it and he was soon caught. The same suspected bank robber was also implicated in a theft of money from the cooperative during the time he worked there. The known thieves are the same, but their activities on Caye Caulker are now bank robberies and embezzlement rather than boat motors and tools.

Dubious forms of banking also seem to be on the rise. This began in 1990, when the International Business Corporation Act set up a kind of hybrid certificate of deposit account that is tied to U.S. interest rates (Rea 1996). Assets in this kind of account are as protected as Swiss bank accounts by the Trust Act of 1992. Neither the Belize nor the U.S. government has access to these accounts, and they cannot be seized by the courts. No one can make a claim against assets in these accounts. These offshore banking accounts are of advantage only to investors from abroad, as a way to hide income (e.g., in a divorce, or when divesting).

Offshore banking accounts have led to some pyramid scams advertised on the Internet. These scams are very simple. Basically, a person opens up an offshore account, entices individuals to put their money in it, and is then issued a debit card on the account after paying a fee to enter the account. Whether any of these accounts have been able to find investors is unknown, since any individual can open an offshore account.

There is a great deal of concern that these new accounts, which are untouchable, will be used for money laundering. Belize enacted the Money Laundering Prevention Act in 1996, and the Central Bank of Belize is now participating in a Caribbean Financial Action Task Force to control money laundering (*The Reporter*, 1996j).

INCOME TAX

Belize has no treaty with the United States on income tax; thus, failure to pay U.S. income tax cannot lead to extradition to the United States, although the U.S. government can request a removal order from the Belize government. A U.S. resident living outside the United States can earn U.S.$75,000 and be exempt from U.S. income tax. Unearned income is taxed the same as in the United States. Recently the husband of Belize's consul-general to Canada, Pamela Picon, was arrested at the request of the U.S. Internal Revenue Service for income tax evasion when he accompanied his wife to Canada. The couple had taken out Belizean citizenship and changed their names from Ross to Picon, marrying under their assumed name (*Amandala* 1997a). Since there are many Americans living in Belize, the IRS regularly appears at the U.S. Embassy to give Americans there the opportunity to declare their income, but very few U.S. citizens show up.

Belize has an income tax of its own, but it is levied mainly on wages. It ranges from 10 percent to 55 percent. The primary tax is the new VAT tax of 15 percent, which has been very hard on merchants and consumers. When the VAT was introduced, many people switched to shopping in Mexico or Guatemala. The short-term result of VAT has been to pull money out of the economy.

COUNTERFEIT MONEY

Counterfeit currency became a serious problem in Belize during 1996. In June 1996, new features were added to Belize money in order to make the notes harder to counterfeit, and in July several men were arrested in connection with the production of counterfeit currency. On Caye Caulker, an islander was caught in possession of counterfeit money and was suspected of being part of a counterfeit money scheme. A year later he was shot in the head in Belize City by a hired killer, supposedly for a drug deal gone sour.

It is legal to take any amount of money, in cash or check form, out of the country, as long as it is declared to the government, and up to U.S.$2,500 without declaration. In the summer of 1996, a Taiwanese merchant was caught trying to smuggle money out of the country and had to pay a fine for breaking Belize's currency law.

Although this description of the Belize economy only touches on some of its features, the general picture that emerges is one of an eighteenth-century trade economy based on agricultural exports and manufactured imports that is starting to create finanscapes in the margins of the global economy. At the same time, the loss of USAID funds for development projects and the reduction in the U.S. State Department presence, as well as the impending loss of protected European markets for exported goods, will have a major negative effect on the Belize economy. How Belize will fare in these finanscapes is still uncertain, but the country is moving in the direction of offshore financial institutions, money laundering, and an international drug trade.

12

Belize Communicating with the Globe

Piracy is alive and well in Belize, but it has entered the communications age. In a meeting with the political attaché from the U.S. Embassy in Belize City one day, I asked him what the U.S. interests in Belize were. I suggested that perhaps the heavy flow of drugs through the country and rumors of this flow being orchestrated from government ministries were a concern to the United States.

"No," he mused thoughtfully. "We cannot change geography."

It must have shown on my face that I was temporarily stumped, because he added helpfully, "Belize lies between Colombia and the U.S. There will always be drugs coming through here. What really concerns me is the pirating of our television programs. That, we are going to stop."

For the first time I saw genuine passion in his eyes.

MOM'S CAFÉ

When I went to Belize in 1972, "communications" meant that if you wanted to get a message to someone, you went to Mom's Café, where you could post it . . . or find one posted to you three months earlier. Better yet, you went to Mom's for breakfast and found the person you needed to find right there, just finishing up fry jacks and eggs. Mom was a large, robust woman from the United States who came to Belize around 1970, at the time Belize was being "discovered" by the early adventuresome types from the United States. She set up an American-style café in a dingy warehouse on the triangle by the Central Drug Store and Augusto Quan's hardware store adjacent to the Swing Bridge on Haulover Creek, and provided pancakes, bacon, milk, and coffee to foreigners of all kinds. Instantly, Mom's became the meeting ground, the geographical hub, for all expatriates, backpackers, or adventurers on the way into Belize, to another part of the country, or on the way out. Chocolate ate there every day and collected his passengers for Caye Caulker. All travelers to Caye Caulker went to Mom's to find Chocolate and find out when he was leaving. Anyone who came to Belize and went through Belize City ended up at Mom's. Mom provided information on places to stay, where to find four-inch nails, whether the road to Tikal was passable. People left messages at Mom's for others and found old messages to themselves. When you went to Mom's, you stayed an hour or so because there was always someone you knew—someone cooking up a new scheme, buying or selling land, just arriving with news from old acquaintances. In those heady days, Mom's was the Rick's Café of Belize, a crossroads for American buccaneers with dubious schemes.

Communication was strictly face-to-face. Information was exchanged verbally, stories were told over and over, and rumors abounded. This was a talking culture rather than a reading culture, and the ability to talk your way out of a scrape, talk your way into a scheme, or just tell a good story was highly regarded. Of course there was the "Belize factor," a term used to refer to the necessity to suspend belief about anything one is told unless it is corroborated by at least ten eyewitnesses. Nevertheless, transactions were often arranged on the basis of trust between people. It was possible to entrust a large sum of money to a person to deliver to a merchant who could be trusted to see that the goods were delivered to your house. It was possible because all the parties in the transaction knew each other, even if only by a nickname. Legal names and bills of sale did not count for much; business deals were based on a face-to-face, personal relationship. This may be why in Belize, when the telephone came in, it was common to have the following sort of phone conversation.

(Ring) Hello.

Is Lindsay there?

Yes. (Click)

(Ring) Hello.

Hello, I asked if Lindsay was there.

Yes, I told you he is.

Well, may I speak with him?

Oh, sure. Why didn't you say so?

People assumed that the purpose of a phone call was to find out if someone was there so the caller could come over and talk face-to-face. No one could expect to get anything done by speaking on the telephone.

As communications in Belize began to change, Mom's also changed. After ten years at the pivotal location by the Swing Bridge, Mom moved to Handyside Street, where she expanded her business and set up some rooms for people to stay. Cynthia, who came to Belize to adopt a family of children who had lost their mother, stayed there every time she came to Belize; Mom, and then her daughter Sue, kept up on the progress of the adoption. When Mom took ill, Sue managed the place. And then Mom died. Pressed financially, Sue moved Mom's from Handyside to a place further out, and suddenly no one went there anymore. In 1996 Sue went bankrupt and Mom's folded. The employees, who had all been at Mom's for 25 years, since the day she opened, sued for severance pay and won. The closing of Mom's was the end of the Casablanca era in Belize, the end of face-to-face, word-of-mouth communications in a place where you could not telephone someone or get information except by talking directly to someone who knew something. That person you found at Mom's Café.

Outside hubs like Mom's, communications dwindled to nearly total isolation from the rest of the world. On Caye Caulker, the only contact with mainland Belize was by boat, often a whole day's trip by sail or several hours on the one and only cargo boat running twice a week between Belize City and Caye Caulker. There was no telephone on the island, so when the need was urgent, messages were transmitted twice a day on Radio Belize. These messages were wonderful: "Josephine, your Aunt Dominga is sick and needs you to come to Double Head Cabbage at once." News from outside the country arrived only when someone from abroad came and recounted it. The mail service was incredibly slow, unreliable, and expensive. According to one resident of Caye Caulker at that time:

The pace of mail to Caye Caulker was about six months round-trip for a letter and reply so the average enquiry took me about 2 1/2 years. At an income of about Bz$300 per month [in the late 1960s] between my wife [who taught elementary school] and me [fishing] the $3 for stamps on an envelope was a major expense and meant the children were going to have to do without something. What I remember most was not only the long time involved in trying to find out information (in years) but the cost, about a week's wages in salary, to pay for the stamps. (E-mail, Cap'n Ray)

By 1982 there was one telephone line to the island. The many extensions meant that it was hard to get a call through or receive one, although it was always interesting to listen in on other people's calls. News from the outside, as well as messages from relatives and friends in other parts of the country, still came over the single government-owned radio station, Radio Belize.

Contact with the mainland was transformed by the energetic entrepreneurship of Chocolate, who ran the only reliable daily boat service. It left Caye Caulker at 7 A.M. on the dot and returned after he had breakfast at Mom's Café around 11 A.M. There were many in those days who tried to pretend to be Chocolate, but the tourists always found out they were impostors because they never could attain Chocolate's reliability. Envy of Chocolate was legend, especially since a different gorgeous European woman was with him every time I saw him.

By the 1990s, transportation between Caye Caulker and the mainland was transformed by an organized water taxi service leaving for Belize City four to five times a day (U.S.$7.50 one way), and by regular daily flights to the airstrip that opened in 1992. Three airlines—Island Air, Tropic, and Maya—connect Caye Caulker with all the major inland cities. Caye Caulker is now connected to the Internet, has a telecommunications office with fax service, and is linked by satellite dish to the major cable networks. Tour operators wear beepers and carry expensive cellular phones (a U.S.$600 purchase with fees of $48 per month for service). Caye Caulker is now in touch with the rest of the world.

LETTERS AND BOOKS

Belize skipped the modern era of postal service. Mail service always had been, and still is, basically hopeless. In the summer of 1996, I received a package that had been mailed from the United States three months earlier. The Caye Caulker post office was a quagmire. Picking up your mail was such a major undertaking that most people gave up trying. The postmistress was so uninterested in seeing the mail get to its destination that often it was only after several visits to the post office that you finally found out a letter had been there for several months. She refused to sort the letters into alphabetical order, frequently had no stamps to sell, and would not hand you a letter from the pile on the counter if you were one minute past closing time, even though she was standing there in her shop, which remained open. The villagers got so frustrated with the situation that they finally wrested the mail from her and opened a new post office next to the community rainwater tank. It still shocks me to go there and find it open during the hours posted, and staffed by an employee who will hand over a letter upon request. However, I do feel a tinge of nostalgia about no longer being able to go through everyone's mail and examine the unpaid bills and hopeless missives that would never get to their addressees.

Books were always scarce in Belize, so Belizeans did not have much reading matter easily available and could not rely on printed material for information. According to the chief librarian at the Leo Bradley Memorial Library, when television was introduced in 1981, there was a dramatic reduction in the number of books checked out of the library. She herself was able to see movies she had only heard about, so she spent much more time catching up on movies than reading.

Television seems to have reduced adult reading, but it is not the only factor. Today people want up-to-date information, but this is not available in the library with its small, antiquated collection. The library has 120,000 volumes for the whole country (16,000 volumes for the Belize district), with one branch in each district. The University College library is extremely small, most of it consisting of out-of-date textbooks. In the chief librarian's opinion, the library is used mainly by students for specific school projects. This use drops off after age 14, when many children leave school.

RADIO

With printed information scarce, mail unreliable, and books not available, the radio was a great asset in Belize. Virtually everyone owned a small portable radio and sacrificed to buy batteries (in the pre-electricity days) in order to listen to the nightly broadcast on Radio Belize. Although it was government-owned and -controlled, and the amount of news was very limited, it was the one and only link with the outside world.

Radio broadcasting started in 1937 with transmission primarily around Belize City. In the 1940s Belizeans developed a taste for country-western music by tuning in to radio stations on the Gulf Coast of Texas. By the early 1950s Belize had a national broadcasting station, but it was only around 1963 that Radio Belize was operating fully as a regular radio station. Even in the 1970s the radio was an AM-only service and was regulated by the Ministry of Broadcasting, Information and Health. The most popular programs were Western popular music and reggae (Lent 1989, 17), but the radio was also important for transmitting messages to loved ones: "John, come home. Annie loves you." Everyone listened to the messages and to the evening broadcast for a few tidbits of world news, but more importantly for emergency broadcasts and for the weather. "Tonight the seas are light chop to choppy" was predicted during the weather hour so frequently that a café in Cayo named itself the Light Chop to Choppy Café. Today, Radio Belize has one AM and one FM station, and still is the only national station. Most of the programming is music, but there are also shows prepared by Maya and Garifuna cultural associations, and about 30 percent of programming is in Spanish. Bilingual newscasts, call-in shows, and information from specific government ministries are also available (Lent 1989, 17–19).

Today, Radio Belize is everywhere. Its opening can be heard every day at the regular news hours: "A Caribbean nation in the heart of Central America with the longest barrier reef in the New World and home to many races and cultures. This is Radio Belize." According to one study, almost everyone has a radio (95 percent), and virtually all (98 percent) listen to Radio Belize (Roser et al. 1986, 15). Although other Central American and Mexican radio stations are available and are popular, especially in the Spanish-speaking areas, there is a strong preference for the local station. Radio Belize carries national Belizean news, linking the different parts of Belize with each other.

There are signs that the government of Belize will not be able to control radio for long. In Cayo district, Radio Ritmo—the Voice of the West—is a small community station with limited reach and operated with homemade equipment. Luis Garcia, the general manager who made the equipment and uses his own compact disc collection for the music, has organized numerous community environmental cleanup projects, using the radio to reach small communities in Cayo. His independent voice and willingness to take action have already brought him recognition as an independent voice in an otherwise controlled radio environment. In one case, the local hospital had no sewage disposal system, and Garcia urged his listeners to join him in providing a septic tank for the hospital. When he and a team of volunteers showed up, the Belize Defense Force barred their way, but the next week a septic tank was provided by the local authorities (personal communication, Luis Garcia).

VIDEOS, THEN TELEVISION

The first appearance of TV in Belize was in the mid-1970s, when some Belizeans in Corozal erected huge antennas to pick up Mexican and Guatemalan television. But no one invested in a television station because Belize was considered too small an audience to warrant it (Lent 1989, 19). However, the arrival of the VCR in Belize changed that situation by creating a demand for movies. In 1978, an American entrepreneur in Miami decided to sell VCRs to ten Belizeans and supply them with videotapes by mail, thereby unleashing a boom, within a few months, in the purchase of VCRs and a local system of tape rentals (Lent 1989, 19).

This was a strange time in Belize. In 1980 the first VCR came to Caye Caulker, brought by Belisario Martinez, who promptly set it up his restaurant. That night he announced that he would show the movie *Jaws* for Bz$1 per person. Curious to see their first movie, almost the whole village showed up and packed the bar. Benches were brought in from all over the island for seating, and for an hour adjustments had to be made until everyone could squeeze in. Packed into the airless room, excited at the enormity of the event, we all strained to see the screen perched on the mahogany bar. I had never seen *Jaws*, but I had heard how scary it was, and frankly I dreaded it. But here we were on a small island, and this was the only commercial entertainment we had been offered for years. Besides, the subject was perfect. The men in the bar were all fishermen who had hunted sharks at one time in their lives and had complete familiarity with the ocean just outside our door. The moment of truth arrived, the famous *Jaws* music built up the suspense, and the great white shark rose out of the sea, chomping everything in sight. The entire audience burst out laughing and the Martinez's place disintegrated into total bedlam. One man laughed so hard he rolled off the bench I was squeezed onto, upsetting the balance and sending me into my only frightened moment of the evening as I grabbed the person next to me to get my balance. *Jaws* was a huge success on Caye Caulker that night, although as a slapstick comedy. After that showing, Marin's restaurant decided the competition was at too much of an advantage and immediately got its VCR. It was at Marin's restaurant that I saw my first porno flick (the story line was about a woman who goes to a primitive, jungly place and is used as a sex object by dark-skinned men) while I ate baked lobster drenched in canned margarine.

The video wars were in full rage, but not for long. That same year Emory King and Nestor Vazquez set up the first television earth station in Belize. It taped shows transmitted from the United States via satellite, from which they made copies for rental to VCR owners (Lent 1989, 20). Other earth stations quickly started up, their owners eager to tape American television shows and put them out to rent. It was only a matter of time, the summer of 1981 to be exact, until one earth station began to broadcast programs live to a few wealthy individuals who paid a hefty fee for the service. Although all of this activity was clearly piracy, no one in the government seemed to care. Ever innovative, another Belizean found a way to tap into the signals from the earth station free of charge and make them available to many more. People were hungry for television, and the government, by this time cognizant of the illegal activity, nevertheless turned a blind eye rather than cut off people's access (Lent 1989, 21). Once the word was out that the government was tolerating it, broadcasting stations sprang up like mushrooms, and have continued to pirate American television programs to this day. There are now at least 12 earth stations pirating U.S. television and numerous cable services. By some estimates there are as many televisions in Belize per capita as in the United States, and few places in the world have more widespread use of VCRs (Lent 1989, 23).

Stewart Krohn of the Belize Channel (Channel 5) and producer of Great Belize Productions, stated in an article written in 1981, "Readers may be wondering why it was not until 1981 that someone got the bright idea to bring television to Belize. The reason is that it was illegal—and still is" (Krohn 1981, 18). According to Krohn, the Belize Telecommunications Authority Ordinance of 1972 empowered the government to issue licenses for transmission of reception of any images, but no license had ever been issued. "Why, then," he asked. "if television transmission is illegal, is the Baymen Avenue transmitter allowed to stay open?" His answer refers to the political problem it would create for the government if it limited people's access to television by making it much more expensive (Krohn 1981, 19). No such government would stay in power. Piracy lives in Belize.

Today, all the cable channels are pirated from U.S. and some Mexican TV stations (Warren 1993). Two independent television stations, channels 5 and 7, produce local news and feature programs. Channel 5, the Belize Channel, whose sponsors include the Belize Broadcasting Corporation, the Programme for Belize, the Ministry of Tourism and the Environment, and the Tourist Board, provides a local news program twice a day, sponsors *The Andy Palacio Show* (a local Punta Rock celebrity), produces programs on celebrations such as that of Settlement Day (when Caribs from St. Vincent came to Belize) in Dandriga, and other local artistic programs that lend themselves to the development of a national consciousness.

The documentary programs produced by Channel 5 are of very high quality. More important, they look at both political and environmental issues and matters of human interest. They include documentaries on the mestization of Belize (the ethnic shift from Creole to mestizo); on the controversial move of Guatemalan immigrants from a nature reserve to the Red Bank community in Cayo; on an order of German missionaries called the Pallotine Sisters, who came to Belize in 1913; on the war games of the Belize Defense Force as they train to combat drugs in jungle warfare. There is a profile of Minister Dean Barrow, a program on the discovery of huge Maya pots used for making alcohol in caves in the Cayo district, and an exposé of the blowing up of the reef at Hatchet Caye by an American resort owner.

TELECOMMUNICATIONS

The telephone system that featured one line to the outside world from Caye Caulker in the 1980s, a line that sounded like it was being filtered through the conversations of schools of dolphins as it lay on the ocean bed, has leaped into the twenty-first century, bypassing the era of telephone poles and telephone exchanges. Belize now has the best telecommunications system in Central America and the Caribbean, completely digital with fiber-optic cable. Even the international links to the United States and the cellular system are digital. This state-of-the-art system surpasses any system available to rural North Americans. Once again Belize has skipped modernity and moved straight into the the age of digital technology.

INTERNET

E-mail service to Belize was set up by a VSO (Canadian Peace Corps) volunteer, Brian Candler, who was working on computer education at the University College of Belize. This led to Belize getting full Internet access at the end of 1995. Though still available only with plenty of glitches, the Internet has already become a great boon to Belize and Belizeans. Belizeans living abroad have a home page (LABEN—Los Angeles Belizean Educational Network), a grassroots organization that links them to each other and to relatives and friends in Belize. The Belize government and the University College of Belize have home pages, offshore financial institutions and tourist information sources proliferate on the Internet, and many hotels, resorts, dive operations, and tour services are on-line. The BTL.NET E-mail index has 550 addresses, and Bz-Culture Mailing List is an active talk group on the Internet.

In January 1996, the Internet began to carry information on Belizean citizenship/passports, including Belize as a tax haven, how to enjoy your rights as a citizen of Belize, and the monetary contribution necessary. In February 1966, the Belize Tourist Board went on-line (http://www.turq.com/belize.html) with maps, pictures, and information about the country. Every day there is new information, including old photographs from Belize (Neil Fraser's Heritage Site), all the major newspaper articles published in Belize, *Belize First* magazine (by Lan Sluder), and Belizean recipes.

New projects for getting information on Belize on-line are beginning to be developed. For example, the land office in Belize has always recorded deeds by hand in large books with no indexing system and plenty of dust. This system dates back to the colonial period. To trace a land deed, you must know the book and page number, then look through stacks of teetering books, which regularly fall down and are shoved back on the shelf in no discernible order, to find the appropriate book. This cumbersome system meant that it was almost impossible to access information on registered land titles. Birth certificates, residency cards, and tax records are kept—or lost—using the same "pile" filing system. Today, with a grant from USAID of $400,000, such information will be put into a data bank that will be available on the Internet. Called a conservation and environmental data system, it will compile information from the Ministry of Lands and the Ministry of Natural Resources, as well as from educational institutions such as the Belize College of Agriculture and the National Library Service, and from NGOs, such as the Belize Centre for Environmental Studies (*The Reporter* 1996d, 19).

Unfortunately, the Internet also attracts some dubious investment schemes and on-line betting. For example, in September 1997 the state of Minnesota won a case in the Minnesota Court of Appeals to block on-line gambling run by a Belize-based sports betting firm, Granite Gate Resorts. Although the firm is based in Belize and Las Vegas, it solicits bets in Minnesota, where betting is illegal.

NEWSPAPERS

There is no historical tradition of an independent press, and little attempt to promote it even today. The newspaper-reading public is very small, and most newspapers are sold in Belize City, where there is the greatest concentration of population. In general, although newspapers in Belize have improved and people are reading them more than before, too many newspapers are still self-serving political organs pushing a particular agenda.

Early newspapers in Belize (the first appeared in 1825) were all dependent on outsiders, usually lasted a short time, and consisted mainly of advertisements and descriptions of social events among the colonialists (Lent 1989, 15–16). When Belizeans began to develop their own newspapers, they were, for the most part, begun to promote political causes. An early serious newspaper was *The Belize Billboard*, begun in 1946 as an organ of the labor movement and opposition to the colonial government (Lent 1989, 16). *The Belize Times*, started in 1959, is the official newspaper of the People's United Party, and *The People's Pulse* is the party organ for the United Democratic Party. Each is sold at party supporters' stores or given away to party members. For example, Milo's store, a PUP stronghold in San Pedro, gets 50 to 70 copies of the *The Belize Times* and gives most of them away to party members. *Amandala* was founded in 1969 as the organ of the United Black Association for Development, a cultural movement dedicated to the Black Power and Black Consciousness movements (Tillett 1997). The newspaper's Black Consciousness/Afrocentrism agenda aims to promote the well-being of blacks in Belize and to counter the increased influence of the Hispanic population. This has led to accusations of racism. An opinion piece published in *The Reporter* claimed:

In my opinion, the most exposure I have been granted to racism and bigotry in my life has not occurred on the streets of Belize or in the "ghetto areas", as they are called, but rather in the pages of our largely circulated *Amandala*. I do not mean that *Amandala* is a racist newspaper, but rather that every issue is packed full of articles dealing with the oppression of the black people, and the struggles that still continue every day . . . it seems that the reporting of pertinent and factual news has taken a back seat to this. (Rudon 1997, 26)

The newspaper has a weekly piece written in Creole and advocates pride in the Creole language. There are articles calling for Creole to be taught in the schools and possibly to replace English as the national language of Belize. The newspaper also has articles trying to unite the Garifuna and Creole populations, and to counter their historical enmity. *Amandala* promotes interest in sports, with the aim of getting blacks "off the streets," and is concerned that more blacks are in jail and on drugs than other ethnic groups, a situtation blamed on the United States and the influence of television. It laments the lack of solid families and family discipline, and is worried about the exodus of blacks to the United States. The editor wants the government to do something about it.

    The Reporter supports the current UDP government, though it tries to maintain some independence and is not a party organ. The editor, Harry Lawrence, has an agenda to "improve knowledge about Belize among Belizeans." He publishes regular sections on world news, children, health, and business. His is a "family" newspaper, aiming to get the whole family to read newspapers. *The Reporter*, while trying to take a more independent stance, is generally favorable to the UDP. Thus businesses friendly to the UDP, such as Martha's Hotel on San Pedro and the Center Store on Caye Caulker, sell *The Reporter*.

The Observer, a newspaper that operated for only a few months in 1996, represented an attempt to create a more high-culture paper. It had sections on community service (e.g., Boy Scouts, health organizations), national history and museums, information on legal issues ("Confessions: How can they be made more credible?"), family and children (the Rights of the Children Conference), health ("Mental Health Is Everybody's Business"), sports, book reviews, fiction ("Why the Alligator Has a Short Tongue"), the Internet, and a page in Spanish. Lead editorials have included a questioning of the church by Reverend Oliver Ottley ("Quo Vadis?") and one on the concept of the self ("Who, and What, Am I?"). The readership of *The Observer* clearly was very limited.

FREEDOM OF THE PRESS

It is generally conceded among Belizean newspaper editors and other intelligentsia that there is no freedom of the press in Belize. Information is carefully guarded by the government, with only certain ministers being allowed to give interviews. All other civil servants give out even innocuous information at the risk of losing their jobs. One Belizean reporter told me, "We live in a police state. Only the police can investigate the government, and the government controls the police. So no investigations of the government can take place." Government ministers are not averse to taking censorship matters into their own hands. On March 11, 1995, after a pro-PUP broadcast, two UDP government ministers were charged with entering the Voice of the West radio station in the Cayo district, damaging the equipment, and beating up the staff. The Voice of the West, as mentioned earlier, is a community radio station that urges people to take action on environmental cleanup that the government will not do. The charges against the ministers were later dropped, leading to further media suspicion that freedom to broadcast is compromised in Belize.

There are other indications of government obstacles to freedom of the press. The media, for example, have been told that they cannot report anything about the courts or the legal system, or they will be held in contempt of court. In the fall of 1996, Sir George Brown, the Chief Justice of the Supreme Court, called for a meeting with all media representatives; there he announced that only verbatim reports of court proceedings would be allowed. Any comments on legal cases would be considered contempt because they might be prejudicial to a jury. The *San Pedro Sun* immediately responded with a regular column of verbatim court records that has become a very popular section of the newspaper. The Belize Press Club has protested the limits placed on journalists' rights to report the proceedings of public trials (*San Pedro Sun* 1996, 14).

The U.S. Department of State Report on Human Rights Practices in Belize states that "the constitution provides for freedom of speech and of the press, and the Government generally respects this right in practice" (U.S. Department of State 1996, 3). The report acknowledges that the nominally independent Belize Broadcasting Corporation produces party propaganda for the government, and the Belize Broadcasting Authority, which regulates broadcasting, asserts its right to preview broadcasts with political content and to delete any defamatory material. The report mentions the incident in which a radio station identified with the opposition party alleged that two cabinet ministers broke into the station, beat the owner, and destroyed equipment. The Belize Press Association, formed in 1995, has as a main goal the achievement of increased access to government information. That the Belize government is sensitive to this issue is indicated in Prime Minister Esquivel's Independence Day speech, in which he went to some length to argue that the government promotes free information, and that it is the media that are restricting information.

Free speech is an issue that is not likely to go away soon, and with information restricted in Belize, but available on the Internet, the government of Belize will not be able to impose censorship for long.

WHO IS COMMUNICATING

Perhaps the biggest recent communication changes in Belize are the communication between the different regions, between individual Belizeans both at home and abroad, and between Belizeans and international organizations. Orange Walk and Corozal in the past had more communication with Mexico than with Belize City, but now, with a good road and easy telecommunications, these regions are being integrated with the rest of the country. Even areas that are still remote and hard to access by road, such as Punta Gorda and the Toledo district, are in touch not only with the central government but also with international groups through modern telecommunications. The recently politicized Toledo Maya, for example, are in daily contact with international indigenous rights groups through E-mail and fax, and are probably going to run their own candidates outside of the two main parties in the next elections. Belizeans who had emigrated to the United States are returning to Belize in large numbers and are affecting the political situation, and those still in the United States play an important role in informing Belizeans in Belize about political issues through such Internet channels as LABEN, the Bz-Culture Mailing List, and the Belize Chat Group.

One outcome of the increased communication between Belizeans of different regions and with others outside Belize is the emerging sense of Belize as a nation. Better internal communication, combined with a stronger sense of how others perceive Belize and Belizeans, has helped Belizeans to evolve a much clearer sense of themselves as a nation than ever before. A sense of national identity is not necessarily shared by all ethnic groups in Belize, but there are indications that it is evolving. For example, Richard Wilk has suggested that local goods in Belize began to be produced about the same time that television became available (Wilk 1989, 11). He suggests that the production of local Belizean goods occurred because the advertising of local goods on television diminished the image of "backwardness" that Belizeans often attributed to them. Locally produced clothes and foods, for example, were always viewed as inferior to imported goods, but when local goods were seen in television ads, they could be placed in the present as "traditional" or "Belizean" (Wilk 1989, 11–13).

The introduction of pirated TV has also been held responsible for a number of changes in Belize. For the first time, Belizeans had access to international news and could see images of places they had never imagined. They began to follow sports and became fans of specific teams (Chicago Cubs, Miami Dolphins, Houston Oilers) in the cities that were home to the stations whose signals were being pirated. Instead of their entertainment in the evening coming from going out on the streets to converse with their neighbors and family, people settled in their homes to watch TV. Although the Belizean affinity for American popular culture and goods predates television, the thirst for American goods increased dramatically as people began to want the consumer goods they saw on television programs. Children developed a taste for American toys, and parents were finding it necessary to get relatives abroad to send specific items for Christmas. American sports, fashion, and slang were adopted, as were American ideas of democracy, public debate on the government, and political campaigning. Seeing the world news on TV made people think and talk about politics more as they observed what was happening elsewhere. It also increased ethnic consciousness. The Garifuna and Maya councils came into being, and the issue of ethnic identity and identification of self with one's ethnic group was promoted. Black Americans from the 1960s Black Consciousness movement became active in Belize. Evan X. Hyde preaches its precepts from the pulpit of *Amandala*. Others, such as Mustafa Toure of University College, and various members of SPEAR, also echo Marxist and Black Power sentiments.

American ideas of environmentalism were brought in partly through U.S. television programs on ecology and the Discovery Channel's very popular nature programs. I know many Belizeans who watch the Discovery Channel virtually every night because of a deep interest in the ecology and natural history of their country. As in many places, American westerns and American and British war movies are enormously popular. Mexican and American soap operas and talk shows are also heavily watched. The use of expressions derived from the classic movies cable channel peppers everyday langauge. People speak of being put "in harm's way," and I have overheard someone call three guys who passed by "the good, the bad, and the ugly." Movie theaters had existed in Belize City before the arrival of videos and television, but the rest of the country was put in touch with the American movie industry only through cable television. In a strange homage to a time past, in 1996 a movie theater opened in Belize City in an effort to entice the public to see movies, but it is doubtful that it will succeed.

According to Richard Wilk, however, the

impact of television lies not in the messages carried over the channel, not in the content of the situation comedies and baseball games, but in the concepts of time and distance carried by the immediacy of the medium. . . . The most important change caused by television is the way it changes people's perception of time, distance, and culture. (Wilk 1989, 4)

Wilk goes on to argue that Belizeans' consciousness of their own culture and of the world outside, and of Belize's place in that wider context, has changed the basis of political rhetoric and political legitimacy (Wilk 1989, 4). The timelessness of life in Belize, its isolation in the past, meant that the few educated elite could be the bringers of the outside world, the agents of change in the society (Wilk 1989, 5). This is no longer true. The slow, out-of-pace-with-the-world colonial time has been replaced with an immediacy of contact that puts life in Belize and life in the United States on the same clock. Belizeans, through television, now directly experience the same flow of events that people in the United States experience. Through cable TV they see the same movies and shows that the rest of the world sees, and through sitcoms and advertisements, they see the same fashions and goods to buy (Wilk 1989, 9).

Conclusion

In his book *Millennium: Winners and Losers in the Coming World Order* (1991), Jacques Attali, financial adviser to former French President François Mitterrand, wrote that the forces of globalization were bound to divide the countries of the world into a few winners and many losers. He suggested that France, of course, would be one of the winners, and small countries like Belize, unable to keep up with the pace of the global marketplace, would be losers. The counterview to Attali that I have suggested is that the very margins of the global world system may become the areas of most creative cultural activity, where the construction of sets of local relations and group identities within a deterritorialized, transnational politics may allow individuals to transcend the boundaries of a state in very creative ways. It just might be that the work of the imagination is best undertaken in the margins, on the borders of a global system where the freedom to experiment is greater.

Such experimentation is already taking place in Belize, most obviously in the tension between the transnational environmental movement and the local Belizean context of identity politics and nation-making where the environmentalists have emerged as the new ecocolonialists and ecomissionaries. The issue at stake is partly the same as the colonialist agenda—control of land, people, and resources. But the new ecocolonialism is also about a larger issue: who gets to control nature itself. Here the religiosity cloak is important: when you play God with nature, you need a religious rhetoric to go with it. There is no question that ecocolonialism deals in salvation (saving species and saving land from development), but so did the old colonialism do good when it saved people by bringing Pax Britannica (God, law and order, and education).

Other areas, newer and more tenuous, warrant a close look. The international drug trade, various and sundry financial scams, the selling of citizenship without residency, and trade in bananas to a protected market all point to a repositioning of the local context within the global system.

Perhaps the most significant turn in Belize is the creation of numerous lines of communication. Having bypassed the era of books and printed reading matter, Belizeans have turned to television, videos, and the Internet to access information. Belize today is in touch with the rest of the world, whereas in the past, Belizeans were isolated not only from the global community but, perhaps more important, from each other. And one of the issues Belizeans abroad and Belizeans at home are talking about is: What is Belizean? There is now Belizean cuisine (before, people just ate stew chicken, rice, and beans), a Belizean flag and national anthem, Belizean ethnic goods (Ziracote wood carvings, black coral jewelry, Mayan baskets), Punta Rock (Belize's own music), and Belize beauty pageants (even Mr. Gay Belize). People in Orange Walk, who 20 years ago had never been to Belize City, did not know who lived there, or what people there looked like, now travel there daily on good roads.

Belize is one of the world's truly multicultural nations. Ethnicity was never reduced to race; it has always been a pastiche of collective identities formed through a complex interplay of race, language, history, and culture. Today these diverse identities are being challenged by a nationalist agenda to forge a common national identity. Recent migrations, immigrations, emigrations, and demographic changes in the country will all have a say in how these local identities fit into the larger social realities of global identities. What is clear is that Belize's diasporic identities cut across traditional Latin American and Caribbean boundaries and are influenced by a multitude of global processes. The emergence of local Belizean culture is profoundly influenced by the localization of the global culture.

The present is the end of a history peculiar to Belize, a history in which Belize had a backwater status, with Belizeans isolated from the rest of the world and, due to a lack of communication within the country, from each other. Though there are still pockets of relative isolation, these are rapidly becoming scarce. What is now taking place is an equally peculiar postmodernism that includes instant contact with the rest of the world, star status as an ecotourism destination for American and European environmentalists, and a search for identity among Belizeans themselves. Mediascapes, which came to Belize only in the 1980s, have given a global dimension to local ideas of ethnicity, national identity, the state, the environment, and "others" (American tourists, Central American refugees, Chinese economic citizens). And improved communications between Belizeans are putting the diverse groups within the country in contact with each other for the first time.

But the changes are patchy and uneven. The government consists of a small number of educated, mostly Creole elites who hold multiple, interwoven jobs within the system and are related to each other through kinship and marriage, creating a cumbersome, sometimes corrupt system. While this unwieldy government struggles with financial scams, a powerful international drug trade, fluctuating tourism, soaring national debt, and structural adjustments mandated by the International Monetary Fund, the economy is still based on crops such as citrus, sugar, and bananas, exported to a protected market in Europe. And as one would expect, AIDS is becoming serious in Belize, with one in every 193 males in Belize infected with HIV (500 HIV-positive cases) and 209 people with fully developed AIDS (Novelo 1997a), before a functioning medical system has even been developed. For even minor surgery, Belizeans fly to Merida, Guatemala City, or Miami.

A central question for Belizeans is what cultural and economic niche this tiny nation, situated on the marginalized borders of the global periphery, will occupy. An important part of the answer to this question will be the struggles between the transnational environmental movement in Belize and Belizeans locality. Ancient land issues and title to the land have been preempted by the environmentalists who work within the government ministries and departments, financing and running the show. Is this the new imperialism from the North, or is this the salvation of Belize and its natural resources? For whom is Belize being reserved, and who benefits?

The connection between globalization processes and the creation of social forms and culture is only just now being understood by anthropologists. The old core/periphery model is being replaced with one that emphasizes the creative cultural and economic explosions of colonialism that took place in the borderlands of the core. Belize is a key player in one of those borderlands. A diverse, multicultural society that is cosmopolitan and deterritorialized, searching for new forms of collective expression, identities, movements, and imagined possibilities, Belize has come to the fore at a time when awareness of global social realities is at an all-time high.

Bibliography

Africa. 1985. " 'Belize Breeze' an Ill wind." No. 172 (December): 56.

Amandala. 1995. "Banana Union May Strike Sunday." June 1.

———. 1996a. "A European Farmer Resident in Belize Writes." June 2, pp. 19–20.

———. 1996b. "Banana Belt Tense." August 18, p. 1.

———. 1997a. "Husband of Belize's Consul General to Canada Arrested for U.S. Tax Evasion." January 5, p. 1.

———. 1997b. " 'Bad Baby, Belize,' Says U.S." March 9, p. 1.

———. 1997c. "In Belize, Cocaine Now Comes by the Tons." March 30, p. 1.

———. 1997d. "Belize and the Two Chinas." June 8, p. 27.

———. 1997e. "Poachers Charged for Firing on Forest Rangers." July 20, p. 24.

———. 1997f. "The First Family: Instant Winners in the $2.5 Million Polaroid Sweepstake." Paid advertisement. July 27, p. 3.

Anderson, Benedict. 1983. *Imagined Communities: Reflections on the Origin and Spread of Nationalism.* London: Verso.

Appadurai, Arjun. 1990. "Disjuncture and Difference in the Global Cultural Economy." In Mike Featherstone, ed., *Global Cultures*, pp. 295–310. London: Sage.

———. 1996. *Modernity at Large: Cultural Dimensions of Globalization.* Minneapolis: University of Minnesota Press.

Attali, Jacques. 1991. *Millennium: Winners and Losers in the Coming World Order.* New York: Random House.

Barber, Benjamin R. 1992. "Jihad vs. McWorld." *Atlantic Monthly* 269, no. 3 (March): 53–63.

Barham, B. L. 1992. "Foreign Direct Investment in a Strategically Competitive Environment: Coca-Cola, Belize and the International Citrus Industry." *World Development* 20, no. 6: 841–857.

Barry, Tom. 1992. *Inside Belize: The Essential Guide to Its Society, Economy and Environment.* Albuquerque, NM: Inter-Hemispheric Education Resource Center.

Belize: Recent Economic Developments. 1996. IMF Staff Country Report no. 96/40. Washington, DC: International Monetary Fund.

Belize Times. 1996a. "Rio Bravo Ecotourism Workshop." May 5, p. 15.

Belize Times. 1996b. "Banana Watch Urges Fyffes to Move on Belize." October 27, p. 9.

Blackhurst, Chris, and Phil Davison. 1996. "Judge Dreadful? Chris Blackhurst and Phil Davison Report on Death-Row Battles in a Former British Colony." *The Independent,* December 1, pp. 1–17.

Bolland, O. Nigel. 1986. *Belize: A New Nation in Central America.* Boulder, CO: Westview Press.

Boyce, Rubert. 1906. *Report to the Government of British Honduras Upon the Outbreak of Yellow Fever in That Colony in 1905.* London: J. & A. Churchill.

Brace, C. Loring. 1996. *Race and Other Misadventures.* Dix Hills, NY: General Hall Press.

Bradbury, Alex. 1994. *Guide to Belize.* Old Saybrook, CT: Globe Pequot Press.

Burdon, Sir John Alder. 1931. *Archives of British Honduras.* Vol. 1, *From the Earliest Date to A.D. 1800.* London: Sifton Praed & Co.

Butler, R. W. 1980. "The Concept of a Tourism Area Cycle of Evolution: Implications for Management of Resources." *Canadian Geographer* 24, no. 1: 5–12.

Campbell, Mark. 1996. *Beyond the Succotz Tree: Ethnolinguistic Identity in a Maya Village and School in Belize.* Ph.D. diss., Department of Anthropology, University of Toronto.

Cardenas, Elizabeth Joan. 1991. *East Indian Folk Culture in Belize.* Benque Viejo, Belize: BRC Printing.

Carter, Jacque, Janet Gibson, Archie Carr III, and James Azueta. 1994. "Creation of the Hol Chan Marine Reserve in Belize: A Grass Roots Approach to Barrier Reef Conservation." *The Environmental Professional* 16: 220–231.

Clifford, James. 1994. "Diasporas." *Cultural Anthropology* 9, no. 3: 302–338.

Collins, Charles O. 1995. "Refugee Resettlement in Belize." *The Geographical Review* 85, no. 1: 20–30.

Comaroff, Jean, and John Comaroff. 1992. *Ethnography and the Historical Imagination: Studies in the Ethnographic Imagination.* Boulder, CO: Westview Press.

Cook, James. (1769). 1935. *Remarks on a Passage from the River Balise, in the Bay of Honduras, to Merida: The Capital of the Province of Jucatan in the Spanish West Indies.* London: Facsimile of the original, with perspective by Muriel Haas. New Orleans: Midameres Press.

Coral Caye Conservation Newsletter. 1996. "Prime Minister Opens Marine Research Centre" 4: 1.

The Courier. 1995. No. 152 (July/August): 12–32.

Crick, Malcom. 1989. "Representations of International Tourism in the Social Sciences: Sun, Sex, Sights, Savings, Servility." *Annual Review of Anthropology* 18: 307–344.

Dachary, Alfredo, and Stella Burne. 1991. "Tourism Development, the Options and Their Problems: The Case of San Pedro." *Fourth Annual Studies on Belize Conference*, SPEAR Report no. 7. Bengue Vieja, Belize: Cubola Productions, 142–146.

DeGregori, Thomas. 1997. "Technology as Experience." Unpublished manuscript.

Destination Belize. 1997. The Official Guide to Belize. Belize City: Belize Tourism Industry Association.

Dobson, Narda. 1973. *A History of Belize.* Trinidad and Jamaica: Longman Caribbean.

Donziger, Steven. 1987. "Peace Corps Follies: In Belize, Volunteers Find the Easiest Job They'll Ever Hate." *The Progressive* 51 (March): 28–31.

Earthwatch. 1996. "Two Tickets to Paradise. Is Ecotourism an Environmental Boon or Boondoggle?" 15, no. 6 (November/December): 32–35.

The Economist. 1993. "Small Wonder." 327 (26 June): 52.

Emond, Charles John. 1997. *A History of Orange Walk Town.* Belize City: BISRA Occasional Publication 6.

Edmondson, Eddie. 1997. "Black in America." *The Reporter*, March 2, p. 2.

Enloe, Cynthia. 1989. *Bananas, Beaches, and Bases: Making Feminist Sense of International Politics.* Berkeley: University of California Press.

Farah, Douglas. 1997. "Belize by the Sea: Much Coast, Little Guard." *Washington Post*, June 10, World News Section, p. A27.

Featherstone, Mike. 1990. *Global Culture, Nationalism, Globalization and Modernity.* London: Sage.

Few, Roger. 1997. "Within the Coastal Zone of Belize." Paper delivered at the Third Belize Interdisciplinary Conference, International Studies Program, University of North Florida. Belize City, March 6–8.

Foster, Byron. 1986. *Heart Drum: Spirit Possession in the Garifuna Communities of Belize.* Benque Viejo, Belize: Cubola Productions.

———. 1987. *The Bayman's Legacy: A Portrait of Belize City.* Benque Viejo, Belize: Cubola Productions.

———. 1989. *Warlords and Maize Men: Guide to the Maya Sites of Belize.* Benque Viejo, Belize: Cubola Productions.

Friedman, Jonathan. 1990. "Being in the World: Globalization and Localization." In Mike Featherstone, ed., *Global Culture: Nationalism, Globalization and Modernity*, pp. 311–328. London: Sage.

Gillett, Cecil. 1996. "The Importance of English and Spanish in Belize's Rapidly Changing Society." *The Reporter.* April 28, pp. 19–20; May 5, pp. 5–6; May 19, p. 19.

Gilroy, Paul. 1993. *The Black Atlantic: Modernity and Double Consciousness.* Cambridge, MA: Harvard University Press.

Glassman, Paul. 1991. *Belize Guide.* Champlain, NY: Passport Press.

Grant, Cedric H. 1976. *The Making of Modern Belize: Politics, Society, and British Colonialism in Central America.* Cambridge: Cambridge University Press.

Greene, Graham. 1984. *Getting to Know the General: The Story of an Involvement.* New York: Simon and Schuster.

Guderjan, Thomas. 1993. *Ancient Maya Traders of Ambergris Caye.* Benque Viejo, Belize: Cubola Productions.

Gunson, Phil. 1996. "Belize Finds Melting Pot May Be Coming to a Boil: Creole Population Faces Uneasy Changes." *Houston Chronicle,* August 26, p. 14A. Reprinted from *The Manchester Guardian.*

Hannerz, Ulf. 1990. "Cosmopolitans and Locals in World Culture Theory." *Culture and Society* 7: 237–251.

———. 1992. *Cultural Complexity: Studies in the Social Organization of Meaning.* New York: Columbia University Press.

Harborne, A. R., P. J. Mumby, P. S. Raines, and J. M. Ridley. 1995. "The Bacalar Chico Reserve: A Case Study in Government and NGO Collaboration in Conservation Projects." In *Proceedings of the Peaceful Management of Transboundary Resources, Third International Conference, Durham, England,* pp. 301–306.

Haug, Daniel, and Sarah Haug. 1994. "The Process of Social Change: Inter- and Intra-ethnic Resistance in Punta Gorda, Belize." Paper presented at the Eighth Annual Studies on Belize Conference, Belize City.

Higinio, Egbert, and Ian Munt. 1993. "Belize: Eco-Tourism Gone Awry." *Report of the Americas* 26, no. 4 (February): 8–11.

Howard, Michael C. 1975. "Ethnicity in Southern Belize: The Kekchi and the Mopan." *Museum Brief* no. 21 (Museum of Anthropology, University of Missouri at Columbia): 1–19.

Huntington, Samuel P. 1993. "The Clash of Civilizations?" *Foreign Affairs* 72, no. 3: 22–49.

Huxley, Aldous. 1934. *Beyond the Mexique Bay.* New York and London: Harper & Brothers.

"Is Belize up for Sale?" 1985. *Central America Report* 12, no. 45 (November 22): 353–354.

Jones, Grant, ed. 1977. *Anthropology and History in Yucatán.* Austin: University of Texas Press.

Kaiser, Rudolph. 1987. "A Fifth Gospel, Almost: Chief Seattle's Speech(es)." In Christian F. Feest, ed., *Indians and Europe: An Interdisciplinary Collection of Essays,* pp. 505–526. Aachen, Germany: Edition Herodot.

Kerns, Virginia. 1983. *Women and the Ancestors: Black Carib Kinship and Ritual.* Urbana: University of Illinois Press.

King, Emory. 1991. *Belize 1798: The Road to Glory.* Belize City: Tropical Press.

Koop, Gerhard S. 1991. *Pioneer Years in Belize.* Belize City: Country Graphics.

Krohn, Stewart. 1981. "Television Mania! The Stations Turn on, the Nation Tunes in, Will the Government Freak out?" *Brukdown Gazette* 5, no. 6: 15–21.

Lent, John. 1989. "Country of No Return: Belize Since Television." *Belizean Studies* 17, no. 1: 14–41.

Lewis, David, and Michael Day. 1988. "Reporting of Belize by Two International Newspapers." *Belizean Studies* 16, no. 3: 32–41.

Line, Les. 1996. "Advocates of Sustainable Mahogany Harvests Counter Boycott." *The New York Times*, June 4, p. B6.

Lundgren, Nancy. 1993. "Women, Work, and 'Development' in Belize." *Dialectical Anthropology* 18: 363–378.

MacCannell, Dean. 1973. "Staged Authenticity: Arrangements of Social Space in Tourist Settings." *American Journal of Sociology* 79: 589–603.

———. 1976. *The Tourist: A New Theory of the Leisure Class.* New York: Schocken Books.

Mahler, Richard, and Steele Wotkyns. 1991. *Belize: A Natural Destination.* Santa Fe, NM: John Muir Publications.

Mallan, Chicki. 1991. *Belize Handbook.* Chico, CA: Moon Publications.

Marks, Jonathan. 1995. *Human Biodiversity: Genes, Race, and History.* New York: Aldine de Gruyter.

McConabay, Mary Jo. 1997. "On the Chopping Block in Belize." *Amandala*, February 7. (On-line).

McCrea, Jim. 1995. "Going Native." *World Traveler* (November): 40–45.

Moberg, Mark. 1991. "Citrus and the State: Factions and Class Formation in Rural Belize." *American Ethnologist* 18, *no. 2:* 215–233.

———. 1996a. "Crown Colony as Banana Republic: The United Fruit Company in British Honduras, 1900–1920." *Journal of Latin American Studies* 28: 357–381.

——— 1996b."Myths That Divide: Immigrant Labor and Class Segmentation in the Belizean Banana Industry." *American Ethnologist* 23, no. 2: 311–330.

"Narcotic Drugs." 1989. Agreement between the United States of America and Belize. February 9.

Nash, Dennison. 1989. "Tourism as a Form of Imperialism." In Valene Smith, ed., *Hosts and Guests: The Anthropology of Tourism*, pp. 37–52. 2nd ed. Philadelphia: University of Pennsylvania Press.

Nembhard, Jessica. 1990. *The Nation We are Making: A Junior History of Belize.* Benque Viejo: Cubola Productions.

1991 Belize Family Health Survey. May 1992. Final Report. Atlanta: U.S. Department of Health and Human Services, Centers for Disease Control.

Norton, Natascha. 1993. *Guatemala and Belize.* London: Cadogan Books.

Novelo, Angel. 1997a. "One Among Every 200 Males Infected with HIV." *The Reporter*, March 9, 1, 3.

———. 1997b. "Makings of a Chinese Harem, John Han Is at It Again!" *The Reporter*, March 23, p. 1.

The Observer. 1996. "Central Bank Launches Coin Design Schools' Competition: Proceeds of sale to restore old prison building" October 16, p. A.

Paik, Felicia. 1997. "Private Properties: Caribbean Flings." *Wall Street Journal*, January 10, Section B, p. 8.

Palacio, Joseph. 1990. *Socioeconomic Integration of Central American Immigrants in Belize.* SPEAR Report 2. Benque Viejo, Belize: Cubola Productions.

———. 1994. "And They Would Not Be Slaves: The Garifuna of Central America." Paper presented to the Eighth Annual Studies on Belize Conference, Belize City, October.

———. 1996. "Is There Any Future for Africanness in Belize?" *Journal of Belizean Affairs* 1, no. 1: 34–47.

Pariser, Harry S. 1992. *Adventure Guide to Belize.* Edison, NJ: Hunter Publications.

Percy, Walker. 1981. *The Loss of the Creature: The Message in the Bottle.* New York: Farrar, Strauss and Giroux.

Price, Richard, and Sally Price. 1995. "Executing Culture: Musee, Museo, Museum." *American Anthropologist* 97, no. 1: 97–109.

Profile of Belize 1989. 1990. SPEAR Report 3. Benque Viejo, Belize: Cubola Productions.

Rabinowitz, Alan. 1986. *Jaguar: Struggle and Triumph in the Jungles of Belize.* New York: Arbor House.

Raines, Peter, et al. 1995. *Coral Cay Conservation Interim Report, April-December.* London.

———. 1997. *Bacalar Chico Marine Reserve Project: Coral Cay Conservation Final Report,* London.

Rea, George. 1996. *Belize: A Guide to Business Investment and Retirement.* Belize City: Offshore Publications.

The Reporter. 1996a. "$30 Million in Cocaine Abandoned as Drug-Running Plane Forced Down." May 5, pp. 1, 3.

———. 1996b. Editorial. June 16, p. 2

———. 1996c. "US Warns: The Gloves Are Off on Drugs, Stolen Cars, Smuggled Aliens." June 30, p. 1.

———. 1996d. "Computer Networking Gives Belize Modern Data System." August 4, p. 19.

———. 1996e. "US Steps up War on Drug Mobsters." September 29, p. 1.

———. 1996f. "Belize's Marine Turtles Fight Back from Brink of Extinction." September 29, p. 4.

———. 1996g. "Environmental Meeting Discusses Biological Corridor." September 29, p. 4.

———. 1996h. "Caribbean Again a Key Transit Route for US-Bound Drugs." September 29, p. 5.

———. 1996i. "Maps Reveal Conflicts between Mayas and Logging Licenses." October 13, p. 4.

————. 1996j. "Central Bank Is Serious about Money Laundering." October 20, p. 21.

————. 1996k. "Breakthrough Achieved in Banana Talks, Says Irish Group." October 20, p. 25.

————. 1996l. "Expert Helps Out on Drugs." October 27, p. 1.

————. 1997a. "Region Unites to Protect Manatees." February 16, p. 21.

————. 1997b. "Belize Outraged at U.S. Criticism, Extradition Proposal Deserves Rebuff." March 9, p. 1.

————. 1997c. "Predawn Fire Devastates Albert and Prince." June 22, p. 1.

————. 1997d. "Chief Justice on the Out! Openings for CJ and 2 Judges." November 23, p. 1.

Ringle, Ken. 1985. "Mildewed Intrigue at Land's End: All That Changes in Belize Are the Fantastic Sun-Baked Schemes." *The Washington Post*, January 27, pp. C1–2.

Ritz, Stacy. 1994. *The New Key to Belize*. Berkeley, CA: Ulysses Press.

Robertson, Roland. 1992. *Globalization: Social Theory and Global Culture*. London: Sage.

Rohter, Larry. 1997. "Central Americans Feel Sting of New U.S. Immigration Law." *New York Times*, April 19, p. 1.

Ropp, Steven Masami. 1995. "Independence, Development and Discontent: Chinese/Belizean Racial and Ethnic Conflict." Paper presented to the Ninth Annual Studies on Belize Conference, Belize City.

Roser, Connie, Leslie Snyder, and Steven Chaffee. 1986. "Belize Release Me, Let Me Go: The Impact of U.S. Mass Media on Emigration in Belize." *Belizean Studies* 14, no. 3: 1–29.

Rudon, Michael, Jr. 1997. "Racism in Belize—the Myth." *The Reporter*, May 25, p. 26.

Salas, Osmany. 1993. "Local Community Involvement in Protected Areas Management." Paper presented at Seventh Annual Studies on Belize Conference, Belize City. October 20–22, pp. 1–18.

San Pedro Sun. 1996. "Environmental Initiatives Taken by the Citrus Industry." October 25, p. 7.

————. 1996–1997. "1996 in Review." December 28, pp. 1, 7–8, 13–15, 17; January 7, pp. 1, 6, 11, 12.

————. 1997. "113 kg Plus of Cocaine Found on Basil Jones Beach, 18 kg Found at Bacalar Chico." February 14, pp. 1, 4.

Shoman, Assad. 1994. *Thirteen Chapters of a History of Belize*. Belize City: Angelus Press.

SPEAR. 1996. "Putting People Back in Democracy." Summit of Civil Society, Conference, Belize City, October 21–24.

SPEAR Reports 3: Profile of Belize. 1990. Benque Viejo, Belize: Cubola Productions, 1–37.

Steagall, Jeffrey, Joseph Perry and Louis Woods. 1997. "An Empirical Analysis of the Macroeconomic Relationships in Belize, 1978–1994." Paper at the Third Belize Interdisciplinary Conference, International Studies Program, University of North Florida. Belize City, March 6–8, pp. 1–17.

Stone, Michael C. 1994. "Caribbean Nation, Central American State: Ethnicity, Race and National Formation in Belize, 1798–1990." Ph.D. diss., University of Texas at Austin.

Sutherland, Anne. 1986. *Caye Caulker: Economic Success in a Belizean Fishing Village.* Westview Special Studies in Social, Political, and Economic Development. Boulder, CO: Westview Press.

———. 1992. "Who Are the Belizeans? I'm Glad You Asked." *Belize Magazine* 1, no. 1: 6–8.

———. 1996. "Tourism and the Human Mosaic in Belize." *Urban Anthropology* 25, no. 3: 259–281.

Tillett, Glenn. 1997. "Racism Does Exist in Belize." *The Reporter*, June 19, p.1.

United Nations Development Programme (UNDP). 1993. *Project Document, Belize: Sustainable Development and Management of Biologically Diverse Coastal Resources.* Geneva: UNDP publishers.

U.S. Department of State. 1996. *Belize Human Rights Practices.* (http://129.81.208.15/bz02004.htm).

Vernon, Dylon. 1997. Opening Plenary Session. Third Belize Interdisciplinary Conference, International Studies Program, University of North Florida. Belize City, March 6–8.

Vix, Cecily A. 1996. "Unrest in the Banana Belt: The Labor Movement of the Banderas Unidas." Unpublished paper.

Wallerstein, Immanuel. 1974. *The Modern World System.* New York: Academic Press.

Walvin, James. 1997. "Chains That Bind." Review of Robin Blackburn, *The Making of New World Slavery. The Times Higher Education Supplement*, June 6, p. 24.

Warren, Derek. 1993. "Public Access to the Broadcast Media." Paper presented to the Seventh Annual Studies on Belize Conference, Belize City.

Weatherford, Jack M. 1988. *Indian Givers: How the Indians of America Transformed the World.* New York: Crown.

Wells, Ken. 1997. "African Game Ranchers See a New Way to Save Endangered Species. Use It or Lose It They Say, Raising Rhinos and Such for Horns—and Profit. Elephants Pulling a Plow." *Wall Street Journal*, January 7, pp. A1, A11.

Wells, M., et al. 1992. *People and Parks: Linking Protected Area Management with Local Communities.* Washington, DC: The World Bank.

Wheat, Andrew. 1996. "Toxic Bananas." *Multinational Monitor* 7, no. 9 (September), pp. 1–10.

Wiegand, Bruce. 1994. "Black Money in Belize: The Ethnicity and Social Structure of Black-Market Crime." *Social Forces* 73, no. 1 (September): 135–154.

Wilk, Richard. 1989. "Colonial Time and T.V. Time: Media and Historical Consciousness in Belize." *Belizean Studies* 17, no. 1: 3–13.

———. 1991. *Household Ecology, Economic Change and Domestic Life Among the Kekchi Maya in Belize.* Tucson: University of Arizona Press.

————. 1995. "Learning to Be Local in Belize: Global Systems of Common Difference." In Daniel Miller, ed., *Worlds Apart: Modernity Through the Prism of the Local*, pp. 110–133. London: Routledge.

Wilk, Richard, and Mac Chapin. 1989. "Belize: Land Tenure and Ethnicity." *Cultural Survival Quarterly* 13, no. 3: 41–44.

Wilkinson, Pete. 1992. "Tourism—the Curse of the Nineties?" *Community Development Journal* 27, no. 4 (October): 386–395.

Willes, Burl. 1990. *Undiscovered Islands of the Caribbean.* 2nd ed. Santa Fe, NM: John Muir Publications.

Wilson, P. 1973. *Crab Antics.* New Haven: Yale University Press.

Woods, Louis, Joseph Perry, and Jeffrey Steagall. 1994. "Tourism as a Development Tool: The Case of Belize." *Caribbean Geography* 5, no. 1 (March): 1–19.

————. 1995. "The Changing Structure and Spatial Distribution of Ethnic Groups in Belize: Differential Immigration and Emigration Patterns, 1980–1991." Paper presented to the Ninth Annual Studies on Belize Conference, Belize City, October.

Zurick, David N. 1992. "Adventure Travel and Sustainable Tourism in the Peripheral Economy of Nepal." *Annals of the Association of American Geographers* 82, no. 4: 608–628.

Index

About the Author

ANNE SUTHERLAND is Professor of Anthropology at Macalester College in St. Paul, Minnesota. Her previous books include *Caye Caulker: Economic Success in a Belizean Fishing Village* (1986) and *Gypsies, The Hidden Americans* (1986).

ISBN 0-89789-579-7

EAN

9 780897 895798

90000>

HARDCOVER BAR CODE

5890